Imagining Persecution

Imagining Persecution

~

Why American Christians
Believe There Is a Global War
against Their Faith

JASON BRUNER

Rutgers University Press

New Brunswick, Camden, and Newark, New Jersey, and London

Library of Congress Cataloging-in-Publication Data

Names: Bruner, Jason, author.
Title: Imagining persecution : why American Christians believe there
is a global war against their faith / Jason Bruner.
Description: New Brunswick, New Jersey : Rutgers University Press,
2021. | Includes bibliographical references and index.
Identifiers: LCCN 2020027534 | ISBN 9781978816817 (paperback) |
ISBN 9781978816824 (cloth) | ISBN 9781978816831 (epub) |
ISBN 9781978816848 (mobi) | ISBN 9781978816855 (pdf)
Subjects: LCSH: Persecution. | Church history—21st century. |
Christians—United States—Attitudes.
Classification: LCC BR1601.3 .B78 2021 | DDC 272/.9—dc23
LC record available at https://lccn.loc.gov/2020027534

A British Cataloging-in-Publication record for this book is available
from the British Library.

♾ The paper used in this publication meets the requirements of the
American National Standard for Information Sciences—Permanence of
Paper for Printed Library Materials, ANSI Z39.48-1992.

www.rutgersuniversitypress.org

Manufactured in the United States of America

Scripture quotations are from the New Revised Standard Version Bible,
copyright © 1989 National Council of the Churches of Christ in the United
States of America. Used by permission. All rights reserved worldwide.

Scripture quotations marked (NIV) are taken from the Holy Bible,
New International Version®, NIV®. Copyright © 1973, 1978, 1984, 2011 by
Biblica, Inc.™ Used by permission of Zondervan. All rights reserved
worldwide. www.zondervan.com. The "NIV" and "New International Version"
are trademarks registered in the United States Patent and
Trademark Office by Biblica, Inc.™

Contents

Preface

At the outset, I would like to ask some forbearance from two groups of readers who might pick up this book. On the one hand could be those who wish to have confirmed the idea that anti-Christian persecution is among the most severe human rights issues presently facing the world community. On the other could be those who would want me to dispel claims of anti-Christian persecution around the globe as mere Christian histrionics, akin to the so-called War on Christmas.

My approach to the subject might very well be objectionable to both of these groups. The broad historical argument that I will develop, along with my questioning of some of the evidence used to support current claims of the extent of anti-Christian persecution, could be seen by the former group as downplaying an egregious contemporary injustice. My insistence that many Christians today remain highly vulnerable as a result of their religious identity might be seen by the latter as an unreasonable bias against other vulnerable minorities.

For these reasons, this book will not resemble many other books on the subject of anti-Christian persecution. It is not filled with graphic accounts of individuals who have suffered because of their faith or religious identity, though some of these stories are included. In short, this is not a book about specific instances of anti-Christian persecution. Rather, it is about how Christians today have come to use persecution to form a new global understanding of their faith.

"Imagining" in the book's title has less to do with believing in something that is not true and more to do with the various ways people might look upon the world and envision persecution.

Imagining Persecution

1

Coming to Terms

Christians, Martyrs, and Persecution

In February 2011, I took a break from my dissertation research to travel back to my childhood home in northern Georgia. While I was there, the mother of a high school friend asked me about my studies. I told her that I was interested in the East African Revival—a Christian movement that spread through Uganda in the mid-twentieth century.[1] Her response came like a reflex: "Oh, we read the Voice of the Martyrs and know about how Christians over there are persecuted."

She assumed, rightly, that I needed no explanation of what the Voice of the Martyrs was. I was well acquainted with its work (through weekly email updates, a website, and a monthly publication) that kept Western Christians apprised of instances of anti-Christian persecution around the world, focusing upon those who are imprisoned, killed, or otherwise physically harmed due to their Christian faith or identity. But I was still caught off guard by her reply.

As a doctoral student in the field of world Christianity, I was being trained to see movements like the East African Revival as laying the foundation for Christianity's numerical success in sub-Saharan Africa.[2] Scholars have estimated that while Africa contained a mere 10 million Christians in the year 1900, it claimed an astonishing 360 million by the year 2000.[3] I was seeing in Uganda a similar historical process of dramatic Christian growth, which is why my friend's mother's response caught me off guard.

Why would someone assume that simply because Christians were "over there" that they would, almost inevitably, be persecuted for their faith?

The idea that Christians are widely victimized today might sound hyperbolic. In the contemporary West, it has been commonplace to connect Christians with the perpetration of violence, such as justifying the Crusades, witch hunts, or colonial massacres. Yet the Center for the Study of Global Christianity (CSGC) claims that there have been 90,000 to 164,000 Christian martyrs *per year* for roughly the past thirty years. Other organizations have published figures with far lower estimates, in the range of 2,000 to 10,000 per year, depending upon the year.[4] But the prospect that millions of martyred Christians are scattered across the globe has captured many Christians' imaginations in the United States and in parts of Western Europe.[5] For them, it has become common knowledge that there were "more Christians martyred in the twentieth century than in the previous nineteen centuries combined."[6] So pervasive is their conviction of this global duress that many Western Christians now speak of "the global war on Christians."[7]

This book is about where the idea that there is a global war on Christians came from, how this idea fits into the broad sweep of Christian history, and why this idea has become a compelling way for many American Christians to think about the global state of Christianity in the early twenty-first century.

Uganda

My friend's mother thought what she did for good reason. The stories that she had read about Uganda from sources like the Voice of the Martyrs (VOM) were dire, often focusing upon the atrocities committed by the Lord's Resistance Army (LRA) in northern Uganda in the early twenty-first century. Take, for example, this quoted vignette from 2008, excerpted from "Alice," who was twelve years old when she was abducted in northern Uganda:

> Rebels emerged from the bush as I was helping my mother harvest groundnuts and abducted me; one of the rebel commanders, called Pope, said he would kill me if I escaped. Although I was put under tight security, I decided to escape one day while going to fetch water. I walked in the forest for two weeks, looking for any place where UN peace-keeping forces could be. I was scared and thought the wild animals would kill me in the jungle. Another boy who had also escaped the rebels joined me but he was killed by civilians in Congo. His head was cut off and the people carried his head, saying rebels were killing people in Congo. I know that other children in the rebel camp want to escape but they are scared of people in Congo. I cry a lot when I imagine how my friend was beheaded and other parts of his body cut up; why do people kill children? We were all abducted and did not want to be with the rebels.[8]

The scale of the LRA's violence has been immense. The LRA Crisis Tracker has calculated over 3,000 civilian casualties and over 8,000 abductions.[9] Additionally, several hundred thousand people in northern Uganda, eastern Democratic

Republic of the Congo, and the Central African Republic have been displaced as a result of the LRA's campaigns.

Though such facts reflect a troubled recent history for this region, they do not capture the whole of Christianity in Uganda, past or present. Uganda, in fact, mirrors the remarkable growth of Christianity across sub-Saharan Africa in the twentieth century. European Christian missionaries arrived in what is now southern Uganda only in the 1870s, yet approximately 85 percent of the country's current population is classified as Christian. Christians in Uganda have been and remain a prominent part of public and political life, while churches and faith-based organizations exert a substantial force in politics, healthcare, and education.[10]

Even with this remarkable growth, the CSGC calculates that there have been 203,095 martyred Ugandan Christians since 1877.[11] It is likely that many Ugandans killed during the civil wars and despotic rules of Idi Amin (1972–1979) and Milton Obote (1966–1971; 1980–1985) contribute to this startling statistic. To be sure, Ugandans do remember particular martyrs from these years, with Anglican Archbishop Janani Luwum (d. 1977) being the most famous. But speaking of martyrs in Uganda more often draws Ugandans' attention to the events of 1884–1886, when forty-five young Anglican and Catholic converts were put to death by the *Kabaka* (King) of Buganda, for which the Catholic martyrs were canonized by Pope Paul VI.[12]

Unlike the generalized violence that resulted in a large number of homicides and deaths during the Amin and Obote regimes of the 1970s and '80s, the Uganda martyrs of the 1880s more closely resemble a pattern that is recognizable in Christian martyrdoms since the earliest centuries of Christian history: Christian individuals are singled out for their religious identity or practice and are called before a powerful figure to answer for it; the Christians refuse to recant, even upon threat of death; and the Christians are then put to death, their faith fully intact.[13]

It is this framework that the VOM story excerpted above has in mind when it states that there is "no direct link to Christian persecution in the article" in Alice's traumatic experience.[14] However, a large percentage of Ugandans in the northern and western regions of the country would be measured demographically as Christians, with Anglican and Roman Catholic being the predominant denominations in the region. For this reason, violence against them would nevertheless contribute to the high martyrdom statistics generated by the CSGC.

Indeed, Alice and many thousands like her have endured horrors that demand the responses of both compassion and justice. I am not calling into question the credibility of the facts of such experiences. What is at stake here is not simply the parsing out of different definitions of "martyr" or "Christian persecution" that are caught between the contrasting methods and priorities of sociology and theology. Rather, what is at stake is how we are asked to imagine the suffering of others. Classifying Alice as a victim of a global war on Christians leads to a different relationship to her, as well as a different form of political (and, for Christians, spiritual) engagement to address the causes, than if one were to regard her as a casualty of poverty and a weakened state infrastructure.

The Persecuted Church

The Voice of the Martyrs includes stories about Uganda sporadically, because its larger mission is to advocate on behalf of a "persecuted family" of Christians worldwide. While VOM is one among several international nongovernmental organizations (NGO) and nonprofit organizations engaged in advocacy and research on anti-Christian persecution (other organizations include Aid to the Church in Need and Open Doors International), it is among the oldest and most pervasive within the United States.[15]

VOM's dedication to the "persecuted family of Christ" has its origins in the experiences of its founder, Richard Wurmbrand. Wurmbrand, a Romanian Lutheran pastor, was imprisoned by the communist regime in Romania for fourteen years from the 1940s to the 1960s.[16] Under his leadership and throughout the rest of the twentieth century, VOM focused on the suffering inflicted upon Christians by communist regimes, particularly those in the USSR, China, and North Korea. Its publications in the past twenty years, however, have shifted to include Christian martyrs in "the Muslim world," which includes regions such as North Africa, the Middle East, South and Southeast Asia, and parts of Central Asia.

Today, it is often to the Christians in these regions that VOM refers with phrases such as the "persecuted family of Christ," the "underground church," or the "persecuted church." These terms represent a way of speaking about Christians who continue to practice and adhere to their faith in the midst of repression. When Christians speak of the "persecuted church," therefore, they are not talking about any one tradition or denomination. The persecuted church is defined by one feature: Christians who suffer because of their faith or religious identity. For this reason, the persecuted church contains Christians as various as Pentecostals and Russian Orthodox, but not all Orthodox or Pentecostal Christians would be included automatically in the "persecuted church." As a result, the phrase is a way of uniting all Christians who suffer from persecution within a single imagined category and spiritual community that transcends borders.

The idea of the persecuted church, as it has come to function within American Christianity, tends to speak of these Christians as possessing a truer, purer, and more authentic faith.[17] As a concept, the persecuted church is also transhistorical, extending throughout all of Christian history. It is common for persecuted Christians to be compared to the earliest Christians, as described in the New Testament book of Acts or in other ancient Christian writings. Many of these writings recount harrowing scenarios in which Christians unflinchingly stood against an imposing Roman Empire.

As Wurmbrand said of the persecuted Christians of Eastern Europe, "Behind the walls of the Iron Curtain the drama, bravery and martyrdom of the Early Church are happening all over again—now."[18] The idea of the persecuted church carries with it the assumption that authentic Christians, be they ancient or modern, stand firm in their faith in the face of persecution. This theological and rhetorical move can separate—however subtly—"true Christians" from Christian doctrine, or the official teachings of particular Christian traditions and denominations. Within this way of understanding Christianity worldwide, the purity of certain Christians' faith is seen only in their faithful endurance of persecution rather than in the precision of their grasp of Christian doctrine or the regularity of their church attendance.

Those who speak about the "persecuted church" usually distinguish between "true Christians" (that is, those who suffer for their faith) and those who might be referred to as "nominal" or "cultural Christians." In cases of persecution, "nominal Christians" might be used to refer to those who were or are not willing to suffer faithfully or who sought to avoid persecution altogether, perhaps by cooperating with local or national governments.

In this sense, the purity of faith of those who are persecuted is not simply connected to the presence of persecution, but also to the kind of simplicity of faith and practice that often becomes more necessary in the face of harsh repression. Wurmbrand, for example, spoke of the ways that the Communist Party "lopped off branches of credulous superstition" that had accumulated in Orthodox and Catholic traditions in Romania.[19] Wurmbrand's accounts of Orthodox priests who were imprisoned with him often focused upon the ways that they were unable to perform their rituals according to tradition, due to the lack of resources. Wurmbrand, however, does recount an imprisoned Orthodox priest who, in his view, improvised meaningfully amid the deprivation: "For the communion service, bread was needed and many were ready to sacrifice their ration. But the Orthodox ritual requires that the bread be consecrated over an altar containing a relic from the body of a martyr. There was no relic. 'We have living martyrs with us,' said Father Andricu. They consecrated the bread and a little wine in a chipped cup."[20]

One could conclude that these notions, which infuse the larger idea of the persecuted church, are more reminiscent of evangelical Protestant spirituality than that found in other Christian traditions—particularly liturgical ones, like Orthodoxy.[21] There is certainly truth to such a conclusion. The emphasis upon the simplicity of worship, the relative unimportance of the creeds or of dogma in lieu of the purity of a basic confession of Christ, and of the logistical impossibility (in prison, for example) of maintaining the full liturgical tradition all can combine to make the individual's encounter with Christ paramount in contexts of severe persecution—a feature that is often more characteristic of Protestant spirituality.

To return to the core of this book, however, if Christians are not primarily defined by what they believe but by the mere fact of persecution based upon their perceived identity or institutional affiliation, then how is one to determine who gets to count as Christian? I do not ask this question as a means of arguing about the doctrine of salvation in general or of the state of any person's soul per se. This question here has direct relevance to the issue of whether counting martyrs is a meaningful way to determine the extent of Christian persecution, as has become common over the last three decades and will be discussed in detail in chapter 4.

Who Counts as Christian?

Most of us, if asked to define a religious community, would likely begin with those things that a community believes or the texts a community holds as sacred. At its most basic level, it might sound something like this: "Christians believe in Jesus (or the Trinity) and read the Bible. Muslims read the Qur'an and believe that there is one God and that Muhammad is God's prophet."

Most of us, however, would also recognize the ways that this definition is insufficient. What about people who are illiterate (and Christian history is full of them), or people for whom the Bible is not available in their native language? Or those for whom the Bible might not be a relevant part of how they understand their faith? What of those groups who identify as Christian but are not Trinitarian? What happens when one's Christian identity is not readily distinguishable from an ethnic or familial identity?

Of course, attempting to determine who should be regarded as a Christian is only slightly younger than Christianity itself. In the New Testament Gospels, Jesus was cautious about the possibility of separating the "wheat" from the "weeds" (metaphorical references to those who, respectively, responded to the "good seed" of his words versus "those of his enemies"; Matt. 13:24–30). Early Christian authors, however, were often less circumspect. For example, the Apostle Paul railed against "false believers [who] had infiltrated our ranks" (Gal. 2:4), and the occasion for writing 1 John was the pastoral concern about those who "went out from us, but did not really belong to us" (1 John 2:9).

Early Christians, particularly those whom scholars have termed the "proto-orthodox" (a term used to define those Christians whose writings contributed to the formation of the theology that would be affirmed at the councils of Nicaea, Constantinople, Ephesus, and Chalcedon), more often sought to divide the proverbial wheat from the weeds. Councils over subsequent centuries would define other groups and beliefs as heretical—that is, placing outside of the Christian community those who believe contrary teachings. In an era in which Christianity was not only tolerated but, by the end of the fourth century C.E., also regarded as the religion of the empire, such a designation carried with it dire political ramifications. The consequences for heresy remained substantial throughout a significant portion of Christian history.[22]

Skipping ahead chronologically to the sixteenth-century Reformation, one finds a markedly different sociopolitical context, but one still shaped by the boundaries of theological truth and heresy. Even if Protestant reformers were condemned by the Catholic Church in edicts and the Council of Trent (1545–1563 C.E.), one can see in their actions a desire to work out what they believed to be at stake in their salvation.[23] The Wars of Religion (ca. 1562–1598 C.E.) that then ravaged Central and Western Europe, however, would show that the Reformation's fissures could never be considered purely theological.

Given the wars' brutality, one cannot imagine the warring Protestants and Catholics pausing to recognize that their confessional identities were, in fact, subordinate to a broader, generically "Christian" identity that they shared with one another. As Protestants and Catholics battled against each other, they certainly would not have seen themselves as equally legitimate victims of a war on Christianity, despite the immense blood shed reputedly on behalf of Christian truth. And even into the twentieth century, one is hard-pressed to find Catholics and Protestants (or Protestants and Orthodox) generally viewing one another as equally Christian, though a few such instances will be discussed in chapter 3.[24]

Two important developments began to change these relationships in the twentieth century. One was the ecumenical movement among Christians. The other was the creation of sociological tools for measuring religious adherence.

The ecumenical movement grew out of the nascent collaborative efforts of various Protestant denominations in foreign missions. (Most of these denominations are comprised of what people often refer to now as the "Protestant mainline denominations.") The Edinburgh missionary conference of 1910 remains a historically significant moment in moving toward formal ecumenical dialogues that sought to reconcile historical ecclesiastical and theological differences among Christian traditions and denominations.[25] There were, of course, limits to this movement, both because of a lack of willingness to participate on the part of some churches (such as fundamentalists and some early Pentecostals) and a lack of invitation extended to others (for example, Mormons).

Still, the early ecumenical efforts had as their goal the institutional reunification of the Christian churches. Toward that end, they hoped to resolve the differences among their ecclesiastical structures and doctrinal teachings through formal dialogues, many of which are still ongoing.[26] Though Christian denominations continued to proliferate through the twentieth century, the goal of the ecumenical movement itself implies that there is something of an essential core that all Christian churches share.

The ecumenical movement (especially as instituted by the World Council of Churches or the National Council of Churches) was perceived by some conservative Christians as being theologically suspect and politically sympathetic toward communism, but other forms of ecumenism developed among these Christians, reflected particularly in phrases such as "Christian America" or the "Judeo-Christian tradition." Such notions spread in the wake of World War II and helped to define the civilizational stakes of the Cold War, creating ideological contrasts between America and the USSR.[27]

The second impact upon the creation of a globalized definition of Christianity is the introduction of sociological survey tools to measure religion, religious adherence or affiliation, and religious belief.[28] Something about religion might seem like it should be simple to measure, but one can get widely varying results based upon what one uses to measure "religion." For example, one way of determining if someone is a Christian is by asking them if they identify as Christian. But do they also have to adhere to a set of beliefs? If so, which beliefs? Is baptism a good marker of Christian identification? In the case of minors, should they also be counted as a Christian if their parents describe themselves as Christian? What if someone claims a Christian identity but only attends worship services at a church rarely or never?

When the Pew Research Forum states that there are 2.3 billion Christians in the world (approximately 31 percent of the total global population), this large research group certainly did not individually ask a large portion of the world's population whether they identify as "Christian."[29] Massive research projects such as those conducted by the Pew Forum or the CSGC count as "Christian" many groups whom some Christian denominations or individual Christian believers might not consider Christian. For example, both Pew and the CSGC count Mormons as Christian just as they count Roman Catholics or evangelical Protestants as Christian.

While theological differences still prevent full communion among many denominations (such as Southern Baptists and Roman Catholics), a research group like the Pew Forum does not really concern itself with those differences, except in studies that are specifically tracking denominational affiliation. As a result, the category of "Christian" as it is employed in large statistical references can often be at odds with many individual Christians' understandings of their faith because the sociological definition is often broader.

If statisticians ask individual Christians to perhaps set aside their denominational or theological inclinations when they read statistics such as "2.3 billion Christians," they also ask them to leave these beliefs aside when they report that there are some 100,000 (or more) Christian martyrs per year. This is a figure that necessarily must include the complete swath of people who are defined in sociological terms as "Christian." It also, as will be shown in chapter 4, is a figure that must include a wide range of perpetrators and causes of death.

American Christians at Home, in Exile

From the outset, I want to point out a fuzzy conceptual border with respect to Christian persecution. One can easily find statistical evidence to support claims that Christianity is the most persecuted religion in the world, as many do.[30] But one is sometimes also confronted with the reality that statistics might become relevant in these instances because they support a perception, or what some Christians believe or feel to be true about the world they live in.

A few months ago I test-drove a car. As I steered the car onto the road, the salesman—an older white man I estimated to be in his early seventies—sitting in the passenger's seat, asked, "What is it that you do for work?" I told him I teach the history of Christianity. He paused for a few seconds and then quietly asked, "Does it seem to you like it's getting tougher to be a Christian?"

Perhaps my salesman would have been among the 57 percent of white evangelical Americans who, according to a 2017 Public Religion Research Institute poll, say that there is "a lot of discrimination" against them when compared to Muslims in America. To be sure, white evangelicals were the only measured demographic group in the survey who perceived greater discrimination against them than against Muslims.[31] This finding reflects a trend over the last decade or so, as it has become common for American Christian leaders to express a feeling of living in exile.[32] The Supreme Court's 2015 *Obergefell v. Hodges* decision, which resulted in the legalization of same-sex marriage within the United States, seems to have intensified the perception among conservative Christians that they are "strangers and exiles in American culture."[33]

This feeling of Christian belittlement—or my salesman's sense that it has been "getting tougher to be a Christian"—does not stop at the borders of the United States. As demonstrated by my friend's mother who spoke to me about the persecuted Christians in Uganda, the stories and statistics on global Christian persecution allow American Christians who are otherwise separated by lines of tradition, doctrine, and geography to imagine themselves as being part of a global community of Christian suffering. A shared religious identity that extends worldwide and transcends the boundaries of nation and even conflicting Christian doctrines means that those who are believed to suffer because of their Christian beliefs and identity are held in special regard. When viewed in this way, they are believed to be the most spiritually righteous among the world's Christians; their faith is described in one recent book on anti-Christian persecution as "raw, first-century Christianity."[34]

In this book, I am asking that we not take these developments for granted. Rather, I contend that these beliefs are the outgrowth of three major historical developments. One is that ancient Christian ideas about persecution and martyrdom had (and continue to have) a direct role in shaping how Christians have made sense of both the world and Christian traditions and doctrine (chapter 2). The second is that over the course of the twentieth century, religious persecution has increasingly been understood by American Christians in ecumenical terms, meaning that suffering has become a way of uniting Christians who are otherwise separated by doctrinal, ethnic, and institutional differences (chapter 3). The third is that the "global war on Christians" narrative casts all of this religion as being both singular and in a common state of embattlement (chapter 4). These three chapters are intended to give a broad historical overview of how Christians throughout history have used these terms, contextualizing the essential conceptual shifts that have happened within American and world Christianity in the twentieth and twenty-first centuries.

CHAPTER 2

This book starts with the earliest Christians and their beliefs about persecution and martyrdom. These sources of Christian spirituality and theology form the enduring categories and sensibilities that condition how later Christians understand their own and others' suffering and persecution. This chapter highlights the fact that categories such as "martyr" were more often understood within particular Christian traditions and sects. These understandings make clear the boundaries of Christian communities and traditions rather than opening up those communities and traditions to a larger, more ecumenical understanding of Christianity. I also start with the early church because literature that engages Christian suffering and persecution implicitly and explicitly places that suffering in relation to Christian persecution throughout history. In doing so, activists, chroniclers, and scholars are performing transhistorical theological work in which contemporary and past Christian suffering are connected as part of a continuous narrative. Chapter 2 examines how Christians have used persecution to determine who counted as truly Christian from their earliest history up to the seventeenth century. This survey will help to make clear the real shifts that occur in the terms and in their application over the course of the twentieth and twenty-first centuries.

CHAPTER 3

Though chapter 3 covers material that is chronologically sequenced after chapter 2, it also serves a slightly different purpose within the book. Chapter 3 seeks to account for why the "global war on Christians" discourse largely arose within the context of American Christianity. I argue that American Christians' sensibility of being (or having been) persecuted within the United States is related to the ways that the global war on Christians literature has developed. For this reason, chapter 3 not only examines the emergence of the awareness among American Christians of a sense of global Christian persecution, but it ties that awareness to conflicts regarding religious freedom and religious persecution within the United States.

CHAPTER 4

The content of chapter 4 is somewhat different from chapters 2 and 3, because it examines the quantitative evidence that has been offered in support of the claim that there is a global war on Christians. These claims have been made using data from the Commission on International Religious Freedom, the Pew Forum, and, perhaps most importantly, from the Center for the Study of Global Christianity. My analysis of this data prioritizes the challenges raised earlier regarding the difficulties of quantifying Christianity, suffering, and especially martyrdom. In general, I argue that some of the most common statistics employed in the service of the global war on Christians narrative are deeply problematic and without clear comparative references with respect to other religious traditions. These statistics are, nevertheless, easily incorporated into a narrative of extreme global Christian duress.

CHAPTER 5

Chapter 5 is directed most specifically to Christian readers, and for that reason, it might strike others as peculiar. It is my intention not to leave my contribution to this important and contentious subject merely at the level of description and critique. Rather, I conclude with what I believe to be at stake theologically in the question of whether or not there is a "global war on Christians." I view the issue as a matter of where we are being asked to see the suffering of Christ. This is also a question, therefore, of where Christ's suffering might be made invisible to us, including in the very ways that we as American Christians are perpetrating that suffering.

Many Christians now look at the world with a conviction that their Christian faith creates a distinct obligation to attend to Christians who are being persecuted worldwide. This disposition to anti-Christian religious persecution can make visible some forms of suffering that have not necessarily been highlighted by governmental agencies, NGOs, and human rights monitors. There is a beauty to claiming, as many Christians do, that suffering can be shared through some form of spiritual communion, such as prayer. But viewing the world in this way can also produce its own blind spots.

On January 27, 2011, just a couple of weeks before I returned to Georgia to visit my family, David Kato was killed in Mukono, Uganda, by a man who beat him to death with a hammer. Though by certain metrics (not necessarily self-identification), Kato could be counted as a Christian, his death would not have been among the ones that my friend's mother read about in the Voice of the Martyrs. Neither Kato nor the many other LGBTI Ugandans who have been harassed, beaten, ostracized, jailed, and killed would be regarded as "Christian martyrs" or as part of the "persecuted church" by such groups.

The official investigation into Kato's murder claimed that it was carried out by a disgruntled male prostitute. But many human rights organizations and international government officials thought that the murder was more likely due to Kato's outspokenness on behalf of LGBTI Ugandans in an increasingly hostile and homophobic atmosphere—an atmosphere that had been fostered by conservative Christians within Uganda in conjunction with Christians in the United States.[35]

Whose suffering are we to imagine when we hear about "how they are persecuted over there"? Whom do we assume is responsible for the persecution? Who is the victim? These questions get to the issue of proximity, which is at the heart of the idea that there is a global war on Christians. In other words, in a world filled with suffering, how and why are we made to feel as though some forms of suffering ought to matter to us more than others?

2

Christians, Martyrdom, and Persecution from the New Testament to the Reformation

In the late 1990s, it became common for activists who raised the alarm regarding the severity of anti-Christian persecution to claim that there were more Christian martyrs in the twentieth century than in the previous nineteen centuries combined.[1] It was not always clear, however, who counted as a "Christian" or a "martyr" in this statistic, either in the present or throughout history. Did it include Arian Christians, condemned as heretical at the Council of Nicaea in 325 C.E.? Or, during the Reformation, did it include Catholic, Protestant, and Anabaptist martyrs of Central and Western Europe, nearly all of whom were killed at the hands of fellow Christians? If so, then the definition of both "Christian" and "martyr" is not one that various Christians of the fourth or sixteenth centuries, respectively, would recognize. In this sense, the historical consciousness that has been fostered by anti-Christian persecution activists moves in two directions simultaneously, pulling early Christian texts, vocabulary, and spirituality through history up to the present, even as they use the present to make claims about that history.

What follows in this chapter is an overview of how Christians have written about martyrs and martyrdom from the time of the New Testament through the Reformation in the sixteenth century. Readers more familiar with one or more of the time periods or traditions covered in this chapter might not find altogether new information with respect to that period. My goal in this chapter is to show how martyrdom has largely served as a means of drawing proverbial lines in the theological sand, separating Christians of different traditions from one another and bolstering their existing theological claims and traditions. In short, I intend to show in this chapter that the concept of martyrdom did not serve to create an ecumenical imagination of Christianity, an argument that I will then contrast with developments from the nineteenth century to the present that are the subject of chapters 3 and 4.

Christianity's first centuries are often associated with the Roman Empire's persecution of the new religion. A cursory reading of the New Testament makes clear that the Christians to whom these texts were written had no expectations of having an easy time of it. And even if one argues that the Christians needed stories of persecution rather more than the Roman Empire needed to persecute them, it is not an overstatement to claim that Christians "largely [constructed] their identity around suffering."[2] This does not mean, however, that Christians invented accounts of persecution out of whole cloth. Rather, this chapter aims to examine how Christians found theological truth and spiritual meaning in these persecutions. In writing about their martyrs, Christians have connected their suffering not only to the suffering of Christ but also to the theological traditions of which they are part.

Moving from late antiquity into the Middle Ages, one can see these traditions taking shape, as well as new dynamics that emerge with respect to the history of Christian martyrdom—namely, the definition of orthodoxy in the ecumenical councils of the fourth through the seventh centuries and the expansion of Islamic empires from the mid-seventh century. Most importantly, the sharply divided Christian traditions largely failed to recognize one another's suffering and persecution. I argue that Christian martyrdom and suffering were not generally seen as experiences that transcended Christian traditions but rather were more frequently used to solidify these boundaries. Such an impulse is especially clear in the Reformation. Catholics and Protestants, for example, did not see in their attacks upon one another a more encompassing persecution of "Christians." This is because Catholics were often responsible for Protestants' persecution, and vice versa.

The New Testament Gospels

The New Testament Gospels were likely written in the last third of the first century of the Common Era (c.e.).[3] Together they constitute four different accounts of the life of Jesus, focusing upon his relatively brief public ministry of teaching and healing, and his conflicts with Jewish religious authorities, which led ultimately to his death and resurrection. While the Gospels focus in various degrees upon Jesus' actions, miracles, and teachings, they also collectively capture the difficult conditions Christians faced in the first century. There can be little doubt that the theological imagination found in these early Christian texts was "fashioned in the heat of persecution."[4] That does not mean, however, that the Gospels or other New Testament writings share a common view of that persecution or how Christians might respond to it.

The Gospel of Mark, which most scholars agree was the first of the four canonical Gospels to be written, frames the issue with that Gospel's characteristic terseness: "Everyone will hate you because of me" (Mark 13:13). Matthew's Gospel, which likely drew upon Mark, elaborated this warning in the Beatitudes (Matt. 5:11–12): "Blessed are those who are persecuted for righteousness' sake, for theirs is the kingdom of heaven. Blessed are you when people revile you and persecute you and utter all kinds of evil against you falsely on my account." Indeed, these predictive descriptions were not merely about people's emotional disposition to Jesus's early followers. In Matthew (10:21–22), Jesus goes on to warn his disciples of a coming time when "brother will betray brother to death, and a father his child, and children will rise against parents and have them put to death; and you will be hated by all because of my name." In the Gospel of John (15:18)—a Gospel that bears evidence of a deep antagonism between Jews and early Christians—Jesus encourages his disciples with these words: "If the world hates you, keep in mind that it hated me first." He then proceeds to make a difficult promise to those who followed him (16:2): "They will put you out of the synagogues. Indeed, an hour is coming when those who kill you will think that by doing so they are offering worship to God."

Based upon the evidence in the Gospels alone, it is clear that early Christians were shown the stakes of the decision they were asked to make in joining the early church. In these matters, Jesus was not asking his disciples to take on challenges that he himself refused to meet, for true discipleship would result in sacrifice, following his example. Turning the proverbial other cheek was not all that was required of those who would become his disciples: "If any want to become my followers, let them deny themselves and take up their crosses and follow me" (Matt. 16:24, Luke 9:23). Others' hostility became a measure of Christian devotion, and endurance amid this opposition would result in salvation. Suffering for one's faith in Christ was a trial, for "the one who endures to the end will be saved" (Matt. 24:13).

With respect to persecution and suffering, the New Testament Gospels have had two significant influences upon later generations of Christians: one, true Christians ought to expect suffering and persecution on account of their faith; two, Jesus's endurance of suffering became the paradigm of a righteous death. Indeed, as the "Lamb of God" (John 1:36), Jesus was depicted as being innocent before men. He was unjustly killed (Luke 23:47) and even refused to respond to the taunts of those crucified around him ("Let God deliver him now, if he wants to; for he said 'I am God's Son'"; Matt. 27:43). Instead of lashing out, Jesus asked for the forgiveness of his tormentors (Luke 23:34). The New Testament book of Acts—a history of the early Christian church and its leaders—recapitulated Christ's sacrificial model in the death of Stephen, Christianity's first martyr (Acts 6:8–15). In these texts, early Christians established the example that later Christians would seek to emulate and whose death theirs would need to resemble in order to be regarded as martyrs. Importantly, these narrative characteristics of Jesus' death not only created a model for his later followers to emulate in the face of persecution but also established the composition of texts as central documents for memorializing martyrs' sacred deaths.[5]

Suffering in Other New Testament Texts

APOSTLE PAUL

The author of the Gospel of Luke and the related Acts of the Apostles records that a man named Saul stood by and looked on approvingly as Stephen, the first Christian martyr, was stoned sometime after Jesus' death. This is the same Saul who would, following a dramatic encounter with the resurrected Christ, take the name Paul and become the "apostle to the Gentiles" (Gal. 1:1–24). Paul repeatedly wrote of the suffering he endured in that role, which took him on numerous dangerous missionary journeys around the northeastern Mediterranean.

Suffering on behalf of the gospel could join together bodily affliction and hardship taken on willfully for the sake of Christ, as well as suffering that was imposed as a result of one's identification with Christ and the early Christian movement. Take, for example, Paul's boasts in his second letter to the Corinthians (11:23–27, 30) about the hardships he had endured:

> Are they ministers of Christ? I am a better one: with far greater labors, far more imprisonments, with countless floggings, and often near death. Five times I have received the forty lashes minus one. Three times I was beaten with rods. Once I received a stoning. Three times I was shipwrecked; for a night and a day I was adrift at sea; on frequent journeys, in danger from rivers, danger from bandits, danger from Gentiles, danger in the city, danger in the wilderness, danger at sea, danger from false brothers and sisters; in toil and hardship, through many a sleepless night, hungry and thirsty, often without food, cold and naked. . . . If I must boast, I will boast of the things that show my weakness.

In Paul's view, shipwrecks, hostile Gentiles, nearly drowning in rivers, and enduring Jewish opposition to his preaching were not hardships sent by an evil Satan but rather were experiences to be praised for showing Paul's own weakness. For in such things, Paul assures the Corinthians, Christ's power was made perfect (2 Cor. 12:9). It is this promise of spiritual power, of the possibility of Christ's power dwelling within the otherwise "weak" bodies of Christians, that infused Paul's descriptions of his suffering. Paul's theology of suffering draws upon his understanding of the crucifixion and resurrection, connecting the shame of Christ's death on the cross with the triumph of Christ's empty tomb.[6] This theology of divine power will later be developed through Christian martyrologies.

For Paul, Christ's resurrection made possible a new life in God, which could be experienced through baptism and by joining in the new people of God, the church, which Paul described as the "body of Christ." As he wrote in his first letter to the Corinthians (12:12–13), "For just as the body is one and has many members, and all the members of the body, though many, are one body, so it is with Christ. For in the one Spirit we were all baptized into one body—Jews or Greeks, slaves or free—and we were all made to drink of one Spirit." He goes on to explain that "God has arranged the body [so that] the members may have the same care for one another. If one member suffers, all suffer together with it" (1 Cor. 12:24–26).

Even though Paul's letters almost certainly preceded the writing of the Gospels, Paul took up a model of suffering and self-sacrifice that was predicated upon Christ's death and resurrection. Paul used his difficult life to make clear to the churches he visited the unexpected correlation between weakness and strength, suffering and salvation. Paul, then, worked out the redemption of others through his own suffering, a suffering that was shared with Christ and all those who were part of the nascent Christian church.

The letter of 1 Peter was addressed "to the exiles of the Dispersion," with the implication being that their exile was due to their faith in Christ. In giving guidance, the author offered social and household codes reminiscent of others that circulated around the first century C.E., advising Christians to "accept the authority of every human institution, whether of the emperor as supreme, or of governors. . . . Honor everyone. Love the family of believers. Fear God. Honor the emperor" (1 Pet. 2:13–14, 17). The basis of this advice was the model of Christ's willing self-sacrifice. Taking Christ's death as a fulfillment of Isaiah 53:7 ("Like a sheep he was led to the slaughter, and like a lamb silent before its shearer, so he does not open his mouth"), 1 Peter (2:21–23) implored Christians to "follow in [Christ's] steps. 'He committed no sin, and no deceit was found in his mouth.' When he was abused, he did not return abuse; when he suffered, he did not threaten; but he entrusted himself to the one who judges justly." The ethical household codes that are on either side of this passage, therefore, suggest that Christians ought to live innocently according to their social surroundings, yet should also expect that their innocence will not be sufficient to prevent hostility and unjust suffering at the hands of government officials and neighbors.

HEBREWS

The Epistle to the Hebrews was written as a sermon to a community of early Christians who had experienced persecutions: "But recall those earlier days when, after you had been enlightened, you endured a hard struggle with sufferings, sometimes being publicly exposed to abuse and persecution, and sometimes being partners with those so treated. For you had compassion for those who were in prison, and you cheerfully accepted the plundering of your possessions, knowing that you yourselves possessed something better and more lasting" (Heb. 10:32–34).

Such encouragement comes to a dramatic culmination in chapter 12, urging the Christians to consider their sufferings as a form of divine discipline that will "later [yield] the peaceful fruit of righteousness" (12:11). In this understanding, suffering ultimately comes from a God who wishes for the redemption of those who have faith in the hoped-for resurrection. This theology requires of Christians a form of embodied memory: "Remember those who are in prison, as though you were in prison with them; those who are being tortured, as though you yourselves were being tortured" (13:3).

REVELATION

If 1 Peter presents Christians as obedient subjects unjustly targeted, and Hebrews casts persecution as coming from an ultimately benevolent God, Revelation depicts the suffering and persecution of the early churches as due to the forces of evil. These forces of darkness were at war with the righteous saints, leading to the apocalyptic destruction of God's people who would, nevertheless, triumph in the end. The dramatic scene of Revelation 20:4 promises the first resurrection to "those who had been beheaded for their testimony to Jesus and for the word of God" so that they could triumphantly reign with Christ for a thousand years. In contrast to both 1 Peter and Hebrews, Revelation's portrayals of the persecutions of Christians under Emperors Nero and then Domitian, which seem to be described in apocalyptic style, are presented as evidence that the evil Antichrist was undeniably at work in pagan Rome, the heart of the empire, which was bent on the destruction of the Christians.

In one sense, early Christians could hardly be viewed as imposing. They took as their guide a Jewish peasant prophet who had a relatively short-lived public ministry and was killed on the periphery of the Roman Empire. It would take several decades in some places for the Romans to see Christians as discernibly different from Jews, and the earliest persecution of Christians seems to have come from Jews rather than from Romans. These conflicts among Jews and early Christians appear to have been local and, in some cases, represented theological and textual disputes that would carry on well beyond the first century. Still, members of the tiny Christian sects were noticeable enough to famously attract the attention of Nero and his eventual successor, Domitian. The ensuing persecutions under their reigns were not empire-wide, though texts such as Revelation make clear that they were devastating to at least some early churches, who lived the heartbreaking prophecy of "brother betraying brother" to death.[7]

If one can see in the book of Revelation an apocalyptic description of the Roman Empire aligned with the forces of evil, other early Christians had different ways of theologizing the dichotomy between the demands for the spread of the gospel and the reality that one was taught to expect persecution for doing so. The Acts of the Apostles, for example, viewed the early persecutions as a providential means of Christian expansion: "Now those who were scattered because of the persecution that took place over Stephen traveled as far as Phoenicia, Cyprus, and Antioch" (11:19). Still, Acts ends with Paul's symbolically significant journey to Rome with an expectation, as predicted in the Gospel of Luke, that from Rome the gospel would be taken "to the ends of the earth."

Christian faith tended to maintain that true disciples should expect suffering. Theologies of suffering created models for the early persecuted Christians to emulate. Biblical examples, therefore, became mimetic sources—texts that directly impacted how persecuted Christians perceived and interacted with those who were persecuting them. In these ways, martyrs became woven into the larger life of the church's structure, theology, and liturgy.[8] One can see the spiritual allure of an early Christian combination of liturgy and martyrdom in the letters of Ignatius, a Christian bishop of Antioch who was arrested in the early second century and sent to Rome.[9] On his way there, he wrote a series of letters to other Christians, some of which are notable for the intensity of Ignatius's expressed desire for a martyr's death. Writing to the church in Rome, he fiercely proclaimed,

> I am corresponding with all the churches and bidding them all realize that I am voluntarily dying for God—if, that is, you do not interfere. I plead with you, do not do me an unseasonable kindness. Let me be fodder for wild beasts—that is how I can get to God. I am God's wheat and I am being ground by the teeth of wild beasts to make a pure loaf for Christ. . . . Come fire, cross, battling with wild beasts, wrenching of bones, mangling of limbs, crushing of my whole body, cruel tortures of the devil— only let me get to Jesus Christ![10]

It is this sensibility that many Romans—and even some later Christians—would find repulsive and potentially subversive. Yet texts from the second century attest to the gradual expansion of Christianity as well as Christians' courage in the face of death.

If early Christians understood these persecutions with respect to their beliefs, it is not always clear that that is how they were perceived by those who were doing the persecuting. In the often-cited early-second-century letter from Pliny the Younger, a provincial governor, to the Roman emperor Trajan, it is not clear that he knows who or what, exactly, he is persecuting, other than a group that was disrupting social order under his jurisdiction.[11]

> They assured me that the main of their fault, or of their mistake was this: That they were wont, on a stated day, to meet together before it was light, and to sing a hymn to Christ, as to a god, alternately; and to oblige themselves by a sacrament [or oath], not to do anything that was ill: but that they would commit no theft, or pilfering, or adultery; that they would not break their promises, or deny what was deposited with them, when it was required back again; after which it was their custom to depart, and to meet again at a common but innocent meal, which they had left off upon that edict which I published at your command, and wherein I had forbidden any such conventicles.[12]

What Pliny describes here is information gotten from people who had been brought before him on libelous allegations that they were Christian. While Pliny was obviously concerned about the spread of this sect within his province, his response to its presence seems measured and, modern sensibilities notwithstanding, fair:

> I asked them whether they were Christians or not? If they confessed that they were Christians, I asked them again, and a third time, intermixing threatenings with the questions. If they persevered in their confession, I ordered them to be executed; for I did not doubt but let their confession be of any sort whatsoever, this positiveness and inflexible

obstinacy deserved to be punished. There have been some of this mad sect whom I took notice of in particular as Roman citizens, that they might be sent to that city. After some time, as is usual in such examinations, the crime spread itself and many more cases came before me.[13]

In keeping with common practice, Pliny observed the rights of Roman citizens who were accused of being part of the Christian sect, and he was not unreasonably severe with everyone who was brought before him. In light of leaders who faced a brutal death with such an unwavering disposition as had Ignatius, one might appreciate the legitimacy of Pliny's concern with respect to the Christians within his province. Punishing a few Christians who would not recant their faith surely cannot be taken as a plenary persecution of Christians as a whole. Nevertheless, Pliny imagined Christianity to be a contagion that was both in the cities and the countryside, the real threat of which seemed to be how it detracted from the worship of the image of the emperor.[14]

It was the worrisome thought of a world infused with an unwelcomed group of fanatics like Ignatius or the Christians put to death by Pliny that a second-century Christian, Methetes, believed to be responsible for Christians' persecution at the hands of Roman authorities. In a letter to Diognetus, he wrote,

For Christians are not distinguished from the rest of mankind either in locality or in speech or in customs. For they dwell not somewhere in cities of their own, neither do they use some different language, nor practise an extraordinary kind of life. . . . [They] dwell in cities of Greeks and barbarians as the lot of each is cast, and follow the native customs in dress and food and the other arrangements of life, . . . In a word, what the soul is in a body, this [is what] Christians are in the world. The soul is spread through all the members of the body, and Christians through the divers cities of the world.[15]

Methetes invited Diognetus to imagine a world infused with Christians. It was the diffuse universality of Christians, Methetes argued, rather than the numerical size of their communities, that accounts for their universal revulsion. Methetes was not interested in conviviality among "religions," and he offered no model for pluralism. Rather, in the spirit of the 1 Peter passage quoted above, Methetes demonstrated the utter injustice of this state of affairs while also showing that this injustice was to be expected. It was an injustice, however, that stemmed from the logic of his own theology: if the soul permeates all parts of the body and the body is inclined to war against the soul, and Christians are the "soul" within the "body" of society, then those societies will naturally revolt against the example shown to them by Christians' "extraordinary kind of life."[16]

Though Methetes's claim that Christians inhabited all the "cities of the world" was more aspirational than descriptive, it nevertheless reflects an important sensibility among early Christians: they imagined themselves in relation to a network of belonging that transcended geographical and linguistic boundaries, seeing themselves as a righteous soul in a sinful world that could not help but war against it. As a result, it seems impossible that Methetes could imagine a world that would not battle against Christians. For Christians like him, to speak of persecution was also to describe a normative form of pure Christianity—that is, a sense of what it meant for Christians to be in the world. This act of imagination has frequently formed bonds of communion among Christians who are otherwise separated by vast geographical, linguistic, political, and cultural differences.[17]

Theologians from the second century onward tell us that many Christians lived up to the high standards of early Christian discipleship, and Christianity's first centuries are often still associated with the gruesome, heroic, and spectacular accounts of those who suffered at the hands of a Roman Empire that was described as being inherently opposed to Christian belief and practice.[18] One can take the martyrdom of Perpetua and Felicity, written after the persecution led by Septimus Severus in the early third century c.e., as exemplifying these dynamics. Perpetua was a young woman from a well-to-do family, and Felicity was a slave; both were converts to Christianity. Here is the gripping description of their final moments:

> The other [Christians] took the sword in silence and without moving, especially Saturus, who being the first to climb the stairway was the first to die. . . . [Perpetua] screamed as she was struck on the bone; then she took the trembling hand of the young gladiator and guided it to her throat. It was as though so great a woman, feared as she was by the unclean spirit, could not be dispatched unless she herself were willing.

> Ah, most valiant and blessed martyrs! Truly are you called and chosen for the glory of Christ Jesus our Lord! And any man who exalts, honours, and worships his glory should read for the consolation of the Church these new deeds of heroism which are no less significant than the tales of old.[19]

Early Christian writers who composed accounts like these sought to show that imprisonment, torture, and even death could not tamp down the Christian movement. They also wanted to show how these Christians' deaths illustrated the

Apostle Paul's theology: that in Christ, God uses the weak (in this case, Christian women) to shame the strong (Roman Empire).[20]

Martyrdom so consumed the imagination of early Christians that some early Christian theologians wrote extensive treatises on the matter. Many of these were apologetic in nature and sought to defend martyred Christians against attacks from learned Greeks that their embracing of death was something more than insanity. As Clement of Alexandria (mid-second century–ca. 215 C.E.), a Christian philosopher and theologian, wrote, "We call martyrdom perfection, not because the man comes to the end of his life as others, but because he has exhibited the perfect work of love."[21]

Tertullian, a Christian theologian from Carthage who lived from the mid-second century to the mid-third century, once warned a Roman official by using a story that transpired under the rule of Arrius Antoninus (Roman proconsul of Asia in 78–79 C.E.). Arrius had sentenced some Christians to death, only to discover yet more Christians who readily offered themselves before him. He asked the Christians if they "have not crags and halters" to throw themselves off of if they so desired death. Tertullian recounted this story to suggest to a later official that he might be creating more of a problem for himself than he realized in persecuting Christians.[22]

Other early Christian theologians and ecclesiastical leaders, however, were concerned with the suicidal connotations of examples like the one Tertullian mentioned. Some Christians were so desirous of a martyr's death that early church leaders sought to distinguish legitimate martyrdom from an undue courting of death. In this process, "martyrs" came to be defined in quite narrow terms, needing to meet certain expectations so as to show that their symbolic deaths were not illegitimately sought out. Not every Christian, therefore, who was persecuted and died ostensibly for their faith would have been regarded as a martyr by early Christians.[23] Clement of Alexandria, for example, made the following distinctions between, on the one hand, those who disdain the need for bloody martyrdoms and those, on the other, who seem all too eager to meet death:

> Now some of the heretics who have misunderstood the Lord, have at once an impious and cowardly love of life; saying that the true martyrdom is the knowledge of the only true God (which we also admit), and that the man is a self-murderer and a suicide who makes confession by death; and adducing other similar sophisms of cowardice. . . .

> Now we, too, say that those who have rushed on death (for there are some, not belonging to us, but sharing the name merely, who are in haste to give themselves up, the poor wretches dying through hatred to the Creator)—these, we say, banish themselves without being martyrs, even though they are punished publicly. For they do not preserve the characteristic mark of believing martyrdom, inasmuch as they have not known the only true God, but give themselves up to a vain death.[24]

Clement placed those who would eagerly give themselves up to be killed not only outside the sacred category of martyr but outside of Christianity altogether. In fact, he developed a notion of nominal Christian ("sharing the name merely") directly in response to what he judged to be an unholy disposition to death and, therefore, one's God-given life.

In condemning such deaths as "vain," theologians such as Clement sought to define true Christian martyrdom as something that must conform to particular expectations.

The death could not be sought out, nor could it be shied away from. Rather, the believer was taught to conform to the model of Christ's death. It was in that identification with Christ and the apostles—not so much in the exact replication of the crucifixion, but in the acceptance of whatever suffering would come as that which needed to be endured for the sake of one's faith—that the spirituality around martyrdom drew its power and appeal.[25]

If Tertullian's famous quip—"The blood of the martyrs is the seed of the church"—highlights the central irony of early Christian persecution, it also suggests that perhaps the early Christians felt a greater need to be persecuted than the Roman Empire felt compelled to staunch the movement. Yet there still exists a perception that the early church was constantly beset by Roman persecution. The truth is, in historian Robert Louis Wilken's words, that "suppression of Christianity in the Roman Empire was spasmodic and infrequent, usually prompted by local circumstances."[26]

The first empire-wide attempt at suppression came in the year 250 under Emperor Decius. The preceding decades had witnessed calamities in harvests and on battlefields. When he entered Rome at the end of 249, Decius seemed driven by a conviction that the growing Christian churches were undermining the solidity of the empire. He required of each subject a certificate (*libellus*) indicating that the individual had completed a formal public ritual that would ensure the beneficence of the gods.[27] What followed was a rending of Christian churches as people fled, offered the sacrifice, or otherwise compromised their faith. It was also during this period that one sees the category of "confessors" (i.e., those who were tortured for their faith but did not die) entering into the politics of the church. Those Christians who had lapsed in their faith during the persecution sought the aid of confessors in returning, leading to confrontations and challenges from formal sources of ecclesiastical authority, such as Cyprian, the bishop of Carthage, who vehemently opposed such changes to church polity. Indeed, similar issues would resurface a half-century later when Diocletian and Galerius issued in the Great Persecution of the early fourth century, a calamity from which Christians felt rescued by the miraculous conversion of Constantine.[28]

Eusebius

By the time Eusebius, post-Constantine Christianity's quintessential historian, started writing in the middle of the fourth century, several transformative developments had taken place. Eusebius lived at a time when Christianity was intellectually and politically ascendant within the Roman Empire. Following a period of intense persecution in the early fourth century, Constantine's armies had marched on Rome, where they famously defeated Maxentius at the battle of Milvian Bridge. Following these events, Constantine joined with Licinius Augustus to sign the Edict of Milan in 313, "so that we might grant to the Christians and others full authority to observe that religion which each preferred."[29]

Eusebius's writings did theological work for Christians who wanted to make sense of both the whiplash change in Roman policy over the course of less than a decade and the expansion of orthodox Christianity (as defined by the Council of Nicaea in 325) under Constantine's reign. Eusebius, in his *Life of the Blessed Emperor Constantine*, described the emperor as a new Moses, a man who was appointed by "no mortal man" so that he could "liberate [Christians] from the yoke of tyranny."[30]

In *Ecclesiastical History*, Eusebius worked to separate true Christianity from what he believed were aberrations and heresy by compiling dramatic snapshot accounts of Christian martyrs from across the Roman world. Eusebius placed hundreds of accounts of Christian martyrdoms within a larger narrative of God's providential movements through history, culminating in the rise of a Christian Roman emperor. Talking about martyrs, therefore, drew a clear, eternal line in the sand, and for this reason, martyrdoms are not often marked by their geopolitical complexity. For Eusebius, the persecuted early Christians were righteous, innocent victims who held firm to the faith that the pagan Romans had tried to eradicate. Church Fathers like Eusebius viewed persecution apocalyptically, seeing it as the confrontation between good and evil; persecution, therefore, had one source (Satan), and Christians were persecuted for one reason (their faith).[31] In the words of Eusebius, martyrs were "the trophies won from demons, the victories over invisible enemies."[32] Experiencing persecution and withstanding it were taken to be a sign that one was righteous before God. As Candida Moss observes, "Readers come away with the impression that the heretics and the demons are in league with one another. The orthodox Christians, the church, are just like the martyrs. The heretics that Eusebius is denouncing are just like the demons that attack the Christians. Even from the beginning, then, Eusebius starts weaving the themes of his history together, so that he can group different sets of opponents into a single class. In this situation martyrs now stand for the church. They become a kind of litmus test for orthodoxy and truth."[33]

From Eusebius to the Rise of Islam

Much had shifted within Christian communities by around the year 500. The most politically significant of these shifts was undoubtedly the transformations that followed in the wake of Constantinian toleration and the increasing support of Christianization that came with it. Before the Edict of Milan, Christians had an enduring, intimate experience of persecution. Christ and the apostles served as models of how Christians ought to comport themselves amid whatever persecutions may come, even unto the point of death. Suffering for one's Christian faith was a form of spiritual identification with Christ himself, and accounts of Christians' brave confrontation of opposition became remembered proof of a miraculous embodied faith. Martyrdom, therefore, brought the spiritual power of Christ's death into subsequent contexts, in which later Christians could testify to the power of God amid severe repression. Still, Clement's hesitations make clear that in order to be a martyr, one needed to be remembered as a martyr, and for that to happen, one's death needed to conform to expectations, theological and historical. In this remembering, the examples of Christ and the apostles weighed heavily.

If early Christians developed ways of remembering suffering and persecution in the deaths of martyrs, they also used those deaths to work out theological disputes. One can see this in the writings of Clement and Eusebius, among others, who sought to leverage the meaning of others' deaths to support the correctness of their theology; sects such as the Gnostics, the Montanists, and, eventually, the Arians were outside of the truth. Eusebius, for example, believed that martyrdoms could distinguish the true church from those who were doctrinally suspect, like the Montanists, a controversial early Christian sect. To Eusebius (following earlier theologians such as Clement), cowardly Montanist heretics hung themselves like Judas, while the orthodox stood firm in the face of Rome's attempts to combat Christian belief through violence.[34] The inverse is also true, meaning that one Christian sect's martyrs were another's illegitimate, foolish dead. The ways that early Christians remembered and disputed martyrs—or violence against heterodox Christian traditions—show that there was not a common Christian identity that transcended what were held as fundamental theological schisms in the imagination of a broader Christian unity.

Generally speaking, by the end of the fifth century, most Christians would have viewed the age of the martyrs as comfortably in the past. That newfound comfort, however, came at a price—not only of transformations within the theology of Christianity itself as it moved from being a persecuted sect to the official religion of the empire, but also because of the theology of suffering, the body, and salvation that had developed within the earlier milieu. How was one to measure the purity of one's devotedness in these new circumstances? *The Life of Anthony*, for example, was an influential account of an early monastic leader written by a fourth-century theologian and bishop, Athanasius of Alexandria. Athanasius writes that Anthony, who had lived an ascetic life, "longed for martyrdom." But "when at last the persecution [under Maximinus] ceased, . . . Anthony departed, and again withdrew to his cell, and was there daily a martyr to his conscience."[35] It is here that monastic practices took on a "white martyrdom" (because there was no blood spilled), representing a sacrifice of the body and its desires that came closest to that encountered in the earlier martyrologies (written accounts of martyrs).

The early fourth century to the mid-seventh century saw Christians coming to terms with their new hold on political power and the uses of that power to further their distinctive claims upon Christian orthodoxy. From the perspective of Catholic and Orthodox historiography, most of the major heresies could be traced to the councils of these centuries that sought to define the mysteries of the Christian gospel. The "Arians" were condemned at Nicaea (325), the "Nestorians" at

Ephesus (431), and the "Monophysites" at Chalcedon (451). Condemned Christians who adhered to these theologies took up residence on the peripheries of the empire, or in the lands beyond its borders, particularly in the east, if they were not already from those regions. Surely many martyrs transcended the divisions of the fourth and fifth centuries; of these, the apostles and Christ were foremost. But it was many of these condemned Christian traditions that would first encounter the dramatic political and religious changes that occurred in the Arabian Peninsula as a result of the Prophet Muhammad in the early seventh century. What follows is a brief description of the largest of these eastern Christian traditions in their own terms.

The Syrian Orthodox Church (Jacobites, or Miaphysites) traces its prevailing theology to three Jacobs: Jacob of Serug in the late fifth century, Jacob Baradaeus in the sixth, and Jacob of Edessa in the seventh and early eighth centuries. Syrian Orthodox Christians are in communion with the Coptic Church and share its emphasis on Miaphysite Christology, which focuses upon the unity of the divine and human natures of Christ. In addition to the Syriac-speaking churches, the regions to the east of the Byzantine Empire were home to the Armenian Apostolic Church, which also adopted a Miaphysite Christology in rejecting the Council of Chalcedon in 451.[36]

The history of East Syrians (Church of the East, or, pejoratively, "Nestorians") has often been traced by Western historians back to Nestorius of Constantinople and his insistence that *theotokos* (God-bearer) ought not be used to describe the Virgin Mary (Nestorius preferred *Christotokos*, or Christ-bearer). Nestorius would be condemned at the Council of Ephesus in 431. Theodore of Mopsuestia (ca. 350–428), rather than Nestorius, was among the most influential theologians who gave an orienting character to these churches. The patriarchal see for these churches was established at Seleucia-Ctesiphon, from which they built a far-reaching missionary network that extended into India and China.[37]

Melkites were those Christians who lived in Islamic lands and spoke Arabic but who followed Byzantine Orthodox theology. Their existence as a distinguishable group (from East Syrians and Jacobites, for example) is a result of the expansion of Islam in the seventh century. "Melkite" referred to Christians who accepted the ecumenical councils through Constantinople III in 681, and they defended their tradition as the only truly orthodox tradition under Islamic rule.[38]

Maronites accepted the orthodox creeds as defined through the Council of Chalcedon (451). Some Maronites periodically adopted a Monothelite theology in the seventh century, which was a controversy regarding how many "wills" (human and/or divine) existed in the person of Christ. Otherwise, Maronites were very much united with Melkites on matters of theology.[39]

From the perspective of Western Christians, Eastern Christians were identified with heterodox ideas or heretical figures who were thought to have some theological affinity with the churches already existing in the East. But the emergence of Islam, and the spread of Islamic armies and empires beginning in the mid-seventh century, would make Christian divisions visible in new contexts. A couple misperceptions regarding Christians and the expansion of Islam need to be addressed. Rather than seeing the expansion of Islam as an attack on a more general "Christianity," many Christians in the Greek and Latin West saw this expansion as duly punitive for the "heretical" Christians who lived in eastern Asia Minor or the Persian Empire. Likewise, many Christians living in the eastern regions of the Mediterranean saw the Byzantines' military defeats in the eastern regions of their empire as having been caused by what they saw as the theological heterodoxy of the Byzantines.

Christians who lived in the regions impacted by early Islamic expansion in the mid-seventh century attested to the destructiveness of the campaigns. But these campaigns did not, in the memory of the churches of these regions, usher in a new era of martyrs akin to the third or early fourth centuries under the Romans. Rather, a more common response was for these various Christian sects to use the new circumstances to legitimize their own traditions and delegitimize others' by often presenting others' bishops and laity in the most negative light possible.

Take, for example, a letter written by Isho'yahb III, an East Syriac Christian, that states, "The Arab Hagarenes[40] do not help those who attribute suffering and death to God [i.e., the Byzantine Orthodox Christians], the Lord of all. If it should happen and for whatever reason they have helped them, if you properly attend to this, you can inform the Hagarenes and persuade them concerning this matter."[41] Isho'yahb's letter evinces the lack of a common Christian identity among Christians living in the East under early Islamic rule. Even in the quote above (i.e., "those who attribute suffering and death to God") one can trace theological distinctions that arose from disputes associated with the ecumenical councils of the fourth and fifth centuries.

The Christians living in these lands seem to have initially viewed the changes in imperial power of the mid-seventh century as a temporary affair but a development that was, unquestionably, destructive. Still, Syriac Christian responses to these developments varied. Many ecclesiastical leaders lamented Christians' apostasy; others used the expansion of Islam to critique rival ("heterodox") Christian traditions in these regions, going so far as to claim that the success of the new Arab armies was divine chastisement for heterodox theology. Others still described the events of the mid-seventh century in apocalyptic terms, though this interpretation appears to have been most common in the late seventh century. The tone of Christian writing across sectarian divides shifted again in the early eighth century, when it became apparent that Arab rule would not be over so quickly and that Christians would need to learn to live in an increasingly Islamic world.[42] As Michael Penn has convincingly argued, Christians living under Islamic rule did not view the coming of these armies and the retreat of the Byzantine Orthodox Christians as a welcome development in itself. Rather, such an interpretation of these religiopolitical changes can only be seen in much later writing of the eighth and ninth centuries, when Christian intellectuals sought to leverage aspects of early Christian-Muslim interactions in quite different political and cultural circumstances. Violence, Christian difference, and persecution, therefore, came to be worked out within a shifting regional political and religious landscape.

What this means is that one looks in vain for a sense of common Christian identity that transcended the confessional boundaries established by the ecumenical councils. The spread of Islam, therefore, cannot be interpreted in monolithic terms, as if there were a singular "Christianity" against which a singular "Islam" could be pitted. Rather, internal Christian theological and ecclesiastical divisions produced different forms of theologizing about the meaning of Islamic conquests, often in a way that contrasts the theologies of the Christian sects. One can see this process at work in a seventh-century text written by a Maronite against Maximus the Confessor. Maximus was known for opposing the doctrine of Monotheletism, which had been developed as a compromise among the continuing Christological controversies. A Maronite author who opposed Maximus's teaching began his treatise on the matter in no uncertain terms: "the history of the wicked Maximus of Palestine, who blasphemed against his creator and whose tongue was torn out." In doing so, the author sought to impugn the reputation of Maximus, who taught contrary to Maronite beliefs. But he went on in the same treatise to track the geographical movements of Arab armies, attributing their early successes to those places where Maximus's teachings had been accepted: "[Arabs] entered Cyprus and Arwad, destroyed them, and took [their inhabitants] captive. They took control of Africa and conquered almost all of the ocean's islands. Following the wicked Maximus, God's wrath punished everywhere that had accepted his error."[43] The conflicts over how Maximus was remembered (to the Orthodox, as a saintly confessor; to the Maronites, as a wicked and erroneous theologian) show again that orthodoxy and memory were deeply intertwined. In short, in order to be a martyr (or confessor, in Maximus's case), one needed to be remembered as a martyr, and whatever contemporary suffering was experienced by seventh-century Christians was confined within particular Christian traditions.

Living within Islamic empires did not simply impact the relationships of Christian sects to one another, but it also changed eastern Christian traditions themselves. For example, Christians learned Arabic and developed robust Arabic philosophical and theological literatures. These processes changed how later Christians living in the East looked back upon the expansion of Arabic armies in the seventh century. East Syrian patriarch Timothy of Baghdad, among later intellectuals who were defining terms of Christian life under Islamic rule, described the conquest not as an apocalypse but rather as a providential—even good—development. In an eighth-century dialogue with Caliph Mahdi, Timothy argued that circumstances for him and his churches became *better* under Islamic rule than under "Roman" (i.e., Byzantine) persecution. In responding to Caliph Mahdi's question "What do you say about Muhammad?" the patriarch proclaimed,

> Who will not praise, honor and exalt the one who not only fought for God in words, but showed also his zeal for Him in the sword? . . . [Muhammad] turned his face from idols and their worshippers, whether those idols were those of his own kinsmen or of strangers, and he honored and worshipped only one God. Because of this God honored him exceedingly and brought low before his feet two powerful kingdoms which roared in the world like a lion and made the voice of their authority heard in all the earth that is below heaven like thunder, viz.: the Kingdom of the Persians and that of the Romans. The former kingdom, that is to say the Kingdom of the Persians, worshipped the creatures instead of the Creator, and the latter, that is to say the Kingdom of the Romans, attributed suffering and death in the flesh to the one who cannot suffer and die in any way and through any process. . . . Who will not praise, O our victorious King, the one whom God has praised, and will not weave a crown of glory and majesty to the one whom God has glorified and exalted?[44]

Despite the swift changes in imperial power that characterized life in this region in the first half of the seventh century, there was not a singular "Christian" response. Rather, these changes, including the increasing Islamicization of the empire, occasioned theological reflection that continued to impact pre-Islamic Christian divisions. The immediate response from Christians was that the expansion of Arabic armies in the mid-seventh century was likely an interruption of short duration that was devastating and not particularly welcomed. Christian leaders often wrote of the apostasy that they frequently associated with heterodox traditions and of the weaknesses of those traditions' leaders.

Within this milieu, Christians offered a variety of interpretations of suffering, persecution, and hardship. It is worthwhile to note that there are very few martyrologies from the early Islamic period, and nearly all of them come from the Melkite communities in Syria. In these narratives, issues regarding the complicated procedures of adjudicating individuals' conversion from Islam to Christianity were central.[45] Despite what can appear, in hindsight, to be a shared disadvantageous context for Christians under Islamic rule in the early medieval period, there does not seem to have developed a common, broad "Christian" identity that encompassed the multiplicity of Christian sects in the East. Instead, most Christians living under Islamic rule first sought to translate the theological particularities of their specific tradition vis-à-vis other Christian sects instead of attempting to develop a common Christian theological discourse in Arabic.[46] Most Muslims seem not to have viewed things in this manner, as a variety of Christian sects were likely to have been lumped together in the references located within the Qur'an and might, therefore, become equally subject to disadvantageous legal codes that commonly impacted all Christian sects under Islamic rule, particularly during the reign of the Abbasid Caliphate (750–1258).[47]

Crusades to Reformation

THE CRUSADES AND CHRISTIAN ECUMENISM

If Christians of various traditions in the East had to come to terms with the spread of Islamic empires, Christians in the West did not necessarily use the sense of embattlement to forge a common Christian tradition or identity with them. Matters of language (i.e., Latin, Greek, Syriac), ecclesiology (papacy, patriarchates), and liturgical theology (the addition of *filioque* ["and the Son"] to the Nicene Creed) set the Latin Catholic West on a different trajectory from the Byzantine Orthodox in the early medieval period. While matters proved perplexing and, occasionally, infuriating, Christians at both ends of the Mediterranean did not always see one another as enemies or heretics either. Rather, relations could shift according to the temperaments and sensibilities of church leaders, political alliances, and shared aims. Perhaps with no other series of events is this complexity born out than with the Crusades.[48]

While relations across much of the tenth century had been amicable between the popes of Rome and the patriarchs of Constantinople, the sources of contention listed above eventually culminated in Cardinal Humbert, a papal delegate to Constantinople, dramatically storming into the magnificent Hagia Sophia in 1054 in order to place a bull of excommunication on its altar as Greek clergy prepared to celebrate the Eucharist.[49] While the condemnation was quickly reciprocated, relations had warmed sufficiently by 1095 that one of the principle motives for Pope Urban II's preaching the Crusade at Clermont on November 27, 1095, seems to have been to bring urgent help to the Christians of Byzantium who were battling with Islamic armies in the eastern regions of their empire.[50] In this action, one can locate a shared Christian tradition and identity—however contested—vis-à-vis the threat posed by Islamic armies. But what followed from the First Crusade was, in Steven Runciman's words, "a melancholy pile of misunderstandings."[51] It does not take much analytical acumen to discern in the 1204 sacking of Constantinople by Catholic Crusaders that whatever shared mission, faith, or allegiance had been part of Urban's initial call had disintegrated a century later.

What began, therefore, as part of Urban's intention to help fellow Christians facing a threat to them as well as to the Holy Lands ended with mutual condemnation and the horrific plundering of an ancient Christian center. In a roundabout way, therefore, a common perceived enemy (i.e., the Islamic Abbasid Caliphate) ended up alienating Christian allies from one another. It should be noted here that such a development is at odds with much of the way a global Christian imagination would later develop in the twentieth century, when Christians would become more likely to see violence done against other Christian communities or traditions as a kind of violence done against themselves.

Urban's preaching of a Crusade seemed to have drawn upon a belief that Byzantines, despite some liturgical and ecclesiastical differences, were nevertheless brothers and sisters in faith. That assumption, however, does not mean that relations were idyllic at the outset of the First Crusade. The author of *Gesta Francorum* (*Deeds of the Franks*), which is among the earliest written accounts of the First Crusade, clearly has no personal affinity for Byzantine leaders. He describes them as suspicious and craven, if not also Christian. For example, he notes how "[the Turks] carried off the children of Christians with them and burned and devastated everything that was of convenience or useful."[52] "Christians" in this passage refers to Byzantine Christians, whose villages were plundered as joint armies of Crusaders pushed Islamic armies to the east.

If the First Crusade could affirm a common Christian identity that linked Latin Catholic and Byzantine Orthodox Christians together, it also established a new model of martyrdom within Christian traditions: the Christian who dies in battle in defense of the faith. This model of Christian martyr contrasts in many ways with early martyrologists, who were at pains to emphasize the righteous innocence of the martyrs of Christianity's first centuries. For example, one can easily note the contrasts between Perpetua and Felicity on the one hand, and the foot soldiers who died in battle against Islamic armies on the other. The crusading soldiers challenge the presuppositions of a martyr as being innocent as well as not having sought out death.

One can, of course, find celebrated examples of early medieval Christians who died in defense of Christendom.[53] There were precedents to this shift, particularly among Northern European Christians who spoke of noble deaths on the field of battle as being in defense of Christ, and hagiographers certainly did much for the reputations of Christian warrior-kings such as Constantine and Charlemagne. But such traditions seem not to have been part of Urban's preaching of a Crusade in 1095. His emphasis was not upon granting slain soldiers of Christ the mantle of martyrdom but upon remitting their penance.[54] Nevertheless, crusading placed their deaths within a sacred context. Again, quoting from the *Deeds of the Franks*: "Many of our men received martyrdom there [at the siege of Nicaea in 1097] and gave up their happy souls to God with joy and gladness, and many of the poor died of hunger for the name of Christ. Triumphing in heaven, they wore the stole of martyrdom they had received, saying with one voice: 'Lord, avenge our blood, which was shed for you.'"[55] What is important to note here is the distinction the author draws between different kinds of death on the same campaign. Those who died in the siege were regarded as martyrs, while those who died of starvation were not. The key difference, it seems, was the shedding of blood. The crusading martyrs' blood became an inverse of the Mass, which celebrates the shedding of Christ's blood for the remission of sin, returning their blood as an offering to Christ.

The sacking of Constantinople in 1204 was the most obvious sign that whatever common goals and faith conjoined Western Crusaders and Byzantine Christians at the end of the eleventh century had utterly dissolved in misunderstandings about what the other was doing and needed with respect to the Holy Land, the governance of pilgrimage sites, and Islamic armies. The sacking and pillaging of the city in April 1204 were a catastrophe for those who lived within the city's walls, as well as for Pope Innocent III's enduring hopes for bringing under his Roman See the Byzantine Christians of the East. Niketas Choniates, a Byzantine Christian, described with horror how the Latin Crusaders spilled the divine body and blood of Christ upon the ground (i.e., the consecrated elements of bread and wine used in the Eucharist), snatched reliquaries, and broke the altar of the Hagia Sophia into pieces to be carried off. The destruction felt apocalyptic—"precursors of the Antichrist"—which recapitulated the egregious injustices done to Christ, in which he was "robbed and insulted and his garments were divided by lot."[56] The suffering of the Byzantine Christians seems much more closely aligned with the model of Christ than does the deaths of those Latin Crusaders engaged in the siege of the city.

To be clear, Pope Innocent III was infuriated by what Latin Crusaders had done at Constantinople. He railed in a letter to the Christian army at Constantinople: "As for those who were supposed to be seeking the ends of Jesus Christ, not their own ends, whose swords, which they were supposed to use against the pagan, are now dripping with Christian blood, they have spared neither age nor sex. . . . They have exposed both matrons and virgins, even those dedicated to God, to the sordid lusts of boys. . . . Under what guise can we call upon the other western peoples for aid to the Holy Land and assistance to the empire of Constantinople?"[57]

Even if the Crusaders themselves disintegrated the common Christian identity that had been leveraged against Islamic "others," one can still see in Innocent's contempt for those who plundered Constantinople a shared Christian identity, which flowed from his deeper desire to have used the Crusades to establish a Christian unity that favored the Latin, Catholic West. This common Christian identity, however, was not extended to those "heretical" Christians living in the East, the Jacobites, Miaphysites, and East Syrian Christians who had lived in these territories and had long negotiated their lives under Islamic rule. One can only selectively find, therefore, an ecumenical, pan-Christian sense of identity that clearly stands in sharp contrast to a singular Islamic identity, at least from the perspective of the Christians coming from western portions of the Mediterranean and Northern Europe.

THE GOLDEN LEGEND

The late medieval period in Western Europe saw an expansion of texts on ancient Christian martyrdoms and performances of passion plays, in which the death of Christ was dramatically depicted. In the performance of passion plays and through the distribution of texts such as *The Golden Legend*, Western Christians were given clear, visceral, and dramatic models of suffering for their faith. *The Golden Legend* was written in the mid-thirteenth century by Jacobus de Voraigne and was the most widely printed and distributed text in Western Europe in the decades preceding the Reformation. The saintly models presented in *The Golden Legend* would not only condition the remembrance of martyrs' deaths in the era of the Reformation but would also impact how Christians who were made to suffer for their faith underwent their suffering.[58]

The martyrological model depicted in *The Golden Legend* clearly takes the death of Christ as establishing a paradigm that later martyrs' deaths recapitulate. Of these, the innocence of the victims and their silence before their accusers is especially clear: "But why and wherefore Jesus in the time of his passion before Herod Pilate and the Jews was thus still and spake not, there be three reasons and causes. The first was because they were not worthy to hear his answer. The second was because Eve sinned by speaking, and Jesus would make satisfaction by being still and not speaking."[59] *The Golden Legend* is not merely concerned with the internal disposition of the suffering saint; rather, it often graphically describes the tearing of flesh, and it uses the physical flesh as a symbol of the spiritual significance of the sinful flesh (cf. Rom. 8:1–17). *The Golden Legend* describes Christ's passion thusly:

> Who is he that is not ravished to hope of affiance which taketh none heed to the disposition of his body? He hath his head inclined to be kissed, the arms stretched to embrace us, his hands pierced to give to us, the side open to love us, the feet fixed with nails for to abide with us, and the body stretched all for to give to us. Fourthly, he was right wise and well advised for to fight against the enemy of the human lineage. Job xxvi.: His wisdom hath smitten the proud man, and after, may ye not take the fiend with an hook? *Jesu Christ hath hid the hook of his divinity under the meat of our humanity, and the fiend would take the meat of the flesh, and was taken with the hook of the Godhead.* Of this wise taking, saith S. [Augustine], our Redemption is come and the deceiver is vanquished. And what did our Redemptor? He laid out his bait to our deceiver and adversary; he hath set forth his cross; and within he hath set his meat, that is his blood. For he would shed his blood not as a debtor, and therefore, he departed from the debtors. And this debt here the apostle

calleth chirographe or obligation, the which Jesu Christ bare and attached it to the Cross.[60]

Drawing upon the theological language of the Apostle Paul, *The Golden Legend* presents Christ here as evidence of the grueling spiritual labor that goes into wrenching the (sinful) flesh from the (pure) spirit. It is this theological truth that is also made clear in the example of the Christian martyrs. Observe how *The Golden Legend* later describes the death of St. Blase:

Then the tyrant did so hang them, and with hooks and crochets of iron did so tear their flesh and all to-rent it. Of whom the flesh was as white as snow, and for blood they gave out milk. And as they suffered these great torments the angel of God descended from heaven and comforted them, and said to them: Have ye no dread, the worker is good that well beginneth and well endeth, and who deserveth good reward shall have joy, and for his work complete he shall have his merit, and for labour he shall have rest, and that shall be the reward. Then the tyrant did do take them down and did so throw them into the burning furnace, which women, by the grace of God issued without taking harm, and the fire was extinct and quenched. And the tyrant said to them, now leave ye your art of enchantment and adore ye our gods. And they answered: Do that thou hast begun, for we be now called to the kingdom of heaven. Then he commanded that they should be beheaded; and when they should be beheaded they began to adore God kneeling on their knees, saying: Lord God which hast departed us from darknesses, and into this right sweet light hast brought us, and of us hast made thy sacrifice, receive our souls, and make us to come to the life perdurable, and thus had they their heads smitten off, and with their souls went to heaven.[61]

In the tortures that St. Blase and the other martyrs must endure are hooks that rend their flesh, revealing a pure milk that pours from them in the process. Blase's (and his companions') holiness is further attested not only by the extraordinary endurance of their tortures but in the miraculous events surrounding their martyrdoms. This account of his death also uses sacramental theology to describe his death, in a manner akin to Ignatius's letters of the early second century. The lives of saints and martyrs retold in *The Golden Legend* emphasize the theological significance of the completion of the act of dying in the model of Christ: silently, innocently, their flesh torn from their spirit, the miraculous made possible through their holy deaths. They also represent the way that liturgical theology, first seen in the letters of Ignatius in the early second century, continued to impact how Christians thought about the spiritual significance of martyrs' deaths and suffering.

The model martyrs that inundated Western Christians' consciousness and spirituality in the years preceding the sixteenth-century Reformation exercised a direct influence on how Protestants, Anabaptists, and Catholics remembered their respective martyrs. Just as importantly, however, texts such as *The Golden Legend* and the New Testament impacted how those who were persecuted approached their impending death. This reciprocal relationship between texts and the socioreligious contexts of early modern Europe is crucial to understanding the phenomenon of martyrdom and its representation in the sixteenth and seventeenth centuries. This means that the deaths that resulted from religious persecution were believed to need to conform to certain models in order to be seen and remembered as true martyrdoms. To say that Catholics, Protestants, and Anabaptists drew upon common literary forms, theological ideas, and spirituality in their presentation of Reformation-era martyrs is not to say, however, that they did so in the same ways.[62]

Martyrdom in the Era of the Reformation

In the period between the ending of the Crusades and the beginning of the Reformation in the early sixteenth century, one can broadly say that the martyrdoms recounted in texts like *The Golden Legend* were read as experiences that would not be expected of ordinary Christians. Rather, these texts were read and shared as mediations of extraordinary faith. Nevertheless, the theological significance of martyrdom, especially as it made clear ideas of righteousness, faith, and persecution, directly impacted the new religious identities that formed in the wake of the sixteenth-century reform movements. What is imminently clear from this contentious period of Christian history is that the sects (Catholic, Protestant, Anabaptist) that were persecuted in the sixteenth and seventeenth centuries did not view their suffering as mutually legitimating. The stakes of orthodoxy, gospel truth, and salvation were simply too high for most Christians to recognize those from a contrasting tradition as genuinely Christian.[63]

Protestants and Anabaptists who experienced persecution in the early sixteenth century had a number of spiritual resources to draw upon. But one important shift that occurred was that reformers began to inhabit a theological world in which suffering, persecution, and martyrdom again became an anticipated component of living according to the gospel, akin to the early Christians.[64] This shift is due in part to the earlier killing of late medieval "heretics" such as John Wycliffe and Jan Hus. French Protestant Pierre Viret clearly captured this sentiment when he wrote, "If our king and sovereign master has been hoisted and hung on wood completely naked, completely bloodied, completely burdened with reproaches, insults, and blasphemies, it cannot be that we wait in this world to sleep always at our leisure, to be exalted with honors and dignities, being dressed in purple, velour, and silk like the rich evildoer, having all our pleasures and sensual delights on this lowly earth."[65] Likewise, Anabaptists imagined their own suffering as being the same suffering endured by the early church under the Romans.[66] In other words, the Reformers understood that martyrdom was not merely in the past but could be demanded of a true disciple in any time, and, like the early church, they took their persecution as a sign of their righteousness and the correctness of their teachings.

Reformers inherited the same expectations for what the death of a true martyr ought to look like, and some of the most gripping texts of the Reformation continue to be the vivid, dramatic accounts of people who endured cruel deaths for their faith. Martyrdom, of course, had first to do with an experience of death, but it then had very much to do with how that death was remembered and given sacred meaning in a literary text. The inheritance of the deeper Christian traditions concerning martyrs and martyrdom likewise conditioned how Catholics, Protestants, and Anabaptists died for their faith—that is, they anticipated being remembered as "martyrs" and, as a result, approached their deaths so that they fit within the parameters of what was required: persecution for religious belief, failure to recant, threat of death, confession, serene death, often accompanied by a miracle of some sort, even if the miracle was one of preservation or endurance. This martyrological type is taken from mimesis of Scripture—reproducing the model of saints who themselves were taken to reproduce the biblical example of Christ. Even though Catholics, Protestants, and Anabaptists were drawing upon similar Christian precedents, the divergence of their traditions also shaped how their co-religionists' deaths were given meaning within those traditions.

Along with these ancient models of martyrdom, Protestants included a focus—even a preoccupation—with a simple confession of faith. One sees in the staunchly Protestant John Foxe's paradigmatic *Acts and Monuments* (commonly known as *Foxe's Book of Martyrs*) no spectacular gushing of milk from a would-be martyr, as one finds in *The Golden Legend*. Rather, whatever miraculous elements are present in Foxe's compilation of Protestant deaths are in service of a simple confession of faith. Many of these elements appear in Foxe's account of the martyrdom of John Hooper, bishop of Worcester and Gloucester:

> As Christ was tempted, so they tempted him. . . . About eight o'clock, on February 9, 1555, he was led forth, and many thousand persons were collected, as it was market-day. All the way, being straitly charged not to speak. . . . Command was now given that the fire should be kindled. . . . In the time of which fire, even as at the first flame, he prayed, saying mildly, and not very loud, but as one without pain, "O Jesus, Son of David, have mercy upon me, and receive my soul!" [A second fire was also lit and burnt out.] The third fire was kindled within a while after, which was more extreme than the other two. In this fire he prayed with a loud voice, "Lord Jesus, have mercy upon me! Lord Jesus receive my spirit!" And these were the last words he was heard to utter. But when he was black in the mouth, and his tongue so swollen that he could not speak, yet his lips went until they were shrunk to the gums: and he knocked his breast with his hands until one of his arms fell off, and then knocked still with the other, while the fat, water, and blood dropped out at

his fingers' ends, until by renewing the fire, his strength was gone, and his hand clave fast in knocking to the iron upon his breast. Then immediately bowing forwards, he yielded up his spirit. . . . Even as a lamb, patiently he abode the extremity thereof, neither moving forwards, backwards, nor to any side; but he died as quietly as a child in his bed.[67]

Similarly, in the martyrdom of Dr. Robert Farrar, death was not an end in itself but rather a form of confession of doctrine: "Concerning his constancy, it is said that one Richard Jones, a knight's son, coming to Dr. Farrar a little before his death, seemed to lament the painfulness of the death he had to suffer; to whom the bishop answered that if he saw him once stir in the pains of his burning, he might then give no credit to his doctrine; and as he said, so did he maintain his promise, patiently standing without emotion, until one Richard Gravell with a staff struck him down."[68]

One can see that the precedents established by earlier martyrs and the biblical texts conditioned how Protestant martyrs approached their deaths; they wanted their deaths to adhere to a set of expectations and standards. The issue is not only that the martyrs needed to live their final moments according to the model set in such examples, but that their way of moving through those moments needed to be recognized by those who witnessed their deaths. Without a common sense of what a martyr should look like, one could not become a martyr. For example, a Spanish Catholic friar witnessed the death of Thomas Cranmer, whose death was sacralized in Foxe's *Acts and Monuments* as a Protestant martyrdom; instead of being awed at Cranmer's faith, however, the friar took his quiet fortitude as a sign of cowardice rather than piety.[69] Catholics and Protestants looked for different virtuous actions in their prospective martyrs.

If one challenge that arose to the shared model of martyrdom among Catholics and Protestants was in what they anticipated of their respective martyrs' final moments, another challenge arose regarding the issue of innocence, which became a theological problem for Protestants arrested and killed under Queen Mary's reign (1542–1558) in England, as well as Catholics arrested and killed under Elizabeth's reign (1558–1603) thereafter. In both cases, the individuals in question might be arrested on charges of conspiracy or treason rather than due to their faith per se. At stake was the necessary component of legal innocence in fitting a biblical model of martyrdom. Martyrologies, therefore, became a genre that had to respond to the longer-term impact of the Reformation. Martyrs—be they Catholic or Protestant—needed to show that they remained purely "religious"—that their deaths were due to their faith. Therefore, even as Reformation-era martyrologists drew upon a common tradition, the forces of the Reformation created ruptures within it—for example, when English Catholics were arrested, tortured, and executed for "treason" rather than for religious belief. This distinction muddled the martyrological genre by questioning the innocence of Catholics arrested in Elizabethan England. Catholic martyrologists who wrote of their persecuted coreligionists then had to counter the legitimacy of the treason charge in order to still claim those Catholics killed as "martyrs."[70]

What remained central for Christians of different confessions was the attempt to single out belief from other contextual factors. Politics and legal questions, therefore, could not be seen as impinging upon the dynamics of the martyr's death, which needed to maintain a righteous purity, unsullied from other dimensions of life. In these issues related to Reformation-era martyrs, one can see the emergence of the fissures that would transform early modern Europe. If one distant consequence of the Reformation was the establishment of the freedom of religion as a part of the formation of the modern nation-state, then another would certainly be the severance of politics from religion with respect to public life in those nation-states. In both cases, one can see the creation of categories that have done much to shape a global liberal modernity. But in the differentiation between aspects of life such as religion, culture, and politics, one can also see the emergence of a challenge of speaking about the suffering of others, and the recognition that the categorization of certain kinds of suffering can have repercussions on how that suffering is understood and, therefore, acted upon.[71]

Conclusion

This chapter has given a broad overview of how Christians from the first century through the Reformation used martyrdom and persecution to imagine themselves in relationship to fellow Christians (of their own tradition), ultimately extending back to a communion with Christ's suffering. What should be clear from the range of historical circumstances that this chapter addresses is that one largely looks in vain for the development of a sustained ecumenical impulse around issues of persecution and martyrdom. Instead, martyrdom drew proverbial lines in the sand between contrasting Christian sects and traditions. In the context of the early church, martyrdom needed to conform to certain expectations, and those early Christians who were either too eager (i.e., Montanists) or those who thought it unnecessary (i.e., Gnostics) were deemed out of line. As the ecumenical councils starting in the fourth century defined Christian orthodoxy within the context of a Christian emperor (Constantine), the suffering and persecution experienced by churches whose theologies were condemned were not viewed by the Latin and Greek churches around the Mediterranean as meriting spiritual sympathy. The difficulties these same churches experienced after the Islamic conquests of the seventh century did nothing to change this perception, which further impacted how later crusading armies of Catholic and Byzantine Christians interacted with them. Whatever ecumenical impulses might have been part of the Crusades seem to have been motivated on the one hand by the pragmatics of military aid, and on the other, from a hoped-for reunion of Byzantine Christians under the auspices of Rome. In the era of the Reformation, one likewise sees martyrdom as serving to solidify the purity of the competing denominations' respective faiths. Such mutual violence was hardly understood by the people of the time as being an assault on fellow, equally legitimate, Christians.

The persecution, suffering, and death of Christians across time and place that this chapter has focused on attests to the inheritance of ancient Christian vocabulary, theological frameworks, and narrative structures. One can clearly see the convergence of these elements in the work of Eusebius and other early Christian theologians.[72] Martyrdom gave subsequent Christians a deep memory and mythos to draw from and place themselves in continuity with. Even as Christians drew upon common deeper theological and historical lines of spiritual affiliation and continuity, going back to the example of Jesus, they did this in a contentious and polemical climate, using such stories to attempt to demonstrate that their traditions were the most righteous, the truest. The long contestations over theological truth included a battle over the legitimacy of one's martyrs.

In the era of the Reformation and early modern Europe, one can see that the mutual martyr-making Protestants and Catholics engaged in seems to have led to a relativizing of their theological claims rather than an establishment of a broader ecumenical fellowship.[73] This relativizing then contributed to the gradual separation of religion and politics in political life and, along with it, the development of modern notions of religious toleration and freedom as rights guaranteed by a nation-state. These dynamics, among others, connect the story of Reformation-era martyrdom to some of the motivations for the settling of the American colonies. This history sets up a recurring tension: How could America, once imagined as a beacon of religious freedom amid a potentially hostile Europe, become an agent of Christian persecution, even within its own borders?

3

Religious Persecution and American Christianity

Few narratives have lodged themselves more indelibly within the American psyche than one that casts America as simultaneously a beacon and a refuge—a city on a hill that became a sanctuary from the intolerance that religious groups such as the Puritans and the Quakers had faced in early modern Europe. But from the beginning, visions of refuge were met with the realities of difference—both that encountered by the Native Americans upon whose land the Europeans settled, and that of new European settlers of contrasting religious convictions. Whatever religious tolerance existed among early American colonists—and it varied by colony, as the experience of Anne Hutchinson's expulsion from the Massachusetts Bay Colony exemplifies—such tolerance was generally limited to Christian denominations.

In both colonial America and the early republic, religious toleration, even among different Christian sects, should not be understood as those sects viewing one another as spiritually or theologically legitimate.[1] Early colonists expressed feeling beset by the Indian "heathenism" that they believed surrounded them. Attempts to remedy the difference could range from missionary conversion efforts—including the establishment of "praying towns"—to massacres.[2] And even later, after the young nation established the rights in the First Amendment, violence against members of religious communities occurred throughout the nineteenth century, with the principle fault line being Catholic versus Protestant.[3] When the First Amendment to the Constitution stated that "Congress shall make no law respecting an establishment of religion, or prohibiting the free exercise thereof," it primarily referred to conflicts among denominational and intellectual rivalries stemming from early modern Europe.[4] The First Amendment did not provide a clear definition of what constitutes "religion" or the "exercise of religion." It did create, however, an enduring legal standard and source of appeal to leverage one's claims within the United States. Despite constitutional guarantees to the freedom of religion, some Americans have felt that the federal government itself is a cause of their persecution on religious grounds. This sentiment, especially among American Christians, is essential for understanding the emergence of a "global war on Christians" discourse at the beginning of the twenty-first century.[5]

This chapter traces two processes as they have developed over roughly the past 150 years in the United States. The first is the expansion of the perception among American Christians that domestic religious discrimination or persecution is part of a global movement against Christians or Christianity. The second focuses upon how American Christians used religious persecution against Christians overseas to create a common Christian identity that is shared among believers who have not otherwise, in a broad historical sense, viewed one another as genuinely Christian. The clearest way to see these developments is by giving attention to particular circumstances in which one can note shifts in perceptions, attitudes, and arguments. The structure of this chapter will oscillate between these two emphases, showing their gradual convergence at the end of the twentieth century.

The Civil War as Religious Persecution

The Civil War was a crisis in American Christianity. The decades preceding the conflict witnessed the fracturing of nearly every Christian denomination over the issue of slavery. But the theological issues raised in the conflict were not simply about biblical interpretation, though the arguments were carried out in those terms. While abolitionists and plantation owners certainly disagreed on whether or not the Bible condoned or condemned chattel slavery, these differences in interpretation revealed deeper conflicts about what, exactly, constituted a righteous society. Following General Robert E. Lee's surrender, therefore, defeated Southern Christians did not need merely to grapple with a supposedly "inaccurate" reading of the Bible. Rather, they had to confront the fact that a perceived godly society had been destroyed by their fellow countrymen and government and, furthermore, that God had permitted such a humiliation to occur.[6]

Northern and Southern Christians generally understood the developments of the war—the early ascendancy of the Confederacy as well as its precipitous defeat—within a theology of Providence, which held that "all things work together for good to them that love God" (Rom. 8:28, KJV). This theology also maintained that God's ways are ultimately unknowable, and to "despise not the chastening of the Lord; neither be weary of his correction: For whom the Lord loveth he correcteth" (Prov. 3:11–12, KJV). It was this shared notion of Providence that President Abraham Lincoln drew upon in his poignant second inaugural address: "Both read the same Bible, and pray to the same God; and each invokes His aid against the other. It may seem strange that any man should dare to ask a just God's assistance in wringing their bread from the sweat of other men's faces; but let us judge not that we be not judged. The prayers of both could not be answered; that of neither has been answered fully. The Almighty has his own purposes." For Lincoln, the brutal vicissitudes of the war and the Union's costly victory were subsumed under an inscrutable divine Providence. But Northern and Southern Christians had markedly different interpretations of how God was at work in the Confederacy's defeat. Northern abolitionists saw the Almighty's purposes as eradicating the evil of slavery; Southern clergymen conceded that God, in his wisdom, sometimes allows "the righteous to be overthrown."[7]

The larger theological malaise faced by Southern Christians lay in discerning God's purposes in leading the Confederacy down a path of defeat. In other words, Southern divines had difficulty distinguishing God's wrath from his benevolent discipline. There were, therefore, differences in Southern theological responses to the Confederacy's defeat in the Civil War. To use a biblical metaphor, they disagreed over whether God, in the course of the war, had fully lopped off a branch that had failed to bear sufficient fruit, or if God was pruning that branch so that it would bear ever more fruit (John 15).

If Southern theologizing during the era of Reconstruction (1863–1877) grappled with the moral question of slavery and its implications for divine judgment, it also had to confront the original rightness of those interpretations as they related to God's will. Some wondered if the defeat was due not to slavery itself, but merely to Southern Christians' failure to sufficiently Christianize their slaves. In general, however, a fundamental questioning of the inherent sinfulness of slavery was voiced by relatively few Southern intellectuals.

John Adger, the editor of the prestigious *Southern Presbyterian Review*, wrote that Southern Christians "retain all our former opinions respecting slavery. . . . It was a good institution, although some abuses were connected with it which demanded reformation, and would have been reformed had the South been let alone of her persecutors." The abolitionists, Adger contended, had "a rationalistic and practically infidel attitude,—for they have set up a morality better than the Bible's, and are impugning the perfectness of Christ's conduct and doctrine. They claim to be more righteous than God, and wiser than his word."[8] Adger's sentiments were a forlorn echo of a eulogy for Stonewall Jackson upon his death in 1863, that Jackson was "the expression of [the Confederacy's] faith in God and in itself, . . . its capacity to smite, as with bolts of thunder, the cowardly and cruel foe that would trample under foot its liberty and its religion."[9]

In the end, of course, the Confederacy failed to smite its foe, a result that carried the weight of a theological fact that needed to be reckoned with. In their reckoning some Southern Christians turned toward the ancient Christian language of martyrdom. Eliza Fain, for example, opined in her diary shortly after her husband—a Confederate soldier— took the oath of allegiance upon General Lee's surrender in 1865: "I believe the Bible teaches slavery is right. If this is true every soldier of the Confederate Army who has fallen is a martyr for the truth and no great truth of God's Holy Word has ever been sustained without the seal of the blood of the Christian being affixed."[10] In a similar vein, Richard Wilmer, a bishop of the Confederate Episcopal Church, would later describe Confederate soldiers as "a noble army of martyrs,"[11] and another clergyman reminded an audience of Confederate war veterans of the "agonies of your Golgotha"—explicitly tying Southern suffering to Christ's crucifixion.[12] These excerpts are not the repentance of the chastened prodigal son.[13] Instead, they connect the fate of the South to a righteous martyr who, in the model of Christ, was unjustly destroyed only to be raised again by God. This theology of the Lost Cause took up the ancient motifs of martyrdom to remember the South and its suffering as virtuous, righteous, and undeserved.

Not all Southerners agreed with Fain or Adger, of course. Martyrs though the Confederate war dead may have seemed to some Southern Christians, lamentations of Southern sinfulness muddied the hagiographical aura in which the Confederate dead were often viewed. Even during the war Southern sins (of miscegenation, of not fully Christianizing their slaves, of drunkenness and moral laxity among its soldiers) had been used to explain Confederate defeats as well as to justify the need for spiritual revival among both soldiers and society in general. Indeed, Northern missionaries who ventured south after 1865 continued to find no shortage of such failings to report.[14] These sins certainly led to calls for repentance. But such repentance was due to Southerners' belief that they had not sufficiently Christianized the society that they had, not that their fundamental vision of society (including slavery) was inherently wrong or sinful in the eyes of God.

While some Southerners saw in the humiliation of Reconstruction the chastening hand of God, others simply could not stomach the thought of God's salvific purposes being accomplished through the federal government. Some clergymen would eventually turn to early Christian apocalyptic narratives to highlight the clear dichotomy between the righteous South and the federal government, which one Southern author deemed the beast of Revelation.[15] As the twentieth century approached, the Southern cause would become more righteous, their sins more difficult to see, their dead more noble. This sentiment would simmer, not always or exclusively defining a Southern response or disposition to the federal government, but nevertheless ready to be heated up should the circumstances warrant.[16]

Armenia

If the Civil War imbued many Southern Christians with the conviction that the federal government could destroy a godly Christian society, war against Christians elsewhere in the world could broaden American Christians' definition of who they regarded as genuinely Christian. The experience of Protestant missionaries in the Ottoman Empire is a pivotal example illustrating how religious conflict could lead to the inclusion of non-Protestant Christians into a more ecumenical, global imagination of Christianity.[17]

The American Board of Commissioners for Foreign Missions (ABCFM) was founded by New England Congregationalists and Presbyterians in 1812. The board sent its first Protestant missionaries into the Ottoman Empire in the early 1820s with an aim to convert Muslims, but the missionaries soon realized that Ottoman Muslims had little interest in adopting American evangelicalism. While not entirely abandoning their original hopes of converting Muslims, ABCFM missionaries set their sights on what seemed to be a more realizable goal: the conversion of the "nominal" Christians who likewise inhabited the region— the Melkite, Maronite, Armenian Orthodox, Chaldean Catholic, and East Syrian Christians who had lived in these lands for centuries. These ancient and variegated Christian traditions stood in marked ecclesiastical, cultural, and spiritual contrast to the form of faith that the New England missionaries hoped to propagate—the bibliocentric evangelical heart religion that had spread with the Second Great Awakening.[18] By the early 1830s, the ABCFM responded to a suggestion to establish Protestant missions among "Nesto-rian" Christians in Persia,[19] using these possible converts to evangelical Protestant Christianity as a "fulcrum to over-turn the Muslim 'delusion.'"[20]

To the American evangelical missionaries, the Christianity observed within Ottoman lands was cold, nominal, and insincere. It seemed to them that the Christians of these ancient traditions performed rote rituals without having cultivated a direct personal faith in Christ. ABCFM missionaries' shift of focus—from Muslims to "nominal" Christians—eventually brought them into conflict with Catholic and Orthodox leaders who saw in the missionaries' efforts both a delegitimization of their faith as well as an insidious attempt at dividing their already precarious communities. Having witnessed a growing number of Protestant converts from both Catholic and Orthodox traditions, Catholic missionaries sent in the 1840s threatened their parishioners: "We will excommunicate you, your fingernails shall be torn out; we will hunt you from village to village and kill you if we can."[21] Similarly, the Armenian patriarch excommunicated Armenian evangelicals in 1846.[22]

An important shift in perception occurred in the late nineteenth century, when Ottoman Muslims carried out a devastating campaign of pogroms against Christians living within the Ottoman Empire.[23] The violence was devastating to the Armenian communities whose homes, businesses, schools, and churches were attacked, destroyed, and seized in the raids. Abraham Hartunian, a survivor of the violence, soberly recounted its cost: "The years of 1894, 1895, and 1896 were years of massacre, rape, and plunder. The order to massacre, issuing from Sultan Hamid, was given at different times for different places. During those years more than 300,000 Armenians perished by either massacre or starvation and disease. Wealth running up to the millions was destroyed. Thousands of orphans and widows were left destitute in misery."[24] In the wake of the violence, however, another sort of ecumenism took place, whereby different Christian traditions—including Orthodox and evangelical Armenians—shared space for prayer and worship due to the destruction of their churches. Hartunian, also an ordained Protestant minister, noted that between 1902 and 1904 "the church services were thronged. Gregorians and even Catholics and Syrians attended. The prayer meetings were inspired."[25]

It was clear that the Ottoman Muslim perpetrators were not especially keen to distinguish evangelical, Catholic, and Orthodox Christians in the raids of the 1890s, subsuming all under a generic Armenian Christian identity. This lack of differentiation would also be characteristic of the intense violence that again targeted these communities during World War I, in what would become known as the Armenian Genocide. Reports of the massacres of Armenian and Assyrian Christians that were published in the United States highlighted this basic religious divide. In one *New York Times* column from 1915, a "traveler" reported, "The Armenians of the interior have been deported in the direction of Mosul. At the time I left Sivas two-thirds of them had gone from the city, including all Protestants, teachers and pupils." The same article shows that the ABCFM attempted to leverage a common Christian identity over and against an Islamic threat in order to motivate a broadly Christian public in the United States and Western Europe to aid in the plight of the Eastern Christians. While the ABCFM stated that "["absolutely reliable" accounts] indicate a systematic, authorized and desperate effort on the part of the rulers of Turkey to wipe out the Armenians," the *New York Times* summarized the matter this way: "Christian cities cease to exist as such and inhabitants are driven far from home."[26] They made no mention, of course, that the very missions that were being used to supply aid to Eastern Christians had been set up decades earlier in order to convert them from their traditional Christianity to evangelical Christianity.

The international campaign that was developed in response to the horrific violence reported and confirmed by American missionaries, diplomats, and travelers proved to be the most elaborate and financially successful philanthropic or humanitarian campaign to date.[27] These efforts emerged out of missionary networks and agencies such as the ABCFM. Even by the end of 1915, Near East Relief (NER) had raised $177,000, though it quickly realized that amount would not begin to cover the catastrophic needs. In 1916, fundraising rose to a remarkable $2.4 million, and donations increased dramatically from there. By 1919, the year NER was chartered by Congress, the organization brought in $19 million.[28] Over its fifteen-year existence, "the missionary-based NER spent a staggering $116 million in assistance," in addition to helping perhaps over two million refugees, training several dozen nurses, and helping to build roads, schools, and other pieces of modern infrastructure in the regions impacted by the genocide.[29] "Because of the missionaries," writes Suzanne E. Moranian, "America had assumed the moral mandate of the Near East."[30]

The effects of the campaign were not simply that missionary networks could be mobilized to raise consciousness about humanitarian catastrophes or to supply aid on behalf of governments. Rather, the campaign also showed the nascent development of a new way of imagining Christianity worldwide, one which depended less upon doctrinal agreements or personal testimonies of conversion to determine who might be regarded as truly Christian. This new concept was based more upon the fact that a group of predominantly non-Protestant Christians had been targeted due to their Christian religious identity. Having been targeted for persecution, they became genuinely Christian in the eyes of the American public, a large percentage of whom were Christian but who might otherwise not regard Catholics or Orthodox as being Christian.[31] This subtle but important process created an internationalized vision of a common Christian identity that extended beyond tradition. Though the "nominal" Christians were earlier the objects of evangelical missionaries' evangelization efforts, with persecution they became common brothers and sisters in the faith, whose suffering carried with it particular spiritual obligations to come to their aid.[32]

Though the shift that the previous paragraph laid out is an important one, it nevertheless had its limits, and these limits highlight the importance of distance and proximity. For example, Armenians who fled the pogroms and settled in the United States were sometimes prevented from buying property due to various legal prohibitions related to race.[33] Their story demonstrates the conditions for being regarded as "Christian" by Americans, and it shows that a common Christian faith would not necessarily result in full inclusion into American public life for those who were otherwise still perceived as "other."

Religious Freedom, Human Rights, and World Christianity

President Woodrow Wilson had the recent history of the Armenian Christians (along with European Jews) in mind when, in the wake of World War I, he pressed for a new international order in the League of Nations that included explicit protections for religious minorities.[34] Wilson's ideas, however, highlighted the tensions between what remained of older European systems and the international order that would not fully come into being until after World War II. In Wilson's proposals, one can see that a new form of national sovereignty was to be determined by agreeing to protections such as religious freedom for minorities. In this model, nation-states created in the wake of World War I would need to agree to these protections and rights in order to be fully welcomed into the League. These same proposals, however, potentially undermined national sovereignty, in suggesting that the status and treatment of religious minorities would be monitored by other nations. Furthermore, such rights were caught between an individualist and collectivist locus of rights: Were religious freedom protections primarily intended to guard the rights of conscience of individuals from a state, or to ensure the viability of certain religious communities as such? Ultimately, of course, Wilson's attempts would be thwarted by both European statesmen and the United States Congress, but they foreshadowed in many respects the liberal order that would develop after the next world war.[35]

The Armenian pogroms and genocide showed that religious persecution could bring foreign issues and incidents to the public consciousness of American Christians. But religious freedom simultaneously served as a way for marginalized groups within the United States to make visible their struggles. In the late nineteenth and early twentieth centuries, Native Americans used the First Amendment to argue that they "had a religion" and, therefore, were entitled to the protections guaranteed to "the free exercise thereof," even though many of their rituals and practices had been legally proscribed in the nineteenth century. By the interwar period, therefore, national and international issues of religious freedom can be considered rather separate, if simultaneous, processes. The international legal and diplomatic framework around freedom of religion contributed to the development of an international consciousness around religious persecution. This framework brought attention to the violation of minority communities' rights. It would take the vast horrors of the Holocaust to create the political will to achieve an international framework that at all resembled Wilson's proposals from a generation prior.[36]

Having fled Poland upon Nazi Germany's invasion in 1939, Raphael Lemkin, a Jewish lawyer, wrote of the need for a new term—genocide—to denote a new kind of crime: the attempted eradication of a people as such.[37] It would not be until the ratification of the United Nations' Convention on the Prevention and Punishment of the Crime of Genocide on December 9, 1948, in which signatory parties agreed "to prevent and punish . . . the following acts committed with intent to destroy, in whole or in part, a national, ethnical, racial or religious group, as such." The means by which this crime could be observed are as follows:

(a) Killing members of the group;
(b) Causing serious bodily or mental harm to members of the group;
(c) Deliberately inflicting on the group conditions of life calculated to bring about its physical destruction in whole or in part;
(d) Imposing measures intended to prevent births within the group;
(e) Forcibly transferring children of the group to another group.

The following day, the UN adopted its Universal Declaration on Human Rights, which guarantees the "the right to seek and to enjoy in other countries asylum from persecution" (Article 14.1) and "the right to freedom of thought, conscience and religion" (Article 18.1).[38]

Created with the recent severe religious persecutions of Armenians, Jews, and other minorities in mind, these documents helped to establish the predominant international legal and moral bar by which future conflicts and possible violations of rights would be measured.[39] But there was controversy even in the formation of the definition of who it should include and why. Political groups could be (and had been) targeted for eradication, but such groups are more fluid in their constitution than ethnic or racial groups. Religious groups, of course, can also be fluid through processes of conversion, apostasy, and methods of defining what, exactly, constitutes a "religion." The USSR was among those nations that abstained from voting on the Universal Declaration of Human Rights. This was probably because Stalin was then engaging in purges of his political enemies.[40] Furthermore, the Soviets did not want to affirm the right of individuals to leave their country (Articles 13, 14), as the declaration coincided with the establishment of the state of Israel in 1948 and raised the prospect of losing a sizeable portion of the Eastern European Jewish population. Ultimately, Article 18 of the declaration attempts to cover both an individualist right of conscience as well as a collectivist sense of religious identity: "Everyone has the right to freedom of thought, conscience and religion; this right includes freedom to change his religion or belief, and freedom, either alone or in community with others and in public or private, to manifest his religion or belief in teaching, practice, worship and observance."[41]

As was the case with Wilson's attempts to advocate for religious freedom for religious minorities in the League of Nations, so too the acceptance of the UN framework would impact how nation-states in an era of decolonization would be welcomed into the international community, as well as how they would be encouraged to regard the communities within their borders. How should states regard population? Are all citizens equal? Are they primarily regarded as individuals before a common law? Or do their group associations as monitored by international protocols mitigate that relationship? These questions suggest an ongoing tension between individualistic and communal rights and protections in what constitutes "religion" and "religious." The category of "religious minority" was not merely descriptive of demographics, but it also created a new way for nation-states to monitor the various people and communities within their borders.[42]

The establishment of the United Nations and its adoption of the Universal Declaration of Human Rights was of a kind with other efforts at repairing a fractured world in the post-Holocaust era. And like the UN and human rights, these other efforts built upon earlier precedents, even extending back before World War I. With respect to Christianity, these efforts were described as the ecumenical movement and resulted in, among other things, the World Council of Churches (WCC) in 1948. Like the analogous work to secure a new international order in the interwar period, this ecumenism was aimed at uniting the world's Christians in light of recent geopolitical chaos.[43] Many Christians understood these attempts at reunification of the world's Christians as constituting an important part of Christ's desire for his followers: "that they may all be one" (John 17:21).

If some Christians viewed these nascent forms of global community as welcome developments in light of the ideological struggles made apparent in fascist nationalist regimes of the 1920s, '30s, and '40s, others saw in the attempts to develop a "world government" and a "world church" dangerous portents of the Antichrist.[44] The theological suspicions toward the formal ecumenical movement notwithstanding, many of these same Christians developed transnational ties and contrasting forms of cross-denominational solidarity outside of the structures of the WCC.[45] The international community that they developed often viewed itself in contradistinction to the efforts of the World Council of Churches or, within the United States, the National Council of Churches. If the WCC's form of ecumenism was institutionalized in theological bilateral dialogues, with the goal of developing formal institutional relations, the latter was mostly constructed through networks that cultivated a shared spiritual imagination, particularly around the suffering and persecution of Christians living in communist nations. American Christians would later come to use the language and apparatuses of this global framework—of rights and genocide—in forging their own responses to violence done against Christians worldwide, particularly those living under communist regimes.[46]

Jim Crow and Civil Rights

Support for the ecumenical movement was not without its detractors. The movement largely excluded Pentecostal and fundamentalist Christians outright, and many evangelicals in mainline churches who held conservative theological beliefs were suspicious of what they viewed as their denominational leaders' attempts to water down the strictures of the gospel.[47] Suspicion of the ecumenical movement's conferences, joint theological statements, and politics was not confined to the southern United States. But Southern suspicion of the ecumenical movement dovetailed with a broader opposition to the World Council of Churches and the United Nations. These institutions were often perceived as portending the erosion of national sovereignty, an unwelcomed drift toward communism, and the loss of theological truth that disproportionately impacted Southern society and religion.[48]

Religious and cultural sentiments that emphasized the uniqueness and exclusivity of Southern Christian society resonated deeply with many Southern Christians. Sometimes termed the religion of the "Lost Cause," these beliefs paired well with a profound sense of Southern grievance against the North for both its defeat in the Civil War and its treatment during Reconstruction.[49] The cultural, social, and racial schisms evident in the erecting of Confederate monuments and veterans' ceremonies, as well as the expansion of the Ku Klux Klan, made clear that whatever lyrical flourish President Lincoln may have put on them, the breaks evinced in the Civil War had seeped into the nation's foundation.[50]

Even if matters of biblical interpretation still found their way into the national spotlight, as they did with the infamous Scopes Monkey Trial, these conflicts could not easily be summarized by pointing to differences in biblical interpretation alone. Nevertheless, the idea of biblical authority based upon a plain sense or literalist reading of the Bible became a shortcut to signaling these deeper differences well into the twentieth century and beyond, as some Southern divines had articulated after the Civil War.[51] They became identified with the effort of recreating a society that would be recognized as similarly godly as the ideals for which the Confederacy fought. These values cannot be understood to be merely "religious" or "cultural" if by those terms one means that which would not influence public life or legal systems. If these values would find new expression in self-consciously fundamentalist religious communities, they would likewise often be brought toward the support of legal inequity established through segregationist Jim Crow laws, and extrajudicially in the thousands of Black men, women, and children who were lynched.[52]

These convictions conditioned the response of many Southern Christians to the early civil rights movement, even in leaders who advocated for a "moderate" position on racial issues and who displayed a reticence to accept full integration as defined by the federal government as biblically sanctioned. For example, L. Nelson Bell, the eventual father-in-law and close advisor to Billy Graham, wrote following the 1954 *Brown v. Board of Education* Supreme Court ruling, "Until the attempts to *force an unnatural situation* are stopped there will be no right solution. . . . There is nothing Christian or natural in *manufacturing* situations for forced relationships whether those relationships be with people of the same race, or some other race."[53] Carl McIntire, a prominent Southern Baptist leader, was more explicit in a letter to President Lyndon Johnson upon the passage of the Civil Rights Act of 1964:

> At this point we are being told that human rights, therefore, are better and greater than private rights and property rights, and to enforce these so-called superior human rights the federal government takes authority. . . . We are very sensitive to increasing federal direction and control over the lives of all our people. We want nothing to interfere with the free exercise of religion, our freedom of speech, and then the reserved rights under the Constitution as individuals, and also to us as States, are a part of the ingredients of liberty. . . . It appears to many of us that what you are asking us to do is to accomplish by law and police force and federal authority that which can only actually be accomplished by the grace of God and the love which God wants us to have for each other.[54]

In these responses from Bell and McIntire, one can see the expression of sentiments whose roots drew from decades of social, theological, and political suspicion of the federal government with respect to Southern Christians and Christianity. The suspicion of the use of "human rights" as a means to legally leverage changes in the structure of Southern and American society was looked upon as impinging on other rights that these Christians deemed to be "natural."

These new measures—legally encoded in the *Brown v. Board of Education* decision and in the Civil Rights Act—were believed to cut against what seemed to these Christians as the natural, biblical, and, therefore, godly structures of Southern segregation. It seemed unnatural to both McIntire and Bell to have the federal government intervening in matters that ultimately had to do with the work of God's grace within the human heart. One decidedly gets the impression from McIntire's response that he was quite sure God's grace would not likely move in such a direction, as it would be out of alignment with the testimony of Scripture. It is these rhetorical moves, which are reminiscent of Southern defenses of racial segregation in the post–Civil War South, that historian Eugene Genovese dismissed as "arguments grounded in politics rather than Scripture."[55] Bell and McIntire, of course, saw the matter differently, perhaps because in their view the Bible (or a "biblical worldview") had come to encompass a web of meaning from which particular biblicist arguments were not as easily extractable as they may seem to have been in the Antebellum South.

One can also observe in the quotes above a sense of how many of these Christians understood America to be a Christian nation that upheld natural rights—such as freedom of religion or individual property rights—that they believed derived from the Bible.[56] They then juxtaposed this vision against perceived legal incursions into it by the federal government. Such a vision of American society served as a counterpoint to communist societies abroad, which were seen to attack both religious institutions, as well as those aspects of society that were believed to naturally accompany religion. Some conservative American Christians, like McIntire, were suspicious of the use of human rights language within the United States, seeing it as a means to erode the freedom of religion. Other American Christians, looking abroad, used the language of human rights and freedom of religion to leverage political power in coming to the aid of beleaguered brothers and sisters in Christ.

Efforts to Aid Eastern European Christians

Human rights language seemed to some American Christians as undermining their freedom of religion within the United States, but this was by no means true of all American Christians. Some leveraged the new international legal rights-based system in order to assist, rescue, and even evacuate persecuted Christians and Jews, especially those living behind the "Iron Curtain" of communism in Central and Eastern Europe.

Efforts on this front built upon transatlantic business and religious networks that can be traced to at least the early twentieth century. These networks of Christian businessmen and church leaders shared broad religious convictions based around a theologically conservative interpretation of scripture and an ideological commitment to democracy and capitalism.[57] Within the United States, these networks were united with a burgeoning Judeo-Christian ideology that held this religious tradition was foundational to Western democratic societies.[58] Even if the rhetoric of "Judeo-Christian" sounded somewhat more ecumenical (in its inclusion of Jews, at least), it could also capture a skepticism of the formal ecumenical efforts of the World Council of

Churches. The case of Richard Wurmbrand, a Romanian Lutheran pastor, shows how these various ideas—of nominal and true Christianity, of persecution and human rights, of Judeo-Christian society and godless communism, and of competing forms of ecumenical imagination—came together and impacted how American Christians understood the suffering of Christians worldwide in the mid-twentieth century. In using a metaphor from the Apostle Paul, American Christians began paying particular attention to their "brothers and sisters in Christ," viewing them as part of the same metaphysical "body of Christ" (1 Cor. 12). Such theological imagery drew their sympathies toward intervening to help fellow Christians suffering under communist regimes.[59]

Wurmbrand's fierce demeanor would broker no compromise with communism, and he eventually spent fourteen years imprisoned on charges related to his Christian ministry and convictions before he was ransomed by a network of Protestant businessmen and Christian leaders in America and Europe. He then made his way to the United States, where he became something of a celebrity due to his vivid descriptions of the brutal ordeals he endured while imprisoned. In May 1965, Wurmbrand recounted his tortures in communist prisons before a Senate internal security subcommittee before going on to publish his experiences in his popular memoir, *Tortured for Christ*.[60]

First appearing in 1967, *Tortured for Christ* quickly sold "more than 3,000,000 copies," as one early edition proclaims. Though the book is part autobiography and part survivor memoir, its heart is ideological. Wurmbrand is desperate to make the case to the American public of the true stakes of the battle against communism: "Behind the walls of the Iron Curtain the drama, bravery and martyrdom of the Early Church are happening all over again—now—and the free Church sleeps."[61]

Wurmbrand's diagnosis is not simply rhetorical. It is also analytically important because it allows him to further distinguish between what he believes to be essential to Christian faith and that which is only concerned with "non-essentials." It is the "underground church" or the "persecuted church" that is most akin to the early church. The underground church, as Wurmbrand describes it, is not coterminous with any particular denomination or tradition. He calls it the "naked" church that can have "no lukewarm members," which is what he imagines the early church was also like; and like the early church, the underground church has "no elaborate theology." He dismisses much of theology as merely "truths about the Truth," whereas in prison he learned to live in only the Truth, which is God.[62] Other religious chaff was burned away in prison, where Wurmbrand said of Orthodox prisoners that there were "no beards, no crucifixes, no holy images," and yet "they found they could get by without all these things by going to God directly in prayer." The persecuted church necessarily leaned Protestant, in Wurmbrand's estimation.[63]

As was the case among the first Christians who did not have many Bibles, in prison, writes Wurmbrand, the "Bible is not well-known." While Wurmbrand, in fact, had memorized quite a lot of the Bible in multiple languages, he says that there came a time during his imprisonment when "hungry, beaten and doped, we had forgotten theology and the Bible."[64] He believes that this forgetfulness ultimately gave Christian prisoners a purer faith—a fascinating statement coming from an evangelical pastor. It also allowed a different kind of spiritual and mystical immediacy, made possible by forgetting that the "outside world" existed at all. It was this combination that made the faith of the persecuted church more authentic and closer to that of the first-century Christians.[65]

It is in the persecuted church in communist lands, according to Wurmbrand, that one can see "the Early Church in all its beauty, sacrifice, and dedication."[66] Persecution, therefore, erased history, making context irrelevant. Persecution also juxtaposed the authentic faith of those who were victimized against what Wurmbrand took to be the languid indifference of Western churches. Never one to understate a point, Wurmbrand claims, "I suffer in the West more than I suffered in a communist jail because now I see with my own eyes the western civilization dying."[67] In Wurmbrand's descriptions of the persecuted church one can easily see what Melani McAlister has termed "enchanted internationalism," or the belief that there is a purer, more authentic faith to be encountered overseas, in the churches of poor, persecuted, or simply non-Western Christians.[68] An orienting philosophy of Wurmbrand's later work on behalf of the persecuted church would take as its spiritual grounding Hebrews 13:3: "Remember those who are in prison, as though you were in prison with them."

Through Jesus to the Communist World, the organization Wurmbrand later founded, he focused upon the evils of communism and highlighted the vast disparities of faith and freedom that existed between the communist and the free worlds, between the "West" and the "persecuted church."[69] This distinction is also found in the literature of the Voice of the Martyrs (VOM), the organization that Wurmbrand used to rebrand his efforts in the early 1980s. In VOM literature, as in Wurmbrand's memoirs, the visceral, physical brutality of persecution—the inflicting of violence upon Christian bodies—is the focus, and it is a focus that conditions the nature of the organization's work. VOM, generally speaking, does not use its literature to highlight violations of religious freedom within the United States or Western Europe. Rather, it sees such things as rather categorically different from the direct, physical suffering of Christians due to their faith or identity, predominantly in communist and Islamic countries. In such an imagination of global Christianity, the expected role for Western Christians is to join in prayer and spiritual solidarity with persecuted Christians worldwide. It assumes, in short, that persecution is "over there" and that Western Christians should join in prayer, aid, or imaginative solidarity with persecuted Christians.

In referring to Christians, VOM uses language that is less doctrinal and more metaphorical, preferring to speak of "brothers and sisters in Christ" or of "the body of Christ" rather than of denominational creeds. Those who experience persecution that is related to their Christian faith, community, or identity are therefore determined to have had genuine faith, regardless of the tradition or denomination they might belong to.[70] Though VOM uses the genre of Christian martyrdom to tell the stories of contemporary persecuted Christians, and often pairs these contemporary instances with ancient accounts of Christian persecution, their sensibilities also change the very tradition that they are drawing from. Whereas martyrologists such as Eusebius or John Foxe wrote of their martyrs as embodying the faith of their tradition (against pagans or Catholics, respectively), groups such as VOM use martyrs to forge an understanding of Christianity that does not neatly cohere to any particular Christian tradition. In fact, Wurmbrand spoke of the ways that the austerities of prison life stripped away the ritual of Orthodox and Catholic tradition; he claimed that in doing so, they were moving towards a purer form of Christian faith.

The idea of the persecuted church carries with it the assumptions of a man who, because of his sufferings, claimed he had "experienced a new form of Christianity, the kind where Christ's love conquers all." This "new form of Christianity" shapes the modern idea of the "persecuted church" itself. The largely nondogmatic, nondoctrinal assumptions of the "persecuted church" are essential to the later mobilization of the 1990s and early 2000s around the issue of anti-Christian persecution because they are premised upon the idea that a global Christian identity transcends geography, confession, and even doctrine.[71]

Since the 1950s, many American Christians have shared concerns about the fate of religious communities under communist regimes, including Christians living in the wake of the Chinese Cultural Revolution, or the fate of religious minorities in the USSR. Western Christians had long been aware of the persecution that Christians and Jews had experienced behind the Iron Curtain. It was, in fact, the fate of Soviet Jewry rather than Soviet Christians that coalesced American Jews, Christians, and human rights activists to pressure the U.S. Congress to pass the Jackson-Vanik Amendment in 1974. The legislation restricted trade with nations that did not adhere to a market economy or allow free emigration. The amendment responded to the USSR's imposition of restrictions that directly targeted Jews wishing to immigrate to Israel. This mobilization showed the possibility of a broad coalition of religious and secular constituents to agree on protecting the rights of Jews in the USSR, where, in Melani McAlister's terms, "human rights, religious freedom, racial persecution, and the Cold War intersected powerfully."[72] It was largely those American Christians who championed the cause of international religious freedom as well as the persecuted church in the 1970s who would later affiliate themselves with the Religious Right of the 1980s. Indeed, this ecumenical political action would serve as a kind of model for the politics of religious persecution that Christian activists hoped to develop well into the 1990s and early 2000s.[73]

The concerns that mobilized the Religious Right in the late 1970s had been brewing for decades and included opposition to the ending of school segregation, the consequent federal incursions into Christian educational institutions, the *Roe v. Wade* Supreme Court decision, free market economics, and a general fear of the consequences of the sexual revolution and a liberal turn in American public life. Many, though not all, of these issues were articulated in relation to a concern about the erosion of religious freedom in the United States.

Fears of incursions into religious life by the federal government in the 1970s sounded similar to those lamentations heard in the era of Reconstruction and in the Jim Crow South.[74] Carl McIntire had earlier articulated this connection in the passage quoted above: "We are very sensitive to increasing federal direction and control over the lives of all our people. We want nothing to interfere with the free exercise of religion."[75] What constituted the free exercise of religion could be expansive. Indeed, the establishment of Christian academies across the South in the wake of the *Brown v. Board of Education* ruling used the logic of the First Amendment and the rhetoric of religious freedom in an attempt to maintain a racially segregated and stratified society.[76] These conflicts often found their way into the courts, and the general principle of religious freedom upon which these decisions were made had broad Christian support that extended well beyond the American South. For example, when Bob Jones University was threatened with the loss of accreditation over its prohibition of interracial dating and marriage, a case that eventually made it to the Supreme Court in 1970, the National Association of Evangelicals (NAE)— the largest ecclesiastical body representing evangelicals throughout the United States—issued an *amicus curia* on the university's behalf, stating, "The ominous threat to religious freedom posed by the decision of the court below compels us to submit this brief. . . . We would not submit this brief on behalf of the University if we had reason to believe that its professed religious beliefs were being used to mask invidious discrimination. . . . Left intact, the decision of the court below will inevitably be used to justify subordination of religious belief to current notions of public policy."[77]

The NAE used similar language when it wrote again to the U.S. Supreme Court on behalf of the Worldwide Church of God (WWCG) later that decade. The WWCG was registered as a religious organization, but the state of California had placed a judge in receivership of it, meaning that the state had acted to remove a religious leader, Herbert Armstrong, as head of a religious organization. In an autobiographical description of the controversy written by one of the leaders of the WWCG, the author concludes with a dire warning that was certainly felt by other Christians in the late 1970s: "Nearly two hundred years later, the need for these [First Amendment] guarantees is more urgent than ever. The wall [between church and state] must stand. If it cracks and shatters, subjecting a small church to State-dictated control and limitation, the state of California will be free to proceed against other churches, synagogues, and religious institutions of all kinds. And then? Once the dike cracks in California, the flood will engulf all of America. The guarantees of the religion clauses of the First Amendment will float away in the torrent."[78] The NAE, joining with a number of other religious organizations, again used the language of religious freedom to defend the WWCG. In an *amici curiae* petition to the U.S. Supreme Court in October 1979, these groups summarized the severity of the threat: "Amici believe that it is not just the rights of the Worldwide Church of God and its members that are threatened by the State of California's action, but those of every religious body and every American. They are concerned that the Attorney General's claimed power to supervise religious institutions will, if upheld, have drastic consequences on traditional religious freedoms and will point the way toward the adoption of state established standards of religious observation and practice."[79]

The threat posed to Christian organizations was further made real in evangelical Christians' minds with the controversy that was occasioned by the application of Title IX to institutions of higher education. Title IX refers to a section of the Education Amendments Act of 1972 that states, "No person in the United States shall, on the basis of sex, be excluded from participation in, be denied the benefits of, or be subjected to discrimination under any education program or activity receiving Federal financial assistance."[80] Title IX is probably most associated with its effects upon women's collegiate sports, but it was not primarily directed at athletics.[81] Universities, colleges, and governmental officials debated the extent of Title IX's reach. Grove City College, a Christian liberal arts college in Pennsylvania, inquired in 1976 whether it needed to fully comply with Title IX across the institution, even if the only federal aid it received came in the form of student grants and loans. The ensuing legal battle likewise made it to the U.S. Supreme Court in 1984 in *Grove City College v. Bell*, which offered an interpretation of Title IX that favored the college, requiring that only admissions and financial aid offices needed to comply with Title IX requirements.[82]

The ruling so curtailed Title IX's interpretation that the U.S. House of Representatives quickly acted to restore Title IX to its pre–*Grove City College v. Bell* status. Due to stalling in the Senate, however, it would not be until 1988 that Congress passed the Civil Rights Restoration Act over President Ronald Reagan's veto, thereby expanding Title IX to encompass the whole of institutions rather than merely the admissions and financial aid offices. Senator Jesse Helms (R-NC) cautioned against the expanded interpretation of Title IX by echoing fears voiced by evangelical Christians in the earlier case of the Worldwide Church of God: "This bill would give the federal government, through several agencies and bureaucracies, the authority to require disruptive affirmative action plans and other unreasonable programs at all levels of state and local government as well as colleges and private enterprises. Moreover, its enactment would pave the way for more control over the lives of American citizens by federal judges."[83] Grove City College, however, ultimately decided not to accept any federal funds or permit its students to use federal financial aid.[84]

There is a perception that the ascendancy of the Religious Right in the 1980s and early 1990s focused American Christians' attention heavily upon the fate of the nation's soul. The movement did mobilize around the perception that the federal government would erode the rights of American Christians without concerted push back, arguing that a "moral majority"—comprised of conservative Christians across denominations and traditions—must rise up and defend the spiritual core of the nation. But this narrative neglects the ways that the movement and its constituents understood themselves globally, including around issues of religious persecution. The evangelical magazine *Christianity Today*, for example, published a number of articles on the devastating effects that the Chinese Communist Revolution had had upon Christians there.[85] Additionally, many conservative evangelicals had joined in the campaign to ensure the release of the so-called Siberian Seven. The success of this mobilization of a broad swath of conservative Christians—Catholics and evangelicals included—meant that many saw in the triumph of the "free world" in the dwindling Cold War further evidence of America's providential role in God's global intentions. That is to say that religious freedom had a distinctly nationalistic ring to it, and many American Christians tended to view this freedom as inherent to American society. At the same time, of course, given the examples described above, they certainly viewed this freedom as being under threat at home. By the mid-1990s, they would join in campaigns attempting to draw attention to the more severe threats to Christians' freedoms abroad.

The 10/40 Window

The Cold War internationalized Americans' consciousness to violations of religious freedom, especially those occurring under communist regimes. The symbolic and political ending of the Cold War ushered in a period of global optimism and interconnectedness—that the world would become "flat."[86] NGOs championed the implementation of the UN's Millennium Development Goals, which they believed would lift former colonial territories out of the mire imposed by structural readjustment programs of the 1970s and '80s. By the end of the decade, the dot-com boom of California's Silicon Valley sought to make good on the earlier promises set forth in the League of Nations or United Nations, fostering connection and understanding among the world's peoples with a vision that was predominantly secular in orientation and that seemed to assume the gradual waning of religion and religious belief in individuals' lives and world affairs.

Even as some political scientists proclaimed "the end of history" (and the consequent triumph of the liberal world

order), others observed an impending "clash of civilizations," defined in religiopolitical terms.[87] Indeed, by the
middle of the 1990s, it had become clear to many American
Christians that though the communist bloc may have disintegrated, what was emerging in its place did not exactly suit
them either. American missionaries had long worked underground in countries such as China, or in parts of Eastern
Europe or the Middle East.[88] The stories these missionaries
sent back to the United States from those regions frequently
highlighted the repression, denials of full religious freedom,
and hardships converts and indigenous Christians might
encounter in their daily lives, such as arbitrary arrests, van-
dalism, corporal punishment, and murder. These accounts
were similar to the stories that had galvanized widespread
public support for humanitarian aid campaigns among the
Armenians in the early twentieth century.

The new literature on global Christian persecution that
emerged in the mid-to-late 1990s collected these stories and
focused them in two important ways. One, while instances
of repression from communist countries persisted (including
especially North Korea, China, and Vietnam), the narrative
increasingly shifted toward "radical Islam" as the chief perpetrator of excessive human rights and religious freedom
abuses against Christians. These stories were geographically
centered upon a region that became known as the "10/40
Window," which referred to a swath of countries between
the 10th and 40th parallels, many of which have large Muslim populations. As Melani McAlister notes, "Officially,
the 10/40 Window was a map of (missionary) opportunity;
in practice, it was also a work of moral and political geography."[89] That is, the term allowed Christians to map the
world according to spiritual need and political action, especially those regions in which Islam was the predominant
religious tradition. Note the echoes of Suzanne Moranian's

observation that due to missionaries, following the Armenian Genocide, "America had assumed the moral mandate of the Near East."[90] Two, the publicizing of these stories drew heavily from both the ancient genre of Christian martyrology and the more recent literature on humanitarian aid, thereby fusing the fight for human rights with the devotional sensibility that Christian martyrs have long fostered. The prophets of Christian persecution proclaimed that the world was living through a Christian apocalypse of unprecedented proportions, much of it focused within the 10/40 Window.

The story of global Christian demographics in the late twentieth century was not simply about a seemingly relentless movement to eradicate Christianity. These decades also witnessed a tremendous shift in the global composition of Christianity (taking an encompassing sociological definition of the term that includes every tradition from Mormons to Syrian Orthodox). Scholars at the Center for the Study of Global Christianity (CSGC) had been developing methods to quantify the global Christian population since the 1960s. Their data showed a tectonic shift that likewise had been noticed by attentive historians and contemporary observers on the ground. In 1900, approximately 90 percent of the world's Christians lived in North America or Europe. By the year 2000, the number of Christians in Africa, Asia, Latin America, and the Pacific Islands had grown so substantially as to constitute approximately two-thirds of the global Christian population.[91]

The reasons for this shift are legion and are the subject of a robust scholarly literature. Some scholars focused upon the important role that translated Christian scriptures and liturgies played in these "younger" churches.[92] Others noted the development of indigenous Christian leaders and church structures, including the expansion of Christian traditions whose origins lay not in Western missionary churches but rather in local prophetic and healing movements.[93] And still others saw in the late twentieth century the emergence of global Christian networks that created opportunities for trans-national community, education, and sharing of resources.[94] The upshot of these developments is that, in the words of the historian and missiologist Lamin Sanneh, "Christianity has not ceased to be a Western religion, but its future as a world religion is now being formed and shaped at the hands and in the minds of its non-Western adherents."[95]

What this shift means for the sake of my argument is that many of these Christian communities, though numer-ous in sum, nevertheless often remained minority commu-nities within their national contexts.[96] Furthermore, the demographic shifts showed not simply the proportional growth of existing denominations, but also the proliferation of independent, evangelical, and Pentecostal expressions of Christianity. These Christians often lived in theological and cultural tension not only with their non-Christian neigh-bors, but also with non-Pentecostal (or non-"born again") Christians, a reality that was described briefly in the sec-tion above on Armenian Christians.[97] In these ways, one can observe how two contrasting narratives—one of global Christian diffusion and demographic success, and another of global Christian persecution and catastrophe—were interlocked and, in some sense, simultaneously pointing to truths observable through the same available data. Both narratives were largely understood in theological terms. On the one hand, global Christian expansion seemed to replicate the cosmopolitan diversity of the book of Acts and the later theological debates of the fourth and fifth centuries.[98] On the other, Christian persecution was taken up as evidence of Christians' perennial suffering for their faith; in the fresh blood of these new martyrs were the seeds of a global church.

The anecdotes that filled the anti-Christian persecution literature from the mid-1990s onward drew heavily from more ancient martyrological genres and Christian theological vocabulary. Indeed, it was not simply that American Christians were turning their backs on fellow Christians, but that, in doing so, they were denying themselves the spiritual communion with those Christians overseas whose lives were filled with the same spiritual power and miraculous potential as the martyrs of Christianity's first centuries. The stories, like their ancient precedents, focused upon the innocence and injustice experienced by individuals, the staid faith that they displayed in the threat of torture, hardship, and death, and the righteous purity of their faith. Absent from these stories are most features of historical contextualization, beyond the basics: religious identity, nation, and the identity of the perpetrator(s). The focus, therefore, moves away from contextual understanding and toward the injustice of what transpired or the spiritual purity of the truths the Christian(s) stood for.

Take, for example, the case of Mary Khouri, a Lebanese Christian whose story was retold in *Jesus Freaks*, a modern remake of *Foxe's Book of Martyrs* published by VOM. Like the dozens of other martyrdom accounts contained within the volume, Mary's story is told in a couple of hundred words, focusing almost exclusively upon her faith. Mary was a teenager during the Lebanese Civil War (1975–1992) when "the leader of the Muslim fanatics who had raided their village waved his pistol carelessly before [the faces of Mary and her family]. His hatred for Christians burned in his eyes." Even with this direct threat and an invitation to avoid violence through converting to Islam, Mary chose to remain a Christian, at which point the man shot her and the rest of her family. She was found two days later, "the only one [of her family] still alive. But the bullet had cut her spinal cord, leaving both her arms paralyzed. They were stretched out from her body and bent at the elbows, reminiscent of Jesus at his crucifixion." Her story ends with her promise to make her life "a prayer" for Muslims. It is telling that on the next page is a quotation from the Apostle Paul (Rom. 12:19, 21, NLT): "Dear friends, never avenge yourselves. . . . Don't let evil get the best of you, but conquer evil by doing good."[99]

Here one can see the ways in which persecuted Christians are presented in a terse genre that draws directly from ancient precedents. Mary and her family are righteous, their persecutors irrational in their hatred. They refuse to recant their faith and suffer the consequences, the effects of which literally connect Mary's suffering with the crucified Christ. Throughout, their innocence is unquestioned and unquestionable. Associating Mary's forgiveness with the verses from the Apostle Paul then directly contrasts what is perceived to be pure Muslim hatred with Christian forgiveness and pacifism. Details of context (Lebanon, a general date, names, religious identities) are kept to a minimum, seemingly as assurances that the event happened, while the weight of the story lies with the spiritual truth it is meant to convey, the purity of the Christian's faith in the confrontation of good and evil. Nothing more is said about the conflict, with the verses from the Apostle Paul's letter to the Romans serving as assurance that Mary was representative of Christians during the Lebanese Civil War. Not mentioned, for example, are the horrific massacres committed by predominantly Christian militias against Palestinian and Lebanese Muslims in the refugee camps of Sabra and Shatila in September 1982, during which as many as several thousand non-combatants were killed, with some having Christian symbols carved into their bodies.[100]

In these ways, and with these elisions, Mary and other Christian martyrs of the 10/40 Window, much like

Wurmbrand and the underground church of the USSR, became imbued with a purity of faith that can only be seen due to the injustice of the suffering they experienced. Their lives (and deaths) are reduced to apocalyptic terms in which Christians can only be innocent, leaving no space for contingency, guilt, complicity, or even the suffering of non-Christians in these same contexts. Suffering Christians are presented as the incarnation of the spiritually pure early church, or even of Christ himself. And it is in relation to the pure Christian faith of persecuted Christians that American Christians are invited to see themselves.[101] A later VOM devotional publication that focuses upon Christians "facing Islamic extremists" makes clear the juxtaposition between the faith as imagined in the 10/40 Window and that of most American Christians: "The Christians being persecuted for their faith in Muslim countries aren't surprised by the reality of sacrifice in their lives. 'After all,' they would have every right to say to us, 'the Bible has told us we would be persecuted. It is an honor to suffer for Christ.' . . . Our brothers and sisters have counted the cost, and they willingly offer themselves to Jesus every day, always living with the knowledge that they may pay the ultimate sacrifice with their lives. What about you? . . . Are you willing to sacrifice everything, if need be, for the cause of Christ?"[102] Despite the attention that these activists hoped to draw the American Christian public to, they often implied that the suffering of Christians overseas—at the hands of Muslims, or at the hands of the Chinese or North Korean governments—was categorically different from that encountered by Christians within the United States.[103]

Such claims were not made in a social or cultural vacuum. The sentiments of a looming destruction of Christian America, of an apocalyptic confrontation between the righteous and the unrighteous, of the dire conditions faced by

Christians worldwide seemed to be confirmed by the 9/11 terrorist attacks.[104] But as the 9/11 Commission Report stated, "The most important failure was one of imagination."[105] It is with respect to the imagination of threat, therefore, that much literature on Christian persecution has focused. This threat has moved in at least two different directions. On the one hand, it has resulted in the proliferation of the ubiquity of possible threats within the United States—a "See something, say something" form of democratized surveillance. The threat seemingly posed by Islamic terrorists within the United States was of a similar kind with that posed from within.[106] In an editorial segment on the "war on Christmas," Fox News host Bill O'Reilly observed that "the USA cannot defeat terrorism and any other evil without a strong, traditional foundation that clearly defines right from wrong. The struggle today is not about Christmas, but about the spirit of our country."[107] But the threat posed to Christians by "Islamic extremists" also resulted in an imagined identification with beleaguered Christians overseas in the 10/40 Window, with the idea that on 9/11 Americans were experiencing something of the daily realities of Christians under Islamic rule. One can see how subtly these perceptions can blur into one another in a short excerpt from a VOM book set titled *I am N.* (The "N" stands for Nazarene and is representative of the Arabic letter "nun," which was painted on the property of Christians living under ISIS): "When Abu and his family members were forced to leave their homes in ISIS-invaded cities of Iraq, it was because of one identity alone: Jesus Christ. . . . In our culture, standing firm in Christ doesn't result in torture or death, but it can have sobering consequences, as business owners and others will attest.[108] Yet it is a matter of allegiance, isn't it? We have been so overwhelmingly loved by our Savior that we can't help but pledge our undying love to him."[109] While making their suffering visible to Americans, passages like the one above have also turned Christians overseas into politicized devotional objects whose experiences and faith are dramatically reduced merely to having been persecuted. We learn little more about them besides the fact that they are persecuted "over there." This is where McAlister's observation that the 10/40 Window was a "work of moral and political geography" again becomes salient.

It is ironic, therefore, that some of the very Christians of the 10/40 Window who have been the objects of these efforts often seem to chafe uncomfortably under the helping hand of others. In an early and influential article on the subject for the *New York Times Magazine*, Jeffrey Goldberg wrote of American Christians' efforts in the mid-1990s to advocate for persecuted Christians in the Middle East and elsewhere. The article opens with a scene shared by both Nina Shea and His Eminence Lufti Laham, the patriarchal vicar for the Orthodox Melkite Church in Jerusalem. "When Shea mentions martyrdom," Goldberg writes, "Archbishop Laham lets out a sigh." He would later walk over to a table that held Shea's book, *In the Lion's Den*, along with Paul Marshall's *Their Blood Cries Out*, and lament, "These titles are not helpful."[110] The archbishop seemed to be recoiling not only at the incendiary wording but at the reduction of his church's ancient tradition to the present issues Christians like him face.

Marshall and other early writers on this topic were clear that Christians do not face a single threat worldwide, nor are they subject to even similar disadvantages globally.[111] But they were clear that Christians should be understood as victims. In fact, however, one sees a wide range of responses by Christians across the globe to experiences of persecution. The Coptic Christians in Egypt have developed a robust international network among Christians and lawmakers in the United States. Other groups of Christians—for example, in Indonesia, Nigeria, and Sudan—have at times taken up arms in response to violence. Furthermore, in some cases, such as in Ethiopia, Eritrea, and parts of Eastern Europe, Catholic and Orthodox churches, who often have a close relationship with the state, can be agents of persecution of independent, evangelical, and Pentecostal churches.[112]

In their efforts to bring global Christian suffering to Americans' consciousness, antipersecution activists have made visible the faith and experiences of Christians overseas that would likely otherwise have gone ignored. But these efforts have also limited the scope of how Americans see the faith of these Christians, which is viewed exclusively through the lens of persecution. This can lead to a circumscribed view of Christianity both in its local and global contexts. In focusing upon those Christians who have been persecuted, their persecution—rather than their traditions, lives, beliefs, or even responses—moves to the center of what we know of them; nearly all else is occluded. By default, the view of global Christianity created by these antipersecution efforts therefore becomes an ecumenical one, overlooking differences of ethnicity, tradition, and theology in favor of collecting instances of anti-Christian persecution. It is this process that leads to evangelical Americans championing the case of Roman Catholic Nigerians attacked by Boko Haram, or of Catholics lamenting the persecution of the Assyrian Church of the East in Syria and Iraq. If some American Protestants were suspicious of the ecumenical movement and the establishment of the World Council of Churches in the early twentieth century, their spiritual descendants have developed their own forms of ecumenism that at least tacitly acknowledge some common Christian identity and faith in traditions that they had viewed as nominal, deficient, or otherwise less than true Christianity.

The presence of Christianity in the New World has seemingly always been fraught. It took hardly any time at all for Puritans to begin lamenting the spiritual state of their settlement.

While lamenting the state of American churches is among the most historically common American Christian pastimes, the recent cries voiced by many American Christian leaders have been raised in the context of the decline in the number of Americans identifying as "Christian" (and the rise of the religiously unaffiliated, those known as "nones," and the related category of the "spiritual but not religious"). These cries reached a fever pitch in the wake of the Supreme Court's 2015 *Obergefell v. Hodges* decision that resulted in the legalization of same-sex marriage in the United States. The court's decision became a revelatory moment for Russell Moore of the Southern Baptist Convention, who wrote in June 2015, "We see that we are strangers and exiles in American culture. . . . We should have been all along."[113] Moore suggests that perhaps the Mayflower Compact was a bad deal after all. By 2016, a substantial percentage of American evangelicals reported that they found American society becoming "more difficult" for them. Nothing less than the viability of Christianity in America seemed to be at stake. But of course, it was a sizeable contingent—81 percent by some measures—of Moore's evangelical "strangers and exiles" who contributed to Donald Trump's presidential victory the following year. As James Dobson expressed in a message of support for Alabama's 2017 GOP Senate candidate Roy Moore, "Last November I believe God gave America another chance with the election of Donald J. Trump." The revivalist's altar call is simply the flip side of his jeremiad.[114]

Perhaps the ubiquity of Christianity in America has, ironically, contributed to a sense of absence, loss, or estrangement, at least for some white American evangelicals, among other conservative and Orthodox Christians.[115] This estrangement has left many of them, not simply Russell Moore, feeling "exiled" in America. David Congdon observes that the ubiquitous use of the theme of "exile" among contemporary white American evangelicals "offers an alternative to the 'culture war' rhetoric of the Religious Right. Instead of a church at war with surrounding culture, a church in exile presents a vision of God's people living peacefully within foreign territory."[116] And that territory, in a physical, cultural, and spiritual sense, is the United States of America.

The fact that, to these Christians, America was "their nation," makes this vision all the more alienating. By the end of 2016, American evangelicals would have their "dream president," as Jerry Falwell Jr., a prominent evangelical leader and son of the noted Baptist preacher, put it.[117] Falwell and others juxtaposed that president against his predecessor, Barack Obama, whom Tony Perkins, now chair of the Council on International Religious Freedom, once deemed responsible for a global increase in Christian persecution.[118] The search for a truer, more authentic Christianity among the "persecuted church" is one result of these ventures. But this feeling of being strangers in their own land is not exclusive to a post–2008 or post–2016 presidential election America. Rather, the sentiment is of a piece with strands of American Christian (especially Protestant) thought in the eras of Reconstruction, Jim Crow, and civil rights, and in the mobilizing ideology of the Moral Majority of the 1980s and '90s. This is the political consciousness fostered by the destruction or erosion of an early, godlier, society.

In this chapter I have sought to show how issues of domestic and international religious freedom have long been related to one another for American Christians rather than being distinct. In this sense, whatever conceptual wall may have existed between the "war on Christmas" and the "global war on Christians" has been dissolved in recent years. One could point to the near simultaneous claim by President Trump that "we're saying Merry Christmas again"[119] with his administration's attempts to "save" Middle Eastern Christians, or of the appointment of Tony Perkins, long a figure of domestic religious freedom issues as the director of the Family Research Council, to head the Council on International Religious Freedom as evidence of this interweaving. In this sense, the "war on Christmas" and the "global war on Christians" have become part of a common imaginary, a feeling voiced by the car salesman I described in chapter 1, that "it's becoming harder to be a Christian." With that feeling, American Christians have joined a global community of suffering.

Along with the dovetailing of domestic and international religious freedom issues is the gradual expansion of the imaginary of concern with respect to other Christians. From the mid-1990s, a new ecumenical understanding of Christianity has been worked out practically and politically. This understanding is based in the conceptual transformations in which Christians of various traditions overseas have essentially become truly Christian in the eyes of American Christians by the fact of their having been persecuted. It is important not to take this development for granted, and its significance can be viewed in contrast to earlier periods of Christian history. For example, one might contrast earlier Catholic and Orthodox responses to the rise of Islam and its impact upon "heretical" Eastern Christians with John Allen Jr., a Catholic journalist, who includes violence against contemporary non-Trinitarian Christian sects as evidence of a global war on Christians.[120] Indeed, what might sixteenth-century Protestant Reformers make of evangelical Protestant uses of the suffering of

Catholic Nigerians at the hands of Boko Haram? What of Richard Wurmbrand's attempts to make visible the suffering of Christians under communist rule by explicitly critiquing the "tradition" in those Christian traditions? In these examples, one can see that confessional tradition has been sublimated in favor of a leveraged common, nondogmatic "Christian" identity, and it is against this perceived common identity that the global war is believed to be waged.[121]

4

A Global War on Christians?

On April 29, 2014, an account associated with the Islamic State (ISIS) tweeted pictures of public crucifixions that ISIS soldiers had carried out in Raqqa, Syria.[1] Those executed were identified as "spies," and their religious identity was not known with certainty. But the brutal use of a Christian symbol resonated with the repression Christians had faced in areas controlled by ISIS. ISIS's violence was so severe that a United Nations commission established in 2016 that ISIS had engaged in genocide against Christian minorities in Syria and Iraq, as well as against Yazidi and Shia Muslims.[2] In light of the grotesque severity of events such as the public crucifixions, as well as various data that attempt to quantify Christian persecution, many Christians and a variety of media have concluded that Christianity is the most persecuted religion in the world, or that there is a "global war on Christians."[3] It has been common in recent years to find social media stories of anti-Christian violence in Africa, Asia, and even the United States by using the hashtag #christiangenocide.

This chapter is not an analysis of particular instances of repression, persecution, or genocide, and I want to be clear that I am not questioning the truthfulness of particular reports of anti-Christian violence. Rather, in this chapter I review the processes by which many Christians in the late twentieth and early twenty-first centuries came to understand that they belonged to a religion that is under global assault or duress. I am interested primarily in two things: (1) the evidence that is used to claim that Christianity is the "most persecuted religion," perhaps having as many as several million martyrs since 1990, and (2) how this conviction has impacted American Christians' view of Christianity as a global community of faith.

The New Politics of Persecution

From the halls of the U.S. Congress to European human rights organizations, Christians have been described as being under attack worldwide.[4] The violence many Christians are experiencing has been made visible due to the documentary work of predominantly Christian researchers, activists, and nonprofit organizations. Since the mid-1990s, a string of books, articles, reports, and, more recently, social media hashtags have sought to make clear the reality of global anti-Christian persecution. Publicizing the harsh realities that many Christians face has its origins in what activists viewed as the neglect of religious persecution against Christians among human rights groups and the media in the 1980s and '90s.

Though there had been international action around issues of religious freedom as early as the 1920s, advocates for persecuted Christians argued that the issue and idea of international religious freedom had become politically occluded by the 1990s. It was, in fact, religious refugees from the USSR who created transnational networks, motivated by a desire to ensure religious freedom for those who were being persecuted, Soviet Jewry in particular. Christians in the West facilitated the emigration of Soviet Jews in the 1970s and '80s, and developed their own networks and methods for helping their co-religionists escape from behind the Iron Curtain.[5] For example, Richard Wurmbrand (see chapter 3) was ransomed and fled through mission networks such as those provided by the European Christian Mission.[6] Those Christians who fled the USSR or other communist countries due to religious persecution became living testaments (or in some cases "living martyrs") to communism's hostility toward religion. In these ways, they argued that the United States could take a different path, positioning itself as "one nation, under God"—a preserver of the "Judeo-Christian tradition."[7] Humanitarian ecumenism was created here in the name of international religious freedom.

Atheistic communism had provided not only an ideological specter against which American domestic politics were contested, but it also produced a certain mental mapping of the world. In this sense, the world became divided into communist and free. For Christians in the West, the challenge was logistically twofold, as they sought to help those Christians in the "underground church" in communist lands, as well as, in some cases, to evangelize communists. Yet, while Christians had mobilized on behalf of Soviet Jewry in the previous decades, Michael Horowitz excoriated Western Christians in the 1990s who had been "so inert and inactive about the suffering of their fellow believers."[8]

Despite some of the efforts that had been made to assist other Christians overseas using the framework of human rights and religious freedom, by the mid-1990s, a contingent of American Christians felt that the level of concern exhibited by their American co-religionists and secular human rights groups was dwarfed by the magnitude of the problem of global anti-Christian persecution. The mid-1990s saw the publication of a number of pamphlets, books, and editorials on the subject of global Christian persecution, efforts that were supported by institutions such as the Institute on Religion and Democracy, Open Doors, Aid to the Church in Need, and the Voice of the Martyrs. This new strand of activism made two fundamental critiques. To one side, the activists argued that a secular ideology among human rights organizations had led to the marginalization of instances of religious persecution, especially those pertaining to Christian persecution. To the other side, these new activists charged fellow Western Christians with neglecting the suffering of their brothers and sisters in Christ who were enduring extraordinary levels of hardship due to their faith.

Those who sought to mobilize American Christians and the American public claimed that the global persecution of Christians was among the most pressing human rights issues of their time. One of the seminal texts that made this case, Nina Shea's *In the Lion's Den*, opens with a stark statistic that would seemingly become gospel truth within a few years: more Christians had been killed for their faith in the twentieth century than in the previous nineteen centuries combined. This claim was elaborated upon in journalistic detail by Paul Marshall in an equally influential text, *Their Blood Cries Out*. The reasons that this rampant persecution and suffering had been ignored by American Christians and the larger world community were several. American Christians, activists argued, had become preoccupied with domestic politics, including domestic issues of religious freedom. Furthermore, they contended that American Christians claimed persecution for things that were, in a broader scale, trivial: there could be no comparison between the criticism experienced by Christians in the United States and the brutal repression faced by Christians in countries such as Sudan.[9] They pointed fingers at a secular world order and human rights NGOs that seemed to not take seriously the enduring presence of religion, religious identity, and religious persecution in the modern world. They criticized a narrative that Christians could only be the persecutors (as in the Crusades, Inquisition, or witch trials), as if these past experiences categorically excluded Christians from being victims at some later point. They lambasted the Washington establishment under President Bill Clinton for not taking up global Christian persecution as a priority in foreign policy.[10]

Calling attention to the global persecution of Christians—whose religion was long associated with the Western world—did not necessarily fit with the generally optimistic geopolitical ethos of the 1990s. Advocates nevertheless pressed their case to American Christians as well as to the U.S. Congress, and their efforts gained a hearing. From the outset of *Their Blood Cries Out*, Paul Marshall makes the stakes clear: "[Anti-Christian prejudice in the United States] could simply be dismissed as my own whining if it weren't for the brutal fact that this prejudice is a barrier to recognizing the suffering of hundreds of thousands of [Christian] children, women, and men worldwide."[11] Marshall goes on to document, often in graphic detail, the "massacre, rape, torture, slavery, beatings, mutilations, and imprisonment" of contemporary Christians overseas.[12]

The politicization of global Christian persecution was not simply left to think-tank conferences. American Christian cultural products carried these messages into the public, especially among evangelical Christians. One can point to examples such as Ray Boltz's 1995 music video, "I Pledge Allegiance to the Lamb," or the following year, to DC Talk's "Jesus Freak" music video. In both cases, contemporary (American) Christian persecution is placed in a deep historical and spiritual framework of previous persecutions (the early church and the Reformation for Boltz, the Armenian Genocide and totalitarian governments for DC Talk). Both videos were imbued with a foreboding sense of a persecution about to be unleashed upon American Christians. It is no accident, therefore, that the Voice of the Martyrs' revised volume of *Foxe's Book of Martyrs*, titled *Jesus Freaks*, opens not with a story of St. Stephen or another early martyr but rather with the story of Cassie Bernall, whose death at Columbine High School in Littleton, Colorado, was attributed to her affirmative response to the shooter's question: "Do you believe in God?"[13]

Cassie's story is notably the only one from the United States included within the volume, but it unquestionably frames the whole of the remaining accounts of martyrdom for American audiences. If martyrdom shows the perennial and ahistorical conflict between good and evil, then there would be no reason to think that such persecution and suffering could be avoided within the United States, much less the contemporary world. Texts like *Jesus Freaks* were published for Christian audiences, while churches were organized around events such as the International Day of Prayer for the persecuted church. First held in 1996 with 5,000 churches and organizations participating, it grew to 70,000 the following year.[14]

The work of activists such as Shea and Marshall had not only taken hold in U.S. churches but had also caught the attention of U.S. congressmen, notably Sam Brownback (R-KS) and Chris Smith (R-NJ). They held hearings on the issue of anti-Christian persecution from 1995, iterations of which continued into the 2010s. Indeed, Senate Concurrent Resolution 71, passed on September 17, 1996, opens with the following statement: "Whereas oppression and persecution of religious minorities around the world has emerged as one of the most compelling human rights issues of the day. In particular, the worldwide persecution and martyrdom of Christians persists at alarming levels." Along with a similar resolution passed in the House of Representatives, the Senate resolution acknowledges the "Statement of Conscience and Call to Action" passed by the National Association of Evangelicals (NAE) in January 1997, in which the NAE requests that the Immigration and Naturalization Services of the United States "process the claims of escapees from such [anti-Christian] persecution with priority and diligence."[15] In turn, the Senate and House resolutions resolve to "initiate a thorough examination of all United States' policies that affect persecuted Christians." By 1997–1998, two different bills were making their way through Congress that sought to address the issue of global Christian persecution. Of the two, the Wolf-Specter bill was more strident, providing for the prioritization of Christian minorities with respect to immigration. Even some advocates for victims of persecution worried about its consequences, including the "emptying out" of Christians from the Middle East.[16] In 1998, the International Religious Freedom Act (IRFA) became law, which established the U.S. Council on International Religious Freedom (CIRF) as well as the creation of an ambassador of international religious freedom.

The activism of the new defenders of Christian religious freedom worldwide was premised upon the perceived disproportionality of anti-Christian persecution. They had a particular eye toward the "advancing jihad" of Islam as a threat to religious freedom in general and to Christians in particular.[17] Contrary to the claims of secular theorists, they argued that religion was indeed enduring and even increasing in global importance such that it deserved to be a national foreign policy priority. But what this should look like was caught in an ideological struggle. Was all of Islam a problem for religious freedom? Or was it selective "radical

Islamic fundamentalists"? Cynically, selected allies of the United States, such as Saudi Arabia, were repeatedly exempted from the list of religious freedom abuses that was compiled as a result of the IRFA. And while CIRF's broad language of religious freedom seemed nonbiased, it was criticized early on for an undue privileging of persecuted Christians. The first ambassador for religious freedom, Robert Sieple, an evangelical who had bipartisan support, left the position because the initiative was "conceived in error and delivered in chaos."[18]

Activists such as Marshall framed anti-Christian persecution as a "worldwide tragedy" in 1997, as indeed it was. His efforts were premised upon the conviction that Westerners were broadly ignorant of the severe human rights abuses against Christians who lived as religious minorities overseas. The events of 9/11 and the subsequent "war on terror" seemed to confirm this analysis, but it also introduced a new sense of imminence, a more pervasive and omnipresent threat. It is on this subtle but important conceptual point that the persecution of Christians went from being a "worldwide tragedy" to a "global war." While John Allen Jr. describes the perpetrators of this "war" as being atheists, communists, Hindus, Buddhists, Muslims, and fellow Christians, one finds that the imagination of the problem is often revealed in simpler dictums, such as in then-presidential candidate Donald Trump's musing, "I think Islam hates us."[19] Such a confession is evidence of the triumph in the American Christian imagination of earlier efforts to define the 10/40 Window as an object of political and spiritual action.

What follows in this chapter is an analysis of evidence on three main points: statistics used to describe Christianity as being severely persecuted in the late twentieth and early twenty-first centuries, the use of these statistics in combination with specific stories, and the proportionality of religious violence against Muslims and Christians, respectively. In pursuing this analysis, I want to make absolutely clear that I am not calling into question the factualness of instances of anti-Christian or anti-Muslim persecution. Rather, my critiques are with the ways in which statistics and stories have become incorporated into narratives that I think are detrimental to the larger purposes they purport to serve.

Counting Christian Martyrs

The quantification of Christian persecution has become central to political efforts on behalf of persecuted Christians. For example, Marshall opens *Their Blood Cries Out* by describing the "spiritual plague" that "affects over two hundred million people, with an additional four hundred million suffering from discrimination and legal impediments."[20] While the scale of the issue has most often been portrayed with numbers, the severity of the persecution is often depicted in the use of singular, horrific accounts of anti-Christian violence. Making the case for persecuted Christians has depended upon a combination of stories and statistics, a method that can create a sense of the global pervasiveness of the persecution.

Large numerical claims have been a consistent part of the tactics for making anti-Christian persecution visible and convincing since the 1990s, when the Center for the Study of Global Christianity at Gordon-Conwell Theological Seminary (CSGC) began tracking annual numbers of "Christian martyrs." The most recent statistics released by the CSGC claim that there have been, on average, 90,000 Christian martyrs per year over the past decade. For the first decade of the twenty-first century, the CSGC estimated 105,000 per year. And for the 1990s, the rate was even higher, claiming as many as 164,000 Christian martyrs per year. These statistics were not relegated to policy reports or white papers but were incorporated into devotional literature. The front jacket flap of the 1999 edition of *Jesus Freaks* reads, "There are more Christian martyrs today than there were in AD 100—in the days of the Roman Empire. Now in the twenty-first century, hundreds of thousands of Christians are martyred around the world every year." And before going into Cassie Bernall's story, the book states, "According to the *World Christian Encyclopedia*, there were close to 164,000 Christians martyred around the world in 1999. An estimated 165,000 will be martyred in 2000."[21]

How can one account for these sobering rates of Christian martyrdom?

The CSGC has been tracking global religious demographics for decades. It estimates the number of martyrdoms from an aggregate total of deaths classified as "martyrs" over a decade and then divides that number by ten to get an annual average across a decade. As other scholars have noted, to get the dramatically high numbers of 90,000 to 164,000 martyrdoms, one must include deaths with a wide range of causes from a wide variety of conflicts, including civil wars, state failure, and ethnic violence.

The CSGC defines martyrs as "believers in Christ who have lost their lives prematurely, in situations of witness, as a result of human hostility."[22] This definition uses the key phrase "in situations of witness" to expand the notion of martyrdom that one would find in early Christian or Reformation-era martyrologies. This qualification is then used to count a wide variety of deaths as "Christian martyrdom." The CSGC's high tallies of Christian martyrs not only have included *all victims* from the Rwandan Genocide (CSGC accepts the Rwandan government's claim of just over one million Tutsi killed), but also a significant percentage of the reported "5.4 million" deaths from the subsequent wars in the Democratic Republic of the Congo (DRC) between 1996 and 2010. Because both of these conflicts have contributed substantially to the alarmingly high numbers of Christian martyrs over the last three decades, they deserve a closer look.

On April 6, 1994, a plane carrying the Rwandan president, Juvenal Habyarimana (a Hutu), and the Burundian president, Cyprien Ntaryamira, was shot down as it approached the Rwandan capital city of Kigali. This event became the catalyst for Hutu extremists to carry out a plot to eradicate the minority Tutsi population from Rwanda. Over the following three and a half months, several hundred thousand Tutsi were killed, along with some moderate Hutu. Determining a precise number of those killed in such a conflict is enormously challenging and fraught with a variety of methodological obstacles.

The Republic of Rwanda's National Commission for the Fight against Genocide claims that there were "1,070,014 Tutsi killed in only 100 days."[23] This is both a high estimate as well as a definition of the genocide's toll that specifically excludes "moderate Hutu," who are usually included in scholarly descriptions of the genocide's victims. These subtle differences are essential in the context of the current Rwandan regime, which has unquestionably politicized the memory of the genocide.[24]

A lower estimate of 800,000 total victims of the genocide is a commonly cited figure. It is significant that the report of the United Nations' independent inquiry into UN actions with respect to the Rwandan Genocide begins with this statement: "Approximately 800,000 people were killed during the 1994 genocide in Rwanda." It goes on to define these deaths as a "systematic slaughter" of both Tutsi and moderate Hutu in the roughly one hundred days of the genocide.[25]

Though the independent inquiry commissioned by the UN does not discuss its methodology, an extensive report from Human Rights Watch (HRW) assesses that the figure of 800,000 includes deaths indirectly attributable to the genocide, such as from malnutrition, illness, or disease. Basing its estimates off of demographic research conducted, respectively, by Gérard Prunier and William Seltzer, HRW reaches a more conservative conclusion that "at least a half a million persons were killed in the genocide," but it does not dismiss Seltzer's higher estimate of 657,000. Even the lower figure would mean the annihilation of approximately three-quarters of the estimated 1994 Tutsi population.[26] Similarly, Marijke Vanpoorten believes 512,000 to 662,000 victims of the Rwandan Genocide to be a reasonable estimate.[27] It is worth noting here that Vanpoorten's analysis includes an estimate of the pregenocide Tutsi population. But even her higher estimate of the *total pregenocide Tutsi population* is nearly 200,000 people less than the Rwandan government's claim of the total number of Tutsi killed between April and July 1994.

These vast disparities are directly relevant to the task of quantifying Christian martyrdoms, because the CSGC takes the highest estimation (1 million) as not only a reliable figure but also as one that counts, in its entirety, toward the rate of "Christian martyrdom" in the 1990s. For example, if one were to take a more modest estimate of 600,000 genocide deaths, this alone would reduce the CSGC martyrdom statistics (estimated at 154,000 to 164,000 per year for the 1990s) by nearly 30 percent.

Removing the 1 million Rwandan Genocide deaths entirely from the CSGC calculations would result in a reduction of approximately 100,000 "martyrdoms" per year across the 1990s. In an article describing their method for establishing a high rate of martyrdom, Todd Johnson and Gina Zurlo argue that the high rate of martyrdom in Rwanda is intended to reflect the fact that a large number of people were slaughtered as they sought refuge on Christian church property. This act, in their view, placed the Tutsi in a "situation of witness" at the time of their death, which is a component of the definition of martyrdom the CSGC uses in its calculations of annual Christian martyrdom. But even the estimates of how many people died in a particular place are fraught with the complex politics of postgenocide Rwanda, as Timothy Longman has convincingly demonstrated.[28] Arguments in favor of a reasonable reduction in the number of victims from the Rwandan Genocide, therefore, would severely reduce the number of Christian martyrs, even if one were still to accept all of the genocide's victims as "martyrs," which is a problematic claim, as I will describe below.

DEMOCRATIC REPUBLIC OF THE CONGO

Nicholas Kristoff, a columnist for the *New York Times*, opened a 2010 op-ed by stating, "Sometimes I wish eastern Congo could suffer an earthquake or a tsunami, so that it might finally get the attention it needs. The barbaric civil war being waged here is the most lethal conflict since World War II and has claimed at least 30 times as many lives as the Haiti earthquake."

If one accepts estimates that the 2010 Haiti earthquake resulted in 230,000 deaths, that would put the death toll for the wars in the eastern DRC at around 6.9 million lives at the time of Kristoff's writing.[29] In what is probably the most frequently cited statistic of the war, the International Rescue Committee (IRC) claimed that there were 5.4 million deaths attributable to the war between 1998 and 2007 (with the remaining 1.5 million deaths in Kristoff's claim coming from 2007 to 2010).[30] The IRC's statistic produced the talking point that Kristoff and many others used to try and convince American audiences that they were bystanders to the "most lethal conflict since World War II."

Because the CSGC counts 20 percent of the DRC war's victims as "Christian martyrs," it is worthwhile to ask how reliable these figures might be in the first place. As with the Rwandan government's claimed death toll from the Rwandan Genocide, the number of 5.4 million deaths between 1998 and 2007 appears to be a very high estimate. The IRC's numerical claim followed from the use of a low prewar crude mortality rate for eastern Congo. A crude mortality rate (CMR) is arrived at by dividing the total number of deaths in a territory in a given period of time (usually measured by month or year) by the total population of that territory. (A low CMR would mean fewer deaths in that time, while a high CMR would mean many deaths.) Since the CMR directly affects how one quantifies the war's impact upon mortality, it determines how many people have died in "excess" due to the wars in the DRC. Statistics such as the death toll of a conflict can vary widely because they often quantify indirect civilian deaths from malnutrition, disease, and the failure of public health institutions, among other factors.[31] What follows are several paragraphs regarding the complexities of quantifying death in the DRC. While these are more technical, keep in mind that the data discussed below is directly relevant to how recent rates of Christian martyrdom have been estimated.

Joshua Goldstein observes that, in order to get 5.4 million victims of the wars, the IRC used a CMR that was an average for all of sub-Saharan Africa in 1998. One of the main problems with this starting point, Goldstein argues, is that the gross domestic product (GDP) for sub-Saharan

Africa, according to the World Bank, was $1,950 per person per year. Congo's GDP, by comparison, was $280 per person per year. Such a dramatic economic difference would have direct bearing on the DRC's CMR, making it significantly higher than in comparatively wealthier regions of the African continent.

According to Goldstein's analysis, one does not see a low CMR in eastern Congo before the outbreak of the war and a spike after the war's inception. Rather, if one accounts for a higher CMR (reflective of the region's economic poverty) before the start of the war, then one would see a less severe spike after the war's outbreak than the IRC has claimed. As a result, deaths attributable to the war would lower substantially, even to the point of being cut in half. Estimates that use a higher prewar CMR for eastern Congo claim that the wars resulted in approximately two million deaths (compared with the 5.4 million claimed by the IRC). The vast majority of these deaths are also indirectly attributable to the violence, meaning that they occurred as a result of disease, malnourishment, or preventable infection.[32]

There is a similar disparity with respect to estimates of violent deaths directly attributable to the wars, but the numbers are far fewer than the above estimates of indirect mortality. Even the IRC's numbers, which Goldstein has criticized for being too high, state that violent deaths account for a mere 0.4 percent of the total mortality. This rate means that, according to the IRC, only 21,600 of the 5.4 million lives lost due to the conflict are regarded as violent deaths. While the IRC's overall estimate of 5.4 million lives might be high, its estimate of 21,600 violent deaths is well below those deaths counted by a UNHCR mapping report that examined direct violent deaths in eastern Congo from 1993 to 2003. From July 1996 to June 2003, the report confirmed 45,278 deaths directly attributable to violence.[33]

To return to the broader estimates of the war's impact upon mortality in eastern Congo, one finds that the war disproportionately impacted the very young. An article by lead author Benjamin Coughlin, who also worked on the IRC study referenced above, concluded that 47 percent of deaths in eastern Congo from January 2006 to April 2007 involved children under the age of five. Coughlin's data included regions that were not impacted directly by the violence in the eastern region of the country. Even still, the study concluded that the CMR remained high throughout the DRC, despite the supposed ending of the war in 2004.

The most common causes of death identified in Coughlin's study were "fever/malaria, diarrhea, respiratory infections, tuberculosis and neonatal conditions." Measles and "preventable infection" also accounted for a significant percentage of deaths in children under five.[34] It was clear that child mortality remained a serious health issue throughout the country in ways that could not be attributable to the violence in the eastern region of the country.[35] What this could mean, though the Coughlin study does not make this claim, is that a very large percentage of the IRC's estimated 5.4 million victims—perhaps as many as 47 percent, or 2.54 million lives—were children under age five who died as an indirect result of the wars.

Let us return again to the relevance of these statistical analyses to the larger question of how Christian martyrdom is quantified. The only way that the CSGC can claim there were over 100,000 Christian martyrs per year in the first decade of the twenty-first century is if one accepts 20 percent of a *high estimate* of Congolese war deaths as being Christian martyrs. Citing IRC numbers, the CSGC states that it takes 20 percent of "4 million" excess deaths (that is, 800,000) in Congo from 2000 to 2010 as being deaths in "situations of [Christian] witness."[36]

It is important at this point to bear in mind three things. First, the definition of martyr used by the CSGC explicitly "*excludes* deaths through accidents, crashes, earthquakes, illnesses, or other causes, however tragic."[37] What the CSGC aims to count are not only incidents that include people overtly testifying to faith in Jesus Christ at the time of their death, but also instances in which "their actions in such situations [in which they were killed] were grounded in, and therefore witness to, their faith."[38] Second, even though it is clear that eastern Congo has been undergoing severe disruption and violence, the number of direct, violent deaths (i.e., those *directly killed*) has been estimated, respectively, by the IRC and the UN at between 20,000 and 45,000 persons for different periods of the conflict. Even if these are regarded as conservative estimates, they represent a very small fraction of the 800,000 counted as martyrs by the CSGC. Third, other scholars who have critiqued the CSGC's high numbers of martyrdom have done so on the assumption that the CSGC numbers capture direct, violent deaths. For example, when Thomas Schirrmacher criticized the CSGC's numbers, he had in mind instances like a church bombing, which could kill people in the church who were visiting but who might not identify as Christian.[39] My analysis above shows that the CSGC statistics are not primarily populated with incidents like church bombings but rather with indirect deaths that should be excluded from the data set based upon the stated definition of "martyr" the CSGC claims to be using.

Following from these observations, one might consider that nearly half of those counted as martyrs (approximately 400,000) between 2000 and 2010 were, statistically speaking, children under the age of five who died due to malnutrition, diarrhea, and infectious disease, among other "indirect" causes, with a large percentage of the remaining

800,000 being older youth or adults who died due to similar causes. The basic point that I wish to make here is that the CSGC's figure of 800,000 Congolese martyrs is a claim that is directly contrary to its own definition of who "counts" as a martyr. Of course, if one were to find a lower estimate of excess deaths from the conflicts, in the range of two million total deaths, to be a more reasonable statistic than 5.4 million, then one would also need to make a similar reduction in the CSGC method of calculating martyrs from the conflict.

Let me be clear here that I am not questioning whether people in Congo (or, in 1994, Rwanda) have endured violence, or whether immense suffering has been experienced and continues to be experienced in eastern Congo. Even the lower reasonable estimates (of 500,000 victims in Rwanda or two million excess deaths in Congo) remain tragically immense. The question here is not whether people have suffered, but rather how that suffering ought to be made visible to Americans, and to American Christians more specifically. Should these deaths be regarded as Christian martyrdoms? If so, why?

It should be fairly obvious at this point that in order to categorize the large numbers of victims from both Rwanda and Congo as "Christian martyrs," one needs to have a definition of "martyr" that is expanded well beyond its Christian theological origins (as discussed in chapter 2).

Statistics and Stories

In both Rwanda and Congo, of course, there have been examples of people whose Christian faith has led them to put their lives at risk for the sake of others or to take a moral stand at the cost of their lives. It is undeniable that the scope of the violence has been horrific, but the question here is whether it is accurate and appropriate to cite the dramatically high figures derived from these conflicts as evidence that there is a global war on Christians costing over 100,000 lives per year.

What I am arguing in this section is for a separation of these stories of horror and trauma from the large statistical claims that are used to contextualize them. In questioning the statistical claims that have been used to quantify Christian martyrdom or Christian persecution, I am not claiming that these specific stories are contrived or fabricated.

Using numbers from either the Rwandan Genocide or the wars in the DRC as statistical evidence of a global war on Christians risks glossing over the fact that the majority of the perpetrators of both conflicts were themselves statistically Christian and that neither conflict can be understood primarily as a battle against Christians or Christianity as such. In fact, one might find quite the opposite, at least in the case of Rwanda, where the Catholic Church was deeply complicit in the establishment of an ethnically based Hutu government.[40] Among the most egregious stories are those in which church officials betrayed Tutsi who had sought shelter on church property.[41] I am sympathetic to Johnson and Zurlo's observation that one must take the Christian faith of the slaughtered Tutsi into account, just as one must take the Christian faith of the Hutu perpetrators into account in assigning blame. Their contention, however, risks overlooking the fact that quite often victims were encouraged to congregate en masse in places like schools, churches, stadiums, and government buildings by perpetrators, who could then centralize the act of killing.[42] But to frame these atrocities as comprising a major part of a global war on Christians neglects how these conflicts are embedded in complex international politics in addition to how ethnicity, resource allocation, regional politics, and other factors have contributed to the development and perpetration of severe violence in the region. And, after the genocide, one also finds that the wars in Congo were fueled and sustained by Tutsi militia (supported by Rwandan president Paul Kagame's regime) searching out Hutu who had fled Rwanda.[43]

Removing all deaths from the Rwandan Genocide and the war in Congo from CSGC's statistics immediately reduces the number of Christian martyrs by approximately 2.5 million over the past thirty years. Simply removing the Congo deaths in the early twenty-first century would reduce the annual rate of martyrdoms from around 100,000 per year to under 20,000, even if one otherwise retained a broad definition of "martyr." Still, news reports continue to repeat claims that in a recent ten-year span "1 million Christians were killed for their faith."[44] As the previous section made clear, a small proportion of these lives were lost due to direct violence.

Who is waging the "war on Christians" in Rwanda and the DRC? Demographically speaking, it is much more likely to be a Christian than someone of another faith. According to the Pew Research Center, just over 96 percent of the DRC is considered to be Christian, a percentage that includes Catholic, Protestant, Pentecostal, and other Christian traditions.[45] Similarly, the overwhelming majority of Rwandans (approximately 90 percent) were considered Christian (the majority of those Catholic) at the time of the 1994 genocide.[46]

Given the circulation of high statistical claims being made about contemporary Christian martyrdom amid the post-9/11 "global war on terror," one often finds a connection made between claims of Christian martyrdom and Islamic extremism. A number of news articles on the subject of Christian martyrdom or global Christian persecution begin with an image that either shows or implies violence committed against Christians by Muslims. These stories make the large statistical claims believable by tying them to undeniable, heartbreaking, and specific atrocities, such as the one this chapter began with.

Over the past decade, for example, Christian news sites have frequently featured headlines such as the following: "'Deny Christ or Die,' Boko Haram Tells Young Christian Woman."[47] The narrative of these stories is that Boko Haram is primarily and fundamentally an anti-Christian movement whose purpose and goal is to eradicate Christians and Christianity, and that Christians, who are persecuted solely because of their faith, are wholly innocent. This is not to say that people in central and eastern Nigeria are not experiencing violence or that Boko Haram is not inflicting violence on Christians there. It is to suggest that this violence has been presented and understood through Christian categories and theology. The result is often an evocative fuzziness in relating specific stories of persecution to statistical claims.

The above narrative neglects the fact that Goodluck Jonathan (a Christian) acceded to the Nigerian presidency through deeply controversial means and that for years before the formation of Boko Haram there were Christian militias organizing in Nigeria's middle states, with one Christian militia alleged to have killed a thousand Muslims.[48] According to Nigeria Watch, the clear majority of Boko Haram's attacks have not been against religious targets but rather against police outposts, government buildings, businesses, and public areas such as bus stations. Nevertheless, Christian news outlets and writers purvey the narrative of righteous Christian innocence and a fundamentally anti-Christian movement in Nigeria.[49]

Take, for example, Johnnie Moore's recent book, *The Martyr's Oath*, which is about global Christian faith and persecution aimed at a broad Christian audience. In introducing several stories from central and eastern Nigeria, Moore writes that Boko Haram is "far more lethal to Christianity than ISIS, to whom Boko Haram has pledged allegiance. Human rights advocates note that Boko Haram killed 6,644 people in 2014—more than even ISIS did."[50] The statistic here is for "people," though Moore's phrasing seems to suggest that these are, perhaps, mostly Christians. In a later chapter, Moore claims that Boko Haram has "focused *almost exclusively* on Christians, whereas ISIS's bloodlust has been extended to all other religious communities in Iraq and Syria."[51]

The first statistic is simply ambiguous; the second one is refuted by evidence provided by Nigeria Watch, which has been tracking comprehensive deaths in Nigeria since 2006. Nigeria Watch records not only that a majority of attacks by Boko Haram have targeted locations such as bus stops, markets, or government-associated buildings, but also that the majority, and perhaps even a significant majority, of the victims have been Muslim rather than Christian. To be fair, Moore later observes that "terrorism and extremism has killed more Muslims than anyone else," though this is never quantified or compared to the statistics provided on Christian deaths.[52] Moore's use of statistics is not coherent or systematic with respect to data or methodology, but that is to miss the purpose of the data in his book. The data here give an impression of sociological support for an underlying apocalyptic theological conviction: There is "a real spiritual war happening," and "Satan himself is playing for keeps," which can be seen in the fact that "[Islamic extremists] are growing stronger; we [American Christians] are growing weaker."[53]

The apocalyptic style and terse, testimonial content of those who, like Moore, advocate on behalf of the "persecuted church" owe much to the literary style of a long line of

Christian martyrologists. One could mistake large swaths of John Allen Jr.'s *The Global War on Christians* or parts of Moore's *The Martyr's Oath* for Eusebius's *Ecclesiastical History* or John Foxe's *Book of Martyrs*. All offer a series of decontextualized snapshots of individuals or small groups who faced opposition, oppression, and even death.

This decontextualization, at least in Moore's case, has a spiritual rationale: "The enemy would like nothing better than for us to keep our focus on our physical circumstances or on our enemies."[54] The use of "our" here is interesting because it implies that American Christians share in this persecution, or at least share a common "enemy" with those Christians who are being persecuted.[55] The remedy to this "real spiritual war" is a kind of globalized politics, in which Christians are reminded in the face of this persecution that "the only thing that truly stops this hatred is the contagion of changed hearts."[56]

Very much *unlike* earlier Christian writers such as Eusebius or Foxe, however, contemporary advocates for persecuted Christians tend to cast a wide net in describing who counts as a "Christian." Those who describe a global war on Christians implicitly adopt a very generous, nondogmatic definition of "Christianity" to cull evidence in support of their narrative. This nondogmatic understanding of Christianity is the result of an "ecumenism of blood," as Pope Francis has termed it, referring to the ways in which a shared common Christian identity is the result of Christians across denominational boundaries commonly being targeted for being Christian.[57] This "ecumenism of blood" also, by virtue of an experience of "persecution," defines as "Christian" those who otherwise might not be regarded as such in a different context. That is, to sustain a narrative of a global war on Christians, it becomes necessary for evangelical Christians to recognize the Christian faith of Orthodox or Roman Catholics, and vice versa.

John Allen Jr. includes non-Trinitarian Christians in Iran to bolster his claim of the global war on Christians (much to Eusebius's chagrin, one imagines). Todd Johnson, who directs the CSGC, argues that Joseph Smith, as well as ancient and medieval Christian heretics, should be regarded as "Christian martyrs." Still, one is hard-pressed to find anecdotes from Allen (or on the websites of relevant advocacy organizations such as Open Doors USA or Voice of the Martyrs) pertaining to Mormons, Seventh-Day Adventists, or Jehovah's Witnesses. These conclusions obviously depend greatly upon how one defines "Christian" or "Christianity" in addition to how one defines "martyr." These differences are not mere matters of semantics. Rather, there are significantly different uses of "martyr" in terms of how persecution is quantified and which stories are told. These differences, which can lead to radically different statistics and conclusions, have seemingly been lost.

This move of including as "Christian" those who experience persecution for their faith or identity has its historical origins in the American Christian responses to the Armenian pogroms and genocide (see chapter 3). But it also begins to place strands of the Christian tradition simultaneously in the role of global persecutor and persecuted. For example, there are Orthodox Christians who oppose Pentecostals in Russia while Orthodox Christians also face violence in Syria.[58] Or Coptic Christians, who have been the focus of much sympathetic Western attention, are also cast as the "enemy" when they oppose evangelicals in Egypt.[59] Or Roman Catholics in Nigeria have had their churches bombed while Catholics in Mexico have become hostile toward evangelicals in southern parts of that country.[60] Or American Christians who were supportive of the Trump administration's efforts to end the persecution of Middle Eastern Christians said little even as the administration deported Iraqi Christians from the United States.[61]

To justify the inclusion of Christian violence on other Christians as evidence of a global war on Christians, John Allen Jr. simply states, "Sometimes the war on Christians is a civil war." But if one uses the high martyrdom statistics from the CSGC, then the last three decades of the global war on Christians would be, numerically speaking, *almost entirely* a civil war.

Comparing Persecution

If one removes the DRC atrocities from the tally of contemporary Christian martyrs, the number drops precipitously for the 1990s and early 2000s. In fact, Thomas Schirrmacher of the World Evangelical Alliance has estimated the number of annual martyrs in this same period to be approximately 7,300, though his exact methodology is not entirely clear.[62] Elsewhere, John Allen Jr., while acknowledging the high CSGC figures, even conceded that there may only be as many as 400 martyrs per year, if one employs a much more conservative theological definition.[63] The so-called global war on Christians, therefore, has between 400 victims and 164,000 victims per year, depending upon one's definition of "martyr."[64]

Allen's goal, however, is not really to track martyrdoms; it is to convince the reader that Christianity *can* be—and is being—persecuted widely. As he states elsewhere, "I think it would be good to have reliable figures on this issue, but I don't think it ultimately matters in terms of the point of my book, which is to break through the narrative that tends to dominate discussion in the West—that Christians can't be persecuted because they belong to the world's most powerful Church."[65]

On this point—making visible a kind of suffering that has often been ignored—I am sympathetic to Allen's goal.

Of course, simply because Christians are powerful in one region does not at all mean that they are equally powerful worldwide. Framing their suffering as a "global war," however, seems to be inhibitive of the supposed goal of easing or ending this suffering. In short, Allen appears to want to have it both ways: to be nuanced and particular in terms of the specific stories that fill his account, while also casting these specific stories in a generic narrative that blankets the globe with anti-Christian persecution. But how do these numbers of Christian martyrdom compare with numbers for other religious groups? Are there other ways that Christian persecution has been quantified? Are Christians disproportionately impacted? The answers to such questions, of course, depend upon where one looks for data.

Open Doors has consistently counted Christian martyrdoms conservatively, often finding between 1,000 and 3,000 annually over the past decade. Its tracking would be regarded by statisticians as a passive tracking, relying heavily upon verified secondhand reports of the details of specific instances. The Pew Forum has tracked some metrics that quantify religious freedom around the globe. Its numbers, both in 2014 and in 2018, measured an "uptick" in "government restrictions on religion." Its most recent report was framed by one Christian publication as indicating that "Christians are the most persecuted religious group in the world."[66] That is true in a sense, but the Pew findings could be interpreted in other ways. Pew found that Christians were "harassed" in 144 countries, Muslims in 142—numbers which, in themselves, do not denote severity. It is also relevant to keep in mind that, although the number of restrictive countries increased and remained nearly even, the number of Muslims worldwide is approximately 73 percent of the global Christian population, making them proportionally more discriminated against.[67]

It is perhaps more telling that there are not really any organizations invested in tracking the number of "martyrs" for other religious communities in the way one finds among Christians. Since Islam is widely regarded as the second-largest global religion, I will make some broad comparative points from available statistics on Muslim deaths. One could point to a source such as the National Counterterrorism Center's 2011 Report of Terror, which stated that in the previous five years (that is, between 2006 and 2011), in instances in which religious identity could be determined, between 82 percent and 97 percent of fatalities caused by terror attacks were Muslims.[68] This is certainly due to the fact that most of the recorded deaths from terrorist attacks in those years were in Afghanistan, Pakistan, Iraq, Somalia, and northern and central Nigeria, countries or regions in which the population is heavily Muslim. This trend continued into 2015, with nearly three-quarters of the 28,328 deaths from terror attacks that year coming in Afghanistan, Pakistan, Iraq, Nigeria, and Syria.

Terrorism, however, is just one form of violence, and many of these countries have a high homicide rate as well.[69] And while deaths from terrorism are not the same as martyrdom, one could make a similar case that victims were targeted for a reason, thus putting them in a "situation of witness" analogous to the definition used in the CSGC's definition of Christian martyrdom.

Using a similar statistical method that the CSGC has used for quantifying Christian martyrdoms, it is possible to reach a similar rate of Muslim martyrdoms in the early twenty-first century. Take a look at estimates of death tolls for the U.S. wars in Iraq, Afghanistan, and Pakistan, and treat them similarly to the way that the CSGC has treated Christian death tolls from mass conflict. Physicians for Social Responsibility has produced a conservative estimate of the total body count (including indirect deaths) of the wars in Iraq, Afghanistan, and Pakistan to be two million people, with some estimates of direct, violent deaths in Iraq (2003–2006) alone going as high as 600,000, according to an earlier study published in the *Lancet*.[70]

To these numbers, one can add 400,000 *direct and indirect deaths* from the war in Syria;[71] 6,000 from the Central African Republic;[72] 15,000 from the war in Libya;[73] 300,000 in Darfur.[74] One could also add to this figure estimates of violent deaths from conflicts in Nigeria (4,400), Mali (300), Indonesia (3,000), Somalia (281,549),[75] and Chad (1,000), as well as death tolls from the Arab Spring uprisings in Egypt, Tunisia, Bahrain, and Yemen (1,550 total).[76] The latter figures above should be regarded as conservative estimates because, with the exception of Somalia, the numbers are limited to confirmed direct, violent deaths in conflict. This combination of data means that there is a higher proportion of direct, violent deaths represented in these figures than in the comparable Christian statistics from the CSGC.

Adding the death tolls from these recent conflicts and their immediate impacts upon the health of these societies amounts to approximately three million Muslim deaths due to conflict from 2003 to 2013, especially if one accepts the higher estimates, as CSGC did with respect to Christian deaths. If one were to take 20 percent of these, as the CSGC has done with Christian figures, and considered them martyrs, then one would get a number of approximately 600,000, which averages out to approximately 60,000 per year over a decade. While that is certainly less than the rate of around 100,000 per year that some Christian-based advocacy groups have used for this period, one should again keep in mind that the global Muslim population is only 73 percent of the global Christian population (taking a very broad definition of each religion).

One could, therefore, use a methodology similar to the CSGC's in order to conclude that Muslims are also being killed or dying prematurely worldwide at a relatively similar (though proportionally lower) rate as some demographers have argued with respect Christians. This conclusion cannot be taken as good news, but it also is not news that can support the claim that Christians are being uniquely targeted or killed at a wildly disproportionate rate over another very large and widespread religious group.

So What?

To these observations, one might ask, So what? What if using hyperbolic statistics for Christian persecution has helped to resolve some instances of religious persecution?

There is no question that some Christians are experiencing severe hardship and even genocidal violence. In 2014, the Islamic State (ISIS) expanded the territory under its control to include parts of Iraq that had sizeable religious minority populations. As early as May 2015, a UN panel on human rights reported that ISIS "may have committed" genocide against the Yazidi, with evidence indicating that they intended "to destroy the Yazidi as a group."[77] So severe was the repression faced by Assyrian Christians and Chaldean Catholics, along with the Yazidi, that the European Union recognized the violence as constituting genocide on February 3, 2016.[78] The United States would do so in a unanimous congressional vote the following month, followed by the U.S. State Department's recognition of the genocide a few days later.[79] Christian advocacy groups were active in campaigning for these public declarations of violence against Christians and Yazidis.[80]

The UN's genocide convention provided the conceptual framework for declaring that ISIS had engaged in genocide, though the violence was not necessarily confined to the years in which ISIS controlled its most expansive territory. Even as recent as 2019 an interim report on Christian persecution to the UK foreign secretary warned, "In some regions, the level and nature of persecution is arguably coming close to meeting the international definition of genocide, according to that adopted by the UN."[81] That same report cited John Allen Jr.'s work on the global war on Christians, along with statistics (discussed above) from Open Doors and the Pew Forum that had quantified aspects of global Christian persecution, such as the number of countries with legal restrictions.

That report had been commissioned in order "make its recommendations for policy and practice" to the UK Foreign Office. But in the United States, where such legal and diplomatic efforts have been carried out since the late 1990s, the effects have been rather mixed. On January 27, 2017, the Trump administration passed Executive Order 13769, "Protecting the Nation from Foreign Terrorist Entry into the United States." While severely curtailing entry from seven Muslim-majority nations, it also made directives "to prioritize refugee claims made by individuals on the basis of religious-based persecution, provided that the religion of the individual is a minority religion in the individual's country of nationality."[82] Such a provision drew directly from the advocacy efforts of anti–Christian persecution activists in the mid-1990s, who then had made the foreign policy proposal to prioritize Christians as religious minorities with respect to immigration to the United States.[83] It was only a few months after this executive order, in May 2017, that Immigration and Customs Enforcement (ICE) conducted raids on Chaldean Christian communities around Detroit, detaining over a hundred people for deportation to Iraq.[84] The State Department issued a statement later that summer that claimed Christians in ISIS-controlled regions of Iraq continued to face genocide.[85] Such dynamics echo the earlier ironies of the international aid efforts extended to the Armenians, some of whom found themselves unable to acquire property in the United States due to legalized discrimination. In doing so, these instances point to the politics of identification, highlighting the importance of considering the conditions in which Christian faith and identity are made to transcend national barriers or reinforce them.[86]

I do not wish to detract from important efforts to ease this suffering or to rectify injustice. Christians' "global war" rhetoric, however, assumes that Christians are always the primary intended target of adverse government policies or violence, a claim that is hard to substantiate in many cases. A U.S. Commission on International Religious Freedom report states that in Indonesia certain blasphemy laws more frequently target Ahmadiyya rather than Christians, as is also the case in Pakistan.[87] And in Iran, there are perhaps several times as many Baha'is imprisoned as Christians.[88]

It was not an unjustly imprisoned Pakistani Ahmadiyya, but Asia Bibi, a Pakistani Christian imprisoned on specious blasphemy charges, who was released after enormous international pressure. And it was not one of the many Baha'is who was released in 2016 after diplomatic pressure, but Saeed Abedini, an Iranian-American evangelical pastor who was imprisoned in Iran. It is doubtful that these Christians would have been freed had not their stories been circulated through networks of Christians who were concerned with global Christian persecution. In these cases, one might argue that good has come from linking specific instances of religious persecution to a general sense that Christians are uniquely and disproportionately targeted.

If select instances of justice for persecuted Christians have come from a concerted international effort to raise awareness about global Christian persecution, herein lie five dangers:

1. *A distorted sense of the proportionality of religious violence.*

   In the case of Nigeria, a report from Nigeria Watch stated that media bias in coverage meant that Christian deaths there were more reported, leading to the impression that Christians faced violent deaths for their religious identity or beliefs at a greater rate than Muslims. This perception, however, was demonstrably false. Elsewhere, Christians and other minorities have undoubtedly been targeted in many instances, as was the case in Syria, with the U.S. State Department declaring that ISIS was engaged in committing genocide against them. Still, by various metrics, one can see that Muslims may experience a greater proportion of violent deaths than Christians and, proportionally speaking, live with greater restrictions on their religious freedom worldwide. Additionally, it would be wrong to simply assume that Christians were targeted for their faith, while Shia, Sunni, and Ahmadiyya Muslims were merely victims of violence rather than targeted due to their religious beliefs or practices. And while bolstering supports for religious freedom can help, it is also the case that American Christians seem to have waning support for guaranteeing the religious freedom of non-Christians.[89]

2. *Western Christians' spiritual obligations to fellow believers become conflated with national foreign policy objectives.*

   Even if one accepts the argument that the United States ought to develop a "tempered" imperial foreign policy in order to protect "minorities" worldwide, there is still no small number of choices that would need to be made as to which minority populations should be prioritized.[90] For example, those advocating on behalf of persecuted Christians have long sought to prioritize Christian minority populations in U.S. immigration—a goal which was policy for a short time under the Trump administration's first draft of Executive Order 13769 in January 2017.[91] Returning to point 1 above, a recent poll conducted among Roman Catholics by Aid to the Church in Need (ACN) found that 58 percent of respondents believed that global Christian persecution is a "very severe" concern. For comparison, climate change was at 57 percent. (The top concerns were human trafficking and poverty.)[92] A direct correlation between very high estimates of Christian martyrdoms and this sentiment cannot be established here, but it does seem relevant that ACN has claimed that Christian martyrdom is happening at a rate similar to that published by the CSGC.[93]

3. *The narrative of a global war on Christians presents Christians worldwide as being primarily victims.*

While many Christians are facing harsh realities, the difficulties they face are not uniform. Many Christians worldwide are responding to poverty, to climate change, to political oppression, to religious opposition, and to famine, to name a few difficulties, and their faith informs how (or if) they respond to these challenges. Christians are not simply sitting and being slaughtered, or passively being taken advantage of. Rather, even in contexts of serious persecution and/or repression, they have found a multitude of ways to respond. In the case of persecution, this response can mean networking with fellow citizens and believers across denominational or religious lines, connecting to international Christian networks, challenging the legality of policies, and even arming themselves to fight back.[94] Christians are not merely victims of violations of their religious freedom or targets of attacks, but rather agents who are also able to respond with the resources of their faith within their local and regional contexts.

4. *Examining particular cases of regional violence and oppression often reveals more complex explanations than simply anti-Christian sentiment.*

Stated another way, would it really help reduce the death rate in eastern Congo to imagine the people there as being victims of a "global war on Christians"? My answer to this is no, because the actual location of the 90,000 to 164,000 Christian martyrs is never (or only rarely) included with the statistic. The statistic separates the martyrs from the places of their martyrdom, ultimately making them decontextualized numbers. John Allen Jr. rightly observes that "two thirds of the 2.3 billion Christians in the world today live . . . in dangerous neighbourhoods. They are often poor. They often belong to ethnic, linguistic and cultural minorities. And they are often at risk. And ultimately I think making that point is more important than being precise about the death toll."[95] But Allen's own rhetoric of a "global war on Christians" is evidence of a tendency to map the world into homogenized identities that makes a more contextualized approach to resolving these issues more difficult. It does matter that these people are Christians, but how their Christian identity or faith relates to their suffering is not uniform, nor are their understandings of their contexts and how they believe they should respond.

5. *A preoccupation with anti-Christian persecution can overshadow the violence committed by predominantly Christian nations.*

The wars in Iraq and Afghanistan surely loom large here, in terms of foreign policy priorities, total lives lost, and the direct consequences unleashed upon Christians and other religious minorities in the Middle East in the succeeding years. But there are less obvious forms of violence, such as the U.S.-backed invasion of Somalia by Ethiopia, or the consequences of U.S. policies with respect to Central American immigration. On a smaller scale, one might point to the armed Pentecostal gangs that have been persecuting religious minorities in Brazil.[96] I am not interested in casting undue blame upon the United States—certainly other nations bear responsibility for the way that they have chosen to treat those who live within their borders. At the same time, however, if one is to presume to act globally, then having a clear global picture of the harms inflicted as well as the justice pursued by a nation is imperative. It is relevant to note here that the Trump administration found itself ignored by those very Middle Eastern Christians it has presented itself as saving.[97]

As Eusebius did in the fourth century (see chapter 2), when Christians speak of their martyrs, they frame conflicts involving Christians as based fundamentally in their Christian belief and/or identity and in their assumption that Christians are wholly and inherently innocent.[98] In part, having recourse to the rhetoric of "global war" reinforces ancient theological notions peculiar to Christianity: you will be persecuted and your persecution will be a sign that you are righteous. The purpose of the statistics, as best I can tell from the ways some Christians have put them to use, are paradoxically both essential and irrelevant. The same point is made using figures of more than 100,000 martyrs per year as is made with 400 martyrs per year over the same chronological span. Statistics of modern Christian martyrdoms (even more modest estimations) help generate this feeling of righteousness.

If we have some reason to be skeptical of Eusebius's presentation of the early Christian martyrs, associated as they were with highlighting Constantine's imperial privileging of Christianity, then we might also have similar reason to be skeptical of those who have followed in his steps. Given how directly some calls for saving persecuted Christians seem to result in military interventions, one wonders whether the blood of today's martyrs may be the seed of American imperialism.[99]

While I think there is truth to this conclusion, I also think it misses an important point. Pope Francis revealed a truth that when someone goes to kill a Christian, they might not first ask if that person is Catholic.[100] Being Christian, the implication goes, is enough. In this sense, one can see that a broader, ecumenical notion of "Christianity"—especially in relation to persecution—is now part of the way that even the most prominent Christian leaders are talking about the faith. This development is due not only to the sociologists of religion who have been using a broad definition of Christianity for decades, but also to Christians themselves, who have reflected upon what the suffering of fellow Christians ought to mean in a globalized world. It is upon this last point that the final chapter will reflect.

5

The Global Politics of the Suffering Body of Christ

Early on the morning of Thursday, May 10, 2018, President Donald Trump greeted three Korean men who had just been released from imprisonment in North Korea and flown to the United States. All three, not coincidentally, were Christians.[1] Later that same day, speaking at the Global Christian Persecution Summit, organized in Washington, DC, by the Institute on Religion and Democracy (IRD), Frank Gaffney reasoned that the three Koreans had been arrested for preaching that "there is some God besides Kim Jong Un." For Gaffney, their release demonstrated that "this Trump administration wants to save persecuted Christians as much as or more than anyone in this room." This was saying something, since the room was filled with several eminent and long-standing activists for international religious freedom, including, among others, Frank R. Wolf, Sam Brownback, and Michael Horowitz.

To look upon the world through the eyes of the conference's panelists and the several dozen people in attendance was to see a world filled with suffering Christians whose duress was being ignored by human rights organizations,

Western nation-states, and the UN. The attendees were already convinced of the reality of global Christian persecution, which was quantified in various ways throughout the day: 215 million Christians are "heavily persecuted," echoing a statistic calculated by Open Doors International; 1.5 million Christians had been displaced from Iraq; there were another 1 million displaced people—many of whom are Christian—in the Nuba Mountains on the Sudan/South Sudan border; "21,000 Christians [had been] killed in Nigeria"; twenty-one Coptic Christians were beheaded by ISIS fighters in 2015; and Andrew Brunson was an imprisoned American pastor in Turkey. Categorizing this wide range of suffering and pain as being "Christian" aggregated these disparate events in order to make them visible. In so doing, these stories and statistics evinced a global anti-Christian pandemic that, the conference maintained, was hidden in plain sight from American Christians, despite more than two decades of activism on the matter. These are the realities that other commenters have asserted amount to a "global war on Christians," though no one at the conference used that specific phrase.

Given this set of facts, the summit was oriented around a pointed question: *Why don't Christians care about Christians?* For the organizers and panelists, the question contained a moral judgment of American churches that bore a striking resemblance to Richard Wurmbrand's strident critiques more than a half-century earlier. American Christians, many speakers lamented, were simply unaware of the "persecuted church"; they failed to grasp the important spiritual reality that "we are one body of Christ" and that a significant percentage of that body was suffering. It was their belonging to a single metaphysical community of the body of Christ that formed the basis for both the judgment and the ethical obligations that were proposed at the summit.

This corporeal metaphor, taken from a variety of New Testament passages (e.g., Matt. 25; Gal. 6) served to make clear a theological truth that the pain experienced by the persecuted church was also the pain of American Christians, for all Christians are "in Christ," and "if one part [of Christ's body] suffers, every part suffers with it" (1 Cor. 12:26, NIV). According to various panelists at the summit, American Christians had become unable to see the suffering body of Christ in the world because of their myopic focus upon denominational differences, a preoccupation with personal salvation, or an acceptance of a "health and wealth" theology of prosperity.

The fact that the suffering body of Christ around the world was invisible to American Christians meant that they could not feel this suffering, and if it could not be felt then it could not be acted upon. In other words, panelists lamented that American Christians had a failure of global imagination. Speaking at the IRD summit, Jordan Allott, a documentary filmmaker, made clear that the visual representation of the persecuted church is crucial in order for Americans to "develop a personal connection" to Christians elsewhere, a connection that will make them "feel like friends or family." Viewing images of the persecuted church could be described in this sense as a "spiritual practice of imaginative identification."[2]

From the mid-twentieth century, the idea of the persecuted church has been inseparable from the images of persecuted Christians. Groups such as the Voice of the Martyrs (not present at the summit) have long distributed jarringly graphic images of tortured and mutilated Christian bodies, always accompanied by harrowing accounts of the genuine faith that endured the brutality. It ought to be noted that over fifty years before, Richard Wurmbrand removed his shirt before a Senate subcommittee in the same building to reveal to U.S. senators "the wounds of Christ" that he bore.[3]

These images of persecuted Christians share much in common stylistically with other photographic genres that attempt to capture and represent pain and suffering, such as is often found in war, humanitarian, or disaster photography. Susan Sontag's *On Regarding the Pain of Others* raises fundamental questions about the direction of this gaze with respect to the capacity of such images to share another person's pain. In both images of disaster and images of persecution, it tends to be "us" in the West who view, passively, the pain of others "over there." For Sontag, such questions evince the gaping distance between an "us" and a "them," a gap that images reproduce more than bridge: "What would they have to say to us? 'We'—this 'we' is everyone who has never experienced anything like what they went through—don't understand. We don't get it. We truly can't imagine what it was like. . . . That's what every soldier, and every journalist and aid worker and independent observer who has put in time under fire, and had the luck to elude the death that struck down others nearby, stubbornly feels. And they are right."[4]

What can we know of the pain of being sold into slavery, of the despair of decades of unwarranted imprisonment, of the horrors of seeing one's family killed—experiences of Christians worldwide that were recounted at the IRD summit? Sontag soberly concludes that the horror of suffering isolates because suffering is ultimately untranslatable. Sontag's conclusion stands in contrast to the assumptions of those who seek to represent the suffering of the persecuted church—through images, stories, or statistics. The gaze that is directed upon the particular suffering of Christians is not the same as that which is cultivated by war or disaster photography. But is there something about suffering due to religious persecution—say, an unjust prison sentence—that distinguishes the suffering from that of those who are imprisoned unjustly for a "nonreligious" reason? Is there something uniquely translatable about suffering endured in religious persecution, or, more specifically, in Christian persecution?

Early Christians were faced with a future that was both precarious and certain. Christ's eminent eschatological victory led them to anticipate a future in which they would be triumphantly welcomed into a holy city where there would be "no more death" (Rev. 21:4). This is a theology that promised salvation to those who would endure to the end. Enduring, especially in the third and early fourth centuries, meant squarely confronting persecution, and Christian martyrs became miraculous examples of extraordinary endurance. Their stories, compelling and singular, made clear the apocalyptic stakes, the confrontation between good and evil that warred for the soul—demanding Christians' capitulation before a recalcitrant empire.

Martyrs helped Christians to see the righteousness of their community, the moral and spiritual purity that was upheld through the integrity and steadfastness of exemplary Christian deaths. These deaths were remembered, preserved, and passed along because of the truths they proclaimed to later generations of Christians. In the wake of Constantine's conversion in the early fourth century, martyrologies took on the double character of both clarifying the devastating evil from which Constantine rescued Christians, as well as the theological truths that the martyrs embodied and adhered to. In these matters, martyrs represented a type of Christ, a sacrifice of pure love for those who were merely fully human and not also fully divine.

To be Christian in the orthodox sense of that term (i.e., those who adhered to the creeds of the fourth- and fifth-century ecumenical councils) meant that one could include martyrs within one's spiritual heritage. These true martyrs were connected to later true Christians—those who adhered to the creeds of Nicaea and Constantinople, and those martyrs whose deaths followed a model that was closest to that of Christ. Martyrs transcended time even as they connected theological truth with Christian memory.

Allowing for some generalizations, these are the models and spiritual inclinations that both Protestant and Catholic reformers inherited and used to cast the persecutions they respectively experienced at the hands of one other. To be sure, neither Catholics nor Protestants nor radical reformers viewed the persecutions and wars of religion that followed the reform movements of the sixteenth century as part of a common war on Christians or on Christianity as such. Rather, their own martyrs served to bolster their claims to be inheritors of the true seed of faith, which they traced ultimately to the early church.

From such a vantage point, it is not difficult to see the dramatic shifts in disposition toward other Christians that various Christian traditions needed to undergo in the intervening centuries since the Reformation. As chapter 4 made clear, both the notion of martyrdom itself as well as the development of a generic, nondogmatic definition of Christianity needed to take place in order to claim that there have been some "1 million Christian martyrs" in recent decades. Furthermore, martyrdom has historically been inseparable from memory: for nearly all of Christian history, there are no martyrs who are not remembered as martyrs. But the new "martyrs" represented in the large statistics exist not as memory but rather merely as data. When I asked some Ugandan Christian (Anglican and Pentecostal) friends what they thought of the fact that an institute in the United States said there were over 200,000 Ugandan Christian martyrs, they let out a disbelieving chuckle before saying that they remembered the early Ugandan martyrs of the

1880s, or the assassination of Anglican archbishop Janani Luwum in 1977. "I don't know anything about the others," one Ugandan friend told me.

Perhaps the move to make martyrdom itself into a statistic makes a certain kind of sense in an age in which metrics have become a new "global sovereign."[5] Statistics like those on annual Christian martyrdom represent what one might call the "collusion of empiricism and the poetic imagination."[6] The numbers give lives—so classified—a meaning that they might not otherwise possess. The way these numbers are employed—the social lives they take on—are almost always in relation to more specific stories. In tragic instances such as the twenty-one Coptic martyrs murdered by ISIS, or of the compelling injustice faced by an individual such as Asia Bibi, one can find a synecdoche of otherwise overwhelming statistics. These numbers and stories, however, do not simply perform analytical work, but theological work as well. The adoption of this high figure of martyrdom represents the ripple of theological shifts and is itself not only indicative of a change in the definition of martyr but in the assumed definitions of Christianity and Christian. Statistics about global Christian persecution are evidence of contemporary theologizing by Christians about their relation to the world. Unlike the early Christians' insistence upon the connection between martyrdom and memory, however, these new metrics of martyrdom do not even allow the possibility of memory. We know them only as noncorporeal numbers.

The theologies and politics of persecution among American Christians might not square with those of Christians elsewhere, including those who are experiencing or have experienced persecution. At the IRD summit, for example, the same "health and wealth" prosperity gospel that was blamed for American Christians' neglect of suffering Christians was never discussed in relationship to Nigerian Christianity itself, where Pentecostal churches preaching a prosperity message have experienced a spectacular growth.[7] In another context, one might recall the scene of the Orthodox patriarch sighing painfully at Nina Shea's framing of the issues his community was facing. In some cases, intervention might be necessary and appropriate, but what seems more pertinent here is to be more attentive to both the local sociopolitical context as well as the variety of Christian traditions present within it in crafting policy responses. Monolithic "global war on Christians" narratives are singularly unhelpful on this point. Religious persecution alone can be a reductive way of presenting the issues certain Christians face, and power dynamics that suggest that Westerners are the only people who can act or intervene leave little space for the agency of the Christians who are the objects of these efforts.[8]

Outrage and compassion—the emotions of humanitarianism—are not the only responses that Christians are asked to cultivate in relation to images of the persecuted church.[9] The most fundamental question images and stories of martyrdom ask of the viewer is not *Can I identify with this pain?*— the goal of so much disaster or humanitarian photography—but rather *What is the state of my soul?* At least, that is a common function of gazing into the "martyr's mirror" throughout Christian history. Scarred faces and broken bodies become evidence of both physical and spiritual survival and are made to become testimonies to the triumphant power of God over evil. Whether in narrative or visual form, describing and representing the pain of the persecuted church has often been intended to make obvious a theological point: the suffering of "brothers and sisters in Christ" is the suffering of Christ.

This difference suggests that questions of the translatability of pain—whether Christians in the West can know the pain of their "brothers and sisters" in Christ—are simply the wrong questions to be asking. When Westerners look to the suffering of the persecuted church, the direction of their gaze is similar: "We"—the West—are looking "over there." But there is at least the potential within a Christian theological framework for the agency of viewer and viewed to be reversed. "They" critique "us" because, as the images of persecuted Christians are framed, *they*—the persecuted—are the ones with more sincere faith, perhaps they even have a sense of the presence of Christ that is unavailable to Christians elsewhere who are looking back via images and stories. They question us rather than simply asking for compassion or anger.[10]

The work of those who advocate on behalf of the persecuted church is premised upon an imagined belonging that makes a particular kind of suffering carry more weight—or at least a distinctive kind of weight. These advocates believe that some suffering can be translated—from raw experience into "religious persecution"—and in being translated it can be shared with those in the West. This conviction, that suffering need not be an inherently isolating experience but something that makes possible a global spiritual communion, is quite beautiful. Indeed, the literature around Christian persecution contains a number of testimonies asserting the power and meaningfulness of that communion. Anti-Christian persecution advocates, therefore, believe that some suffering can be defined not only as pertaining to religion, but also that some suffering is understood to be, in itself, religious. This key move is premised upon the labeling of this pain and suffering as being uniquely "Christian," which then allows that suffering to be made visible to Western eyes and then acted upon. This process has produced a new construction: a global Christianity defined by experiences of persecution over questions of doctrine, which I first described in chapter 3 with respect to the suffering of Armenian Christians in the late nineteenth and early twentieth centuries.

On this point, many of the panelists at the IRD summit referenced Matthew 25 as a way of indicating that it was when fellow believers were hungry, naked, or imprisoned— which was to say "persecuted"—that Christ was present with them. They judged that American Christians are neglecting Christ himself by neglecting the persecuted church, and they tended to pride themselves on being able to locate the myriad ways and places in which Christ is suffering globally, even as the summit was meeting. The question of whether Christ, so understood, might be suffering with those who were not Christian was never considered at the summit.[11]

Since the persecuted church is generally regarded as the righteous, suffering body of Christ enduring the trials of evil, the plight of these Christians is often understood as being explainable without recourse to any factor outside of religious identity or adherence. This is to say that this persecution is largely understood without reference to history. The implications of this analytical conviction are numerous. One panelist, sounding not unlike the Reformation-era martyrologists who had to distinguish between "politics" and "religion," scoffed at the idea of using "socioeconomic" or "cultural" or "political" lenses to explain anti-Christian persecution. In another context, Ambassador Brownback confessed to not really being sure why religious hostilities seem to be rising around the world. And despite the fact that at least three different panelists spoke movingly about the dramatic decline in the Christian population in Iraq "over the last fifteen years" (from approximately 1.5 million to around 200,000), there was not one mention of the U.S. invasion of Iraq. In fact, Sarah Roderick Fitch castigated those who insisted upon a continuous "penance over U.S. imperialism," which she said was a "penance for which Christians in the East are paying the cost." Physicians for Social Responsibility estimated that the total cost of the "war on terror" in the Middle East has been between 1.3 and 2 million "direct and indirect deaths."[12] To be clear, in suggesting that the Iraq War is an important contextual factor here, I am not arguing that there is a moral equivalency between U.S. foreign policy and the Islamic State, though the scale of violence within and around Iraq since 2003 has been unquestionably severe.

The points of U.S. and evangelical history that were referenced at the summit included William Wilberforce and the abolitionist movement, the participation of Jews and Christians in the civil rights movement of the 1950s and '60s, and American mobilization to save Soviet Jewry in the late twentieth century. Historical precedent mattered when it provided evidence of the righteousness of Christians' (and Americans') actions. History could be dismissed when it did not. For most of those present at the summit, to act on behalf of persecuted Christians elsewhere is to act as *American* Christians. But there was considerably less attention given to the fact that their actions occur within history, that they carry the uneven weight of a past that cannot be purely righteous. More to the point: Did Christ suffer with the more than 80,000 peasants who were killed in El Salvador, overwhelmingly at the hands of the U.S.-supported military dictatorship? Or one might ask about the Maya genocide in Guatemala that was tacitly supported because of American Christian support for the Pentecostal president of Guatemala, Efrain Rios Montt.[13] More recently, does Christ suffer as asylum-seeking families—families who are statistically speaking overwhelmingly Christian—are separated at the U.S.-Mexico border?[14]

It was American Christians' responsibilities to their fellow "brothers and sisters in Christ" that was paramount for most panelists at the summit. Luke Moon, for instance, criticized the American Christian leaders who signed an open letter in the *Washington Post* in February 2017 opposing President Trump's so-called "Muslim ban."[15] Moon was irate that these leaders failed to see that the language excepting "religious minorities" in the executive order "was code for Christians," and that by opposing the order these Christians were abandoning the suffering body of Christ.

To see suffering—Christian or otherwise—is not the same as knowing what to do about that suffering, especially if that suffering is conceptualized outside of the categories of nation, economics, politics, culture, and history. Stated in other terms, those people who comprise the living body of Christ also have relationships (as citizens, asylees, or refugees) to particular nation-states. And despite the devotional nature of sharing accounts of martyrdom, organizations that publicize anti-Christian persecution do want one to be moved to compassion upon seeing the widow of a martyr, or to feel outrage at international inaction to help Iraqi Christian refugees. Yet they also want one to use such images to question one's own sense of discipleship—one's relationship to the global body of Christ and, ultimately, of one's soul to Christ. This method muddles the politics of outrage with the disciplining of the soul. This muddling is due to the fact that those of us looking at the images of the persecuted church ostensibly have the power to *do something* about their suffering.

It is not at all clear, however, which foreign policy proposals might alleviate the suffering body of Christ. Should American Christians insist upon a prioritization of suffering Christians overseas? Should they maintain a broader commitment to "international religious freedom" that is fought for on behalf of all people? For those who see global anti-Christian developments as simply a manifestation of evil, how do the politics of metaphysical evil fit into the pragmatic constraints of American foreign policy? In other words, the question of what could be done is made more difficult by the layers of identity among those who are defining the conversation around persecution.[16]

Certain conceptual challenges arise at this juncture. Some of these challenges echo those that were raised in response to President Wilson's attempts to secure religious freedom for minorities in the wake of World War I. Are the rights more about a community or collective group as such? Or are they more oriented toward the protection of an individual's conscience with respect to religious adherence (or nonadherence), conversion, and affiliation? Terms such as "Christian genocide" or "global war on Christians," when used in a generic sense to denote anti-Christian violence or sentiment, highlight the community over individuals. Yet there is a distinct tendency among anti-Christian persecution activists to personalize the issues in figures such as Asia Bibi, Andrew Brunson, or the three Korean pastors who were released from North Korea in the summer of 2018. These kinds of instances highlight violations of an individual's freedoms or human rights. But religion does not pertain merely to individuals.

A religious community of Christians, of course, is by no means static, and people can convert to it or disaffiliate with it, emigrate to another location, or attempt to hide their religious beliefs or identity. And despite the common "Christian" categorization, tens of thousands of denominations and traditions are encompassed within it. I do not raise these issues simply to leave readers with a dilemma, or to suggest that religious freedom is merely something the world community must now go "beyond."[17] Rather, I want to point out the reality that a narrative which casts such issues as part of a "global war" does not provide a solid basis from which one might clearly act to alleviate the suffering so identified.[18] Rather, more contextualized approaches would appear to be a more promising avenue forward. This could mean an emphasis in some cases upon the collective identity or rights of groups of Christians, while in other cases, considering protections for individuals' rights of conscience might be more paramount. In other instances, it may lead to the questioning of whether "religion" is a primary cause of or rationale for violence. It would certainly mean attending to the variety of Christian communities present within a given country, as each of these traditions might have different relations to local political power and global networks. They may well also have different theologies of suffering, including both its sources and how it should be responded to.

From the perspective of the panelists who spoke at the IRD summit, the tragedy was not simply that American Christians were unaware of the plight of their brothers and sisters in the faith elsewhere, but that in their lack of awareness they were unable to leverage their American citizenship on behalf of suffering Christians. Here the gap between New Testament Christians' theology of persecution stands in stark relief with the contemporary possibilities of American foreign policy. The Apostle Paul did not have the ear of his senator; Peter did not preach to his congressmen. The early Christians received no direct word of support from an ambassador. For these reasons, it was striking to hear New Testament texts about caring for persecuted fellow believers while seated in the Dirksen Senate Building at a meeting attended by an ambassador and multiple former and current congressmen. It is worth reflecting on what it means to read New Testament texts about persecution from a position of political power rather than severe marginalization.

Contemporary politics around the suffering "body of Christ" are, therefore, shaped by the ways in which suffering is and has been categorized, and whose suffering is believed to have impacted Christ's body. If there is to be an American form of Christian politics that is organized around the shared suffering of the body of Christ, then we need to be clear about who gets to be included in that body, who is excluded, and why. In other words, any political engagement should first entail a more serious reflection on the disciples' question from Matthew 25: "Where did we see you, Lord?" which, at its best, would seem to make visible acute forms of occluded suffering and to bind people together in a communion around attending to that suffering. But the suffering body of Christ ought not be conflated with suffering that is categorized as religious persecution. Otherwise, this form of political mobilization could easily devolve into a myopic politics of global American righteousness. If it is the latter, there are thousands of murdered Salvadoran Christians—a "crucified people," in the phrase of some Salvadoran theologians—who may very well ask us to remove a proverbial plank from our own eye.[19]

American Christian efforts to draw attention to global Christian persecution have evinced a longing for a faith that is truer, more real, and more transcendent. But the relationship among these people, issues, borders, histories, and communities is not so clear-cut.

In 2016, I was invited by a student to attend mass at an East Syrian church near my home; most of the congregants were asylees or refugees from Syria, Turkey, and Iraq and their children and grandchildren. My former student met me outside the sanctuary, where he was waiting with a police officer the church had hired after receiving threats, along with a number of mosques in the Phoenix metro area. The entire liturgy and homily were in Assyrian Neo-Aramaic, which was the language of heaven, I was told. After the mass, I spoke with the student and his friends about how moved I had been to hear the Lord's Prayer recited in Aramaic and observed how I thought it was remarkable that I would have first heard it in Phoenix of all places. He said he was grateful for the promise of religious freedom in America, as compared with the restrictions Assyrian Christians had long faced in their traditional homelands. His gratitude seemed conditioned by the armed policeman who stood watch behind us. He went on to say that America's religious freedom has meant that his church has realized that it can now fulfill its Christian duty to evangelize, which its members had not previously practiced due to proscriptions on religious activities in their native countries. But he could not really say what evangelism might look like with respect to their tradition, in this place. And yet, he said, the younger generation was learning English rather than Assyrian, seemingly preferring individualistic assimilation to participation in an ancient liturgy. The benefits of American freedom seemed to come with fundamental costs to the tradition.

These are the layers of history and violence present in our conversation: We had participated in a liturgy that was itself a participation with heaven. As we exited, we were guarded by an officer from threats issued on behalf of white Christian nationalism, an idea created through the taking of that same land from the Akimel O'odham (Pima) and the Pee Posh (Maricopa) nations, among others. That same land has been made into a home to others who have fled persecution and has become a place for them of an uncertain welcome. This same land now also houses detention centers full of asylum-seeking Central Americans, nearly all of whom are Christian.

I close with these pieces of my own context because I believe that Christian theology insists upon the mystery of the incarnation—the joining of God to the vicissitudes, contingencies, and histories of a particular time and place in the person of Jesus. If Christ is somehow present in the collective body comprised within and beyond the individual bodies of Christians, as Christian theology likewise maintains, then that metaphysical body likewise exists within other histories and places, including my own in what is now central Arizona. This is my way of asking you to confront the plain reality of Paul's assertion that "if one part suffers, the rest suffers with it," noting that no conditions were placed upon the cause of suffering in order to make it Christ's own. To be an American Christian of whatever denomination or tradition, therefore, is to confront the fact that we, too, have caused Christ to suffer.

Acknowledgments

Many people have helped me bring these ideas into their present form. I have had the privilege to work with a number of students at Arizona State University (ASU) whose questions, interests, and research assistance have been generative and insightful. These include especially Ryan Linde and Amelia Dickey. The Center for the Study of Religion and Conflict at ASU offered the support of Patricia Mabry and BrieAnna Frank, who were both exceptional students in the center's undergraduate fellows program. ASU's Institute for Humanities Research (IHR) supported this work by hosting Ian Bogost and Christopher Schaberg for a writing workshop, which supplied the impetus to keep working on the manuscript. The IHR likewise supported an ongoing writing group that was graciously organized by Chris Jones. This program provided the space for me to complete the manuscript in the fall of 2019.

In some ways, this book flowed out of a long-term collaborative project that has been spearheaded, corralled, and cajoled along by Volker Benkert. That work was funded with grants from the Institute for Humanities Research; the School of Historical, Philosophical, and Religious Studies; the Center for the Study of Religion and Conflict; and the Office of Knowledge Enterprise Development—all of which are at ASU. More significantly for shaping this book, however, was the Project Grant for Researchers that was awarded by the Louisville Institute.

I am grateful to work with a host of inquisitive, kind, and generous colleagues, several of whom deserve special thanks for hearing these ideas in a less refined and coherent form, and for providing feedback, encouragement, suggestions, and criticisms in due course. Among them are Linell Cady, Volker Benkert, Catherine O'Donnell, Blake Hartung, Jacob Affolter, Tim Langille, and Erik Lundin. Friends outside of ASU have been no less helpful, and I'm particularly grateful to David Kirkpatrick, Heath Carter, and David Congdon. I continue to appreciate the mentoring I received at Princeton Theological Seminary, with special thanks to Richard Fox Young. Thank you to Elisabeth Maselli at Rutgers University Press for her support, attentiveness, and reliably good suggestions throughout.

My mother-in-law, Becca Causby, generously read a full rough draft of this manuscript, and her painstaking efforts made the manuscript clearer and cleaner, and saved later editors the headaches of my earlier oversights.

Continuing thanks go to my wife, who was the first to hear these ideas—along with the many false starts, roundabouts, and cul-de-sacs that come with any project—and grant them the kindness of a listening ear.

Portions of this text have appeared elsewhere. Some of the ideas elaborated in chapter 2 and chapter 4 were first presented in an article (co-authored with Ryan Linde) at *Sacred Matters* titled "Eusebius and the Global War on Christians." A second essay, titled "Tortured for Christ in Trump's America" was also published in *Sacred Matters*, and portions of that essay are included in chapter 3. Sections of chapters 3 and 4 were revised from an essay titled "The Evangelical Search for Authenticity" in the *Marginalia Review of Books*.

Notes

Chapter 1   Coming to Terms

1. Kevin Ward, "Tukutendereza Yesu: The Balokole Revival in Uganda," Dictionary of African Christian Biography, accessed April 1, 2019, https://dacb.org/histories/uganda-tukutendereza -yesu/.

2. For representative texts from the field of World Christianity, see Andrew Walls, *The Missionary Movement in Christian History: Studies in the Transmission of Faith* (Maryknoll, NY: Orbis Books, 1996); Lamin Sanneh, *Disciples of All Nations: Pillars of World Christianity* (New York: Oxford University Press, 2008). For a critical introduction to the field, see Joel Cabrita, David Maxwell, and Emma Wild-Wood, eds., *Relocating World Christianity: Interdisciplinary Studies in Universal and Local Expressions of the Christian Faith* (Leiden: Brill, 2017).

3. Philip Jenkins, *The Next Christendom: The Coming of Global Christianity* (Oxford: Oxford University Press, 2002).

4. Thomas Schirrmacher, "A Response to the High Counts of Christian Martyrs per Year," *International Journal of Religious Freedom* 4, no. 2 (2011): 9–13.

5. Patrick Wintour and Harriet Sherwood, "Jeremy Hunt Orders Global Review into Persecution of Christians," *Guardian*, December 26, 2018, https://www.theguardian.com/world/2018

/dec/26/jeremy-hunt-orders-global-review-into-persecution-of
-christians.

6. Nina Shea, *In the Lion's Den* (Nashville: Broadman & Holman Publishers, 1997), 1.

7. John Allen Jr., *The Global War on Christians: Dispatches from the Front Lines of Anti-Christian Persecution* (New York: Image, 2013).

8. "Eyewitness to a Beheading," *The Voice of the Martyrs, Persecution Blog*, updated November 18, 2008, https://www.persecution blog.com/2008/11/eyewitness-to-a-beheading.html.

9. The Crisis Tracker (https://crisistracker.org) is supported by a variety of research groups and nonprofit organizations, including some groups, like Invisible Children, that are faith based. It is widely cited as a credible and reliable resource for tracking LRA violence.

10. Lydia Boyd, *Preaching Prevention: Born-Again Politics and the Moral Politics of AIDS in Uganda* (Athens: Ohio University Press, 2015); Derek R. Peterson, *Ethnic Patriotism and the East African Revival: A History of Dissent, c. 1935–1972* (Cambridge: Cambridge University Press, 2012); China Scherz, *Having People, Having Heart: Charity, Sustainable Development, and Problems of Dependence in Central Uganda* (Chicago: University of Chicago Press, 2014).

11. Todd M. Johnson and Gina A. Zurlo, eds. *World Christian Database* (Leiden/Boston: Brill, accessed January 21, 2017).

12. John Francis Faupel, *African Holocaust: The Story of the Uganda Martyrs* (Nairobi: Paulines Publications Africa, 2007).

13. Elizabeth Castelli, *Martyrdom and Memory: Early Christian Culture Making* (New York: Columbia University Press, 2004); Johan Leemans and Peter Gemeinhardt, *Christian Martyrdom in Late Antiquity (300–450 AD): History and Discourse, Tradition and Identity* (Berlin: De Gruyter, 2012).

14. "Eyewitness to a Beheading," *The Voice of the Martyrs, Persecution Blog*, updated November 18, 2008, https://www.persecution blog.com/2008/11/eyewitness-to-a-beheading.html.

15. Melani McAlister, *The Kingdom of God Has No Borders: A Global History of American Evangelicals* (Oxford: Oxford University Press, 2018), ch. 7.

16. Richard Wurmbrand, *Tortured for Christ* (Bartlesville, OK: Living Sacrifice Book Co., 1967).

17. For two recent examples of this literature, see Johnnie Moore, *The Martyr's Oath: Living for the Jesus They're Willing to Die For* (Carol Stream, IL: Tyndale House Publishers, 2017); Dominic Sputo, *Heirloom Love: Authentic Christianity in This Age of Persecution* (self-published, 2018).

18. Wurmbrand, *Tortured for Christ*, 139.

19. Richard Wurmbrand, *In God's Underground* (Bartlesville, OK: VOM Books, 2004), 137.

20. Wurmbrand, *In God's Underground*, 245.

21. Bishop Kallistos Ware, *The Orthodox Way* (Crestwood, NY: St. Vladimir's Seminary Press, 1995).

22. Henry Chadwick, *The Early Church* (New York: Penguin Books, 1967); Joseph H. Lynch, *Early Christianity: A Brief History* (New York: Oxford University Press, 2010).

23. Carter Lindberg, *The European Reformations* (New York: John Wiley & Sons, 2011); Scott Hendrix, *Recultivating the Vineyard: The Reformation Agendas of Christianization* (Louisville, KY: Westminster John Knox, 2004).

24. This could reasonably be extended into the twenty-first century, depending upon context. See John Hooper and Stephen Bates, "Dismay and Anger as Pope Declares Protestants Cannot Have Churches," *Guardian*, July 11, 2007, https://www.theguardian.com/world/2007/jul/11/catholicism .religion.

25. Brian Stanley, *The World Missionary Conference, Edinburgh 1910* (Grand Rapids, MI: Eerdmans Publishing Co., 2009); Henry Smith Leiper, *World Chaos or World Christianity? A Popular Interpretation of Oxford and Edinburgh 1937* (Chicago: Willett, Clark & Co., 1937).

26. Geoffrey Wainwright, *The Ecumenical Moment: Crisis and Opportunity for the Church* (Grand Rapids, MI: Eerdmans Publishing Co., 1983). For global theologies arising out of this changed context, see Robert J. Schreiter, *The New Catholicity: Theology between the Global and Local* (Maryknoll, NY: Orbis Books, 1997); Stephen B. Bevans and Roger P. Schroeder, *Constants in Context: A Theology of Mission for Today* (Maryknoll, NY: Orbis Books, 2004).

27. Kevin Kruse, *One Nation under God: How Corporate America Invented Christian America* (New York: Basic Books, 2015).

28. Robert Wuthnow, *Inventing American Religion: Polls, Surveys, and the Tenuous Quest for a Nation's Faith* (Oxford: Oxford University Press, 2015). Though she engages with Confucianism, as opposed to Christianity, the issues Anna Sun raises with respect to "counting Confucians" is relevant to my discussion as well. Anna Sun, "Counting Confucians: Who Are the Confucians in Contemporary East Asia?" *Newsletter of the Institute for Advanced Studies in Humanities and Social Sciences of National Taiwan University*, 2009. See also Miguel De La Torre and Gaston Espinosa, eds. *Rethinking Latino(a) Religion and Identity* (Cleveland: Pilgrim Press, 2006).

29. Pew Research Center, "How Does Pew Research Center Measure the Religious Composition of the U.S.?" July 5, 2018, https://www.pewforum.org/2018/07/05/how-does-pew-research-center-measure-the-religious-composition-of-the-u-s-answers-to-frequently-asked-questions/; Pew Research Center, "The Changing Global Religious Landscape," April 5, 2017, https://www.pewforum.org/2017/04/05/the-changing-global-religious-landscape/. (See appendix C for the methodology of the report.)

30. As one example of how these statistics are put into a broader narrative, see Stacy Singh, "Christians #1 Most Persecuted, and Rising," *The Stand*, May 29, 2015, https://afa.net/the-stand/faith/2015/05/christians-the-1-most-persecuted-and-rising/.

31. Daniel Cox and Robert P. Jones, "Majority of Americans Oppose Transgender Bathroom Restrictions," Public Religion Research Institute, March 10, 2017, https://www.prri.org/research/lgbt -transgender-bathroom-discrimination-religious-liberty/.

32. A number of books on the subject aimed at a broad Christian readership include David Platt, *Radical: Taking Your Faith Back from the American Dream* (Colorado Springs, CO: Multnomah, 2010); Rod Dreher, *The Benedict Option: A Strategy for Christians in a Post-Christian America* (New York: Penguin, 2017); Rob Bell and Don Goldon, *Jesus Wants to Save Christians: A Manifesto for the Church in Exile* (Grand Rapids, MI: Zondervan, 2008).

33. Russell Moore, "Why the Church Should Neither Cave nor Panic about the Decision on Gay Marriage," *Washington Post*, June 26, 2015, https://www.washingtonpost.com/news/acts-of-faith/wp /2015/06/26/why-the-church-should-neither-cave-nor-panic-about -the-decision-on-gay-marriage/?utm_term=.fc9fa6d0acca.

34. Moore, *Martyr's Oath*, xi; Jason Bruner and Ryan Linde, "Eusebius and the Global War on Christians," *Sacred Matters*, June 2, 2014, https://sacredmattersmagazine.com/eusebius -and-the-global-war-on-christians/.

35. Boyd, *Preaching Prevention*; Jason Bruner, "Uganda's President Will Sign Anti-Gay Bill. How Did the Nation Get to This Point?" *Religion and Politics*, February 19, 2014, https://religion andpolitics.org/2014/02/18/ugandas-president-will-sign-anti -gay-bill-how-did-the-nation-get-to-this-point/; Katherine Fairfax Wright and Malika Zouhali-Worrall, dirs., *Call Me Kuchu*, Cinedigm Corp, 2012.

Chapter 2   Christian, Martyrdom, and Persecution from the New Testament to the Reformation

1. Chuck Colson, foreword to *In the Lion's Den*, by Nina Shea (Nashville: Broadman & Holman Publishers, 1997), ix.

2. Paul Middleton, "Enemies of the (Church and) State: Martyrdom as a Problem for Early Christianity," *Annali Di Storia Dell'esegesi* 29, no. 2 (December 2012): 166.

3. Raymond E. Brown, *An Introduction to the New Testament* (New York: Doubleday, 1997); Robert A. Spivey, D. Moody Smith, and C. Clifton Black, *Anatomy of the New Testament*, 7th ed. (Minneapolis: Fortress Press, 2013); Bart D. Ehrman, *The New Testament: A Historical Introduction to the Early Christian Writings*, 6th ed. (New York: Oxford University Press, 2016).

4. Middleton, "Enemies of the (Church and) State," 165.

5. Michael L. Satlow, *How the Bible Became Holy* (New Haven, CT: Yale University Press, 2015).

6. Stephen Fowl, "The Primacy of the Witness of the Body to Martyrdom in Paul," in *Witness of the Body: The Past, Present, and Future of Christian Martyrdom*, ed. Michael L. Budde and Karen Scott (Grand Rapids, MI: Eerdmans Publishing Co., 2011), 43–60.

7. Robert Louis Wilken, *Christians as the Romans Saw Them* (New Haven, CT: Yale University Press, 2003).

8. Daniel Boyarin, "Martyrdom and the Making of Christianity and Judaism," *Journal of Early Christian Studies* 6, no. 4 (1998): 577–627.

9. F. Wiedmann, "Rushing Judgment? Willfulness and Martyrdom in Early Christianity," *Union Seminary Quarterly Review* 53, no. 1 (1999): 65–67.

10. "The Letter of Ignatius to the Romans," in *The New Testament and Other Early Christian Writings: A Reader*, ed. Bart D. Ehrman (Oxford: Oxford University Press, 1998), 329; James G. Bushur, "Ignatius of Antioch's Letter to the Romans: The Passionate Confession of Christian Identity," *Logia* 2, no. 1 (2015): 13–18.

11. Middleton, "Enemies of the (Church and) State," 168.

12. "Letters of Pliny the Younger and the Emperor Trajan," *Frontline* ("From Jesus to Christ"), trans. William Whiston, accessed April 1, 2020, https://www.pbs.org/wgbh/pages /frontline/shows/religion/maps/primary/pliny.html.

13. "Letters of Pliny the Younger and the Emperor Trajan."

14. Robert Louis Wilken, *The First Thousand Years: A Global History of Christianity* (New Haven, CT: Yale University Press, 2012), 65–74; Wilken, *Christians as the Romans Saw Them*.

15. "Diognetus," *Early Christian Writings*, trans. J. B. Lightfoot, accessed August 7, 2020, http://www.earlychristianwritings .com/text/diognetus-lightfoot.html.

16. "Diognetus." See also Dale T. Irvin and Scott W. Sunquist, *History of the World Christian Movement*, vol. 1, *Earliest Christianity to 1453* (Maryknoll, NY: Orbis Books, 2001), 92–97.

17. L. Michael White, *From Jesus to Christianity* (San Francisco: HarperOne, 2005), chs. 10, 12, and 15.

18. Irvin and Sunquist, *History of the World Christian Movement*, 137–140; Robert Bartlett, *Why Can the Dead Do Such Great Things?* (Princeton, NJ: Princeton University Press, 2015), 1–10.

19. "The Martyrdom of Saints Perpetua and Felicitas," *Frontline* ("From Jesus to Christ"), accessed April 1, 2020, http://www.pbs .org/wgbh/pages/frontline/shows/religion/maps/primary /perpetua.html.

20. Herbert B. Workman, *Persecution in the Early Church* (New York: Oxford University Press, 1980); Glen W. Bowersock, *Martyrdom and Rome* (Cambridge: Cambridge University Press, 2002); Stuart G. Hall, "Women among the Early Martyrs," in *Martyrs and Martyrologies*, ed. Diana Wood (London: Blackwell Publishers, 1993), 1–21.

21. Clement of Alexandria, Stromata 4.4, accessed April 1, 2020, http://www.earlychristianwritings.com/text/clement-stromata -book4.html; Elizabeth A. Castelli, *Martyrdom and Memory: Early Christian Culture Making* (New York: Columbia University Press, 2004), 25–33.

22. "The Address of Q. Sept. Tertullian to Scapula Tertullus," trans. Sir David Dalrymple, accessed April 1, 2020, http://www .tertullian.org/articles/dalrymple_scapula.htm.

23. Philippe Buc, *Holy War, Martyrdom, and Terror: Christianity, Violence, and the West* (Philadelphia: University of Pennsylvania Press, 2015), 122.

24. Clement of Alexandria, Stromata 4.4.

25. Abraham Gross, *Spirituality and Law: Courting Martyrdom in Christianity and Judaism* (New York: University Press of America, 2005), 1–5.

26. Wilken, *First Thousand Years*, 65.

27. Wilken, 66–67.

28. Irvin and Sunquist, *History of the World Christian Movement*, 160–165.

29. "Galerius and Constantine: Edicts of Toleration 311/313," Ancient History Sourcebook, Fordham University, accessed March 15, 2020, https://sourcebooks.fordham.edu/source/edict -milan.asp.

30. Eusebius of Caesarea, *The Life of the Blessed Emperor Constantine*, ch. 40, Ancient History Sourcebook, Fordham University, accessed March 15, 2020, https://sourcebooks.fordham.edu /basis/vita-constantine.asp.

31. Theofried Baumeister, "Martyrdom and Persecution in Early Christianity," in *Martyrdom Today*, ed. Johanes-Baptist Metz and Edward Schillebeeckx (Edinburgh: T&T Clark, 1983), 3–8.

32. Eusebius of Caesarea, *Church History*, book 5, para. 3–4, New Advent, accessed March 15, 2020, http://www.newadvent.org /fathers/250105.htm.

33. Candida R. Moss, *The Myth of Persecution: How Early Christians Invented a Story of Martyrdom* (New York: HarperOne, 2014), 221; Jason Bruner and Ryan Linde, "Eusebius and the Global War on Christians," *Sacred Matters*, June 2, 2014, https://sacredmatters magazine.com/eusebius-and-the-global-war-on-christians/.

34. Eusebius of Caesarea, *Church History*, book 5, ch. 16.

35. Athanasius, *Life of Anthony of Egypt*, in *Readings in World Christian History*, vol. 1, *Earliest Christianity to 1453*,

ed. John W. Coakley and Andrea Sterk (Maryknoll, NY: Orbis Books, 2009), 137.

36. Sidney H. Griffith, *The Church in the Shadow of the Mosque: Christians and Muslims in the World of Islam* (Princeton, NJ: Princeton University Press, 2012), 134–136.

37. Griffith, *Church in the Shadow of the Mosque*, 131–134.

38. Griffith, 137–139.

39. Griffith, 139–140. See also Michael Philip Penn, *When Christians First Met Muslims: A Sourcebook of the Early Syriac Writings on Islam* (Oakland: University of California Press, 2015); and Michael Philip Penn, *Envisioning Islam: Syriac Christians and the Early Muslim World* (Oakland: University of California Press, 2015). For a history of the theological debates that animated these regions, see Iain R. Torrance, *Christology after Chalcedon: Severus of Antioch and Sergius the Monophysite* (Eugene, OR: Wipf and Stock, 1998).

40. This became the most common term for early Syriac-speaking Christians to refer to Muslims.

41. Isho'yahb III, "Letter 48[B]," in Penn, *When Christians First Met Muslims*, 33.

42. Penn, *Envisioning Islam*, 25–33.

43. Penn, *When Christians First Met Muslims*, 68. For more on Maximus's theology, see Jeremy David Wallace, "Virtue and Knowledge as the Hermeneutical Key for Unlocking Maximus the Confessor's *Quaestiones ad Thalassium*" (PhD diss., Princeton Theological Seminary, 2013).

44. "Apology of Patriarch Timothy of Baghdad before the Caliph Mahdi," in Coakley and Sterk, *Readings in World Christian History*, 232.

45. Griffith, *Church in the Shadow of the Mosque*, 147–151; Jason R. Zaborowski, *The Coptic Martyrdom of John of Phanijōit: Assimilation and Conversion to Islam in Thirteenth-Century Egypt* (Leiden: Brill, 2005).

46. Griffith, *Church in the Shadow of the Mosque*, 156–157.

47. Griffith, 156–157. The Abbasid Caliphate was the predominant Islamic empire of this period and was spread from northern Africa to Central Asia.

48. Jill N. Claster, *Sacred Violence: The European Crusades to the Middle East, 1095–1396* (Toronto: University of Toronto Press, 2009); S. J. Allen and Emilie Amt, introduction to *The Crusades: A Reader*, ed. S. J. Allen and Emilie Amt (Toronto: University of Toronto Press, 2014), xv–xxii.

49. Irvin and Sunquist, *History of the World Christian Movement*, 392.

50. Sir Steven Runciman, "Byzantium and the Crusades," in *The Crusades*, ed. Thomas E. Madden (Oxford: Blackwell, 2002), 211–220; H.E.J. Cowdrey, "Pope Urban II's Preaching of the First Crusade," in Madden, *Crusades*, 16.

51. Runciman, "Byzantium and the Crusades," 215.

52. "The Deeds of the Franks," in *The Crusades: A Reader*, ed. S. J. Allen and Emilie Ant (Toronto: University of Toronto Press, 2014), 57.

53. Bartlett, *Why Can the Dead Do Such Great Things?* 52–56.

54. Colin Morris, "Martyrs on the Field of Battle before and during the First Crusade," in Wood, *Martyrs and Martyrologies*, 97–98.

55. Quoted in Morris, "Martyrs on the Field of Battle," 101.

56. "Documents on the Sack of Constantinople," in *The Crusades: A Reader*, ed. S. J. Allen and Emilie Ant (Toronto: University of Toronto, 2014), 229.

57. "Letters of Innocent III," in Allen and Ant, *Crusades: A Reader*, 232–234.

58. Alice Dailey, *The English Martyr from Reformation to Revolution* (South Bend, IN: University of Notre Dame Press, 2012), ch. 1; Jacobus de Voragine, *The Golden Legend*, Medieval Sourcebooks, Fordham University, accessed December 20, 2019, https://source books.fordham.edu/basis/goldenlegend/.

59. Jacobus de Voragine, "The Passion of Our Lord," in *The Golden Legend*, vol. 1., Medieval Sourcebooks, Fordham University, accessed December 20, 2019, https://sourcebooks.fordham.edu

/basis/goldenlegend/GoldenLegend-Volume1.asp#The%20
Passion%20of%20our%20Lord.

60. Voragine, "Passion of Our Lord"; emphasis added.

61. Jacobus de Voragine, "Here Followeth the Life of S. Blasé, and First of His Name," in *The Golden Legend*, vol. 3, Medieval Sourcebooks, Fordham University, accessed December 20, 2019, https://sourcebooks.fordham.edu/basis/goldenlegend/Golden Legend-Volume3.asp.

62. Dailey, *English Martyr*; Brad Gregory, *Salvation at Stake: Christian Martyrdom in Early Modern Europe* (Cambridge, MA: Harvard University Press, 1999).

63. Bartlett, *Why Can the Dead Do Such Great Things?* 85–91.

64. Euan Cameron, "Medieval Heretics as Protestant Martyrs," in Wood, *Martyrs and Martyrologies*, 185–208.

65. Quoted in Gregory, *Salvation at Stake*, 159.

66. C. J. Dyck, "The Suffering Church in Anabaptism," *Mennonite Quarterly Review* 59 (1985): 5–23.

67. *Foxe's Book of Martyrs*, ch. 16, accessed April 1, 2020, http://www.ccel.org/f/foxe/martyrs/fox116.htm.

68. *Foxe's Book of Martyrs*, ch. 16.

69. Dailey, *English Martyr*, 95.

70. David Loades, "John Foxe and the Traitors: The Politics of the Marian Persecution (Presidential Address)," in Wood, *Martyrs and Martyrologies*, 231–244.

71. Brad Gregory, *The Unintended Reformation: How a Religious Revolution Secularized Society* (Cambridge, MA: Harvard University Press, 2012).

72. Jason Bruner and Ryan Linde, "Eusebius and the Global War on Christians," *Sacred Matters*, June 2, 2014, https://sacredmatters magazine.com/eusebius-and-the-global-war-on-christians/.

73. Brad S. Gregory, "Persecution or Prosecution, Martyrs or False Martyrs? The Reformation Era, History, and Theological Reflection," in *Witness of the Body: The Past, Present, and Future of Christian Martyrdom*, ed. Michael L. Budde and

Karen Scott (Grand Rapids, MI: Eerdmans Publishing Co., 2011), 107–124; William T. Cavanaugh, "Destroying the Church to Save It: Intra-Christian Persecution and the Modern State," in Budde and Scott, *Witness of the Body*, 125–150.

Chapter 3   Religious Persecution and American Christianity

1. Owen Stanwood, "Catholics, Protestants, and the Clash of Civilizations in Early America," in *The First Prejudice: Religious Tolerance and Intolerance in Early America*, ed. Chris Beneke and Christopher S. Grenda (Philadelphia: University of Pennsylvania Press, 2010), 218–240.

2. David Murray, "Spreading the Word: Missionaries, Conversion, and Circulation in the Northeast," in *Spiritual Encounters: Interactions between Christianity and Native Religions in Colonial America*, ed. Nicholas Griffiths and Fernando Cervantes (Birmingham: University of Birmingham Press, 1999), 43–64; Linda Gregerson, "The Commonwealth of the Word: New England, Old England, and the Praying Indians," in *Empires of God: Religious Encounters in the Early Modern Atlantic*, ed. Linda Gregerson and Susan Juster (Philadelphia: University of Pennsylvania Press, 2011), 70–84.

3. John Wolffe, "Anti-Catholicism in Britain and the United States, 1830–1860," in *Evangelicalism: Comparative Studies of Popular Protestantism in North America, the British Isles, and Beyond, 1700–1990*, ed. Mark A. Noll, David W. Bebbington, and George A. Rawlyk (Oxford: Oxford University Press, 1994), 179–197; Allison O. Malcom, "Anti-Catholicism and the Rise of Protestant Nationhood in North America, 1830–1871" (PhD diss., University of Illinois at Chicago, 2011).

4. Jon Butler, Grant Wacker, and Randall Balmer, *Religion in American Life: A Short History* (New York: Oxford University Press, 2003), 142–162.

5. John Allen Jr., *The Global War on Christians: Dispatches from the Front Lines of Anti-Christian Persecution* (New York: Image, 2013).

6. Butler, Wacker, and Balmer, *Religion in American Life*, 247–262.

7. Quoted in Mark A. Noll, *America's God: From Jonathan Edwards to Abraham Lincoln* (New York: Oxford University Press, 2005), 434; Daniel W. Stowell, *Rebuilding Zion: The Religious Reconstruction of the South, 1863–1877* (New York: Oxford University Press, 1998), 33–48.

8. Quoted in Noll, *America's God*, 424.

9. John Esten Cooke, *The Life of Stonewall Jackson* (New York: Charles B. Richardson, 1863), 8.

10. Quoted in Stowell, *Rebuilding Zion*, 42.

11. Charles Raegan Wilson, *Baptized in Blood: The Religion of the Lost Cause, 1965–1920* (Athens: University of Georgia Press, 2009), 42.

12. Wilson, *Baptized in Blood*, 45.

13. The Parable of the Prodigal Son is found in the Gospel of Luke and recounts the story of a son who asks for his inheritance from his father. The son then leaves and ends up squandering the inheritance before returning home to ask for forgiveness from his father, who warmly welcomes him home.

14. Stowell, *Rebuilding Zion*, 130–145.

15. Wilson, *Baptized in Blood*, 64–65.

16. Luke E. Harlow, "The Civil War and the Making of Conservative American Evangelicalism," in *Turning Points in the History of American Evangelicalism*, ed. Heath W. Carter and Laura Rominger Porter (Grand Rapids, MI: Eerdmans Publishing Co., 2017), 107–132. See also Edward Blum, *Reforging the White Republic: Race, Religion, and American Nationalism, 1865–1989* (Baton Rouge: Louisiana State University Press, 2015).

17. The dynamics I describe here are not entirely exclusive to the Armenians or Christians in the Middle East. The Boxer Rebellion in China at the dawn of the twentieth century contained similar dynamics with respect to missionary

publications and violence against Christians, both Protestant and Catholic. Thoralf Klein, "Media Events and Missionary Periodicals: The Case of the Boxer War, 1900–1901," *Church History* 82, no. 2 (2013): 399–404; Karl J. Rivinius, "The Boxer Movement and Christian Missions in China," *Mission Studies* 7, no. 2 (1990): 189–217.

18. Nathan O. Hatch, *The Democratization of American Christianity* (New Haven, CT: Yale University Press, 1989).

19. Among ABCFM missionaries, "Nestorian" seems to have been used generically to refer to a range of non-Protestant Christian traditions in the eastern Ottoman Empire rather than more narrowly using the term only with respect to the East Syrian Church.

20. Joseph L. Grabill, *Protestant Diplomacy and the Near East: Missionary Influence on American Policy, 1810–1927* (Minneapolis: University of Minnesota Press, 1971), 136. See also Peter Balakian, *The Burning Tigris: The Armenian Genocide and America's Response* (New York: HarperCollins, 2003); Deanna Feree Womack, *Protestants, Gender, and the Arab Renaissance in Late Ottoman Syria* (Edinburgh: Edinburgh University Press, 2015).

21. Quoted in Grabill, *Protestant Diplomacy*, 137.

22. Suzanne E. Moranian, "The Armenian Genocide and American Missionary Efforts," in *America and the Armenian Genocide of 1915*, ed. Jay Winter (Cambridge: Cambridge University Press, 2004), 188; Mehmet Ali Dogan, "American Board of Commissioners for Foreign Missions (ABCFM) and 'Nominal Christians': Elias Riggs (1810–1901) and American Missionary Activities in the Ottoman Empire," (PhD diss., University of Utah, 2013).

23. "Americans in Armenia," *Daily Inter Ocean*, December 15, 1894, 12.

24. Abraham H. Hartunian, *To Neither Laugh nor Weep: A Memoir of the Armenian Genocide* (Boston: Beacon Press, 1968), 22; Mugurdich Chojhauji Gabrielian, *Armenia, a Martyr Nation: A Historical Sketch of the Armenian People from Traditional Times to the Present Tragic Days* (New York: Fleming H. Revell, 1916).

25. Hartunian, *To Neither Laugh nor Weep*, 39. Hartunian recounted a similar arrangement in the 1890s with a Gregorian priest and parish (see pp. 22–23).

26. "Mission Board Told of Turkish Horrors," *New York Times*, September 17, 1915, 3.

27. Missionary networks and publications were also very influential in the campaign against the atrocities in Congo. See T. Jack Thompson, *Light on Darkness? Missionary Photography of Africa in the Nineteenth and Early Twentieth Centuries* (Grand Rapids, MI: Eerdmans Publishing Co., 2012).

28. Moranian, "Armenian Genocide and American Missionary Relief Efforts," 194–195.

29. Moranian, 196.

30. Moranian, 196.

31. Charles Jaret, "Troubled by Newcomers: Anti-Immigrant Attitudes and Action during Two Eras of Mass Immigration to the United States," *Journal of American Ethnic History* 18, no. 3 (1999): 9–39.

32. Donald Miller and Lorna Touryan Miller, *Survivors: An Oral History of the Armenian Genocide* (Berkeley: University of California Press, 1999), ch. 1.

33. Earlene Craver, "On the Boundary of White: The Cartozian Naturalization Case and the Armenians, 1923–1925," *Journal of American Ethnic History* 28, no. 2 (2009): 30–56.

34. Anna Su, "Woodrow Wilson and the Origins of the International Law of Religious Freedom," *Journal of the History of International Law* 15, no. 2 (2013): 235–267; David Monger, "Networking against Genocide during the First World War: The International Network behind the British Parliamentary Report on the Armenian Genocide," *Journal of Transatlantic Studies* 16, no. 3 (2018): 295–316; Charlie Laderman, "Sharing the Burden? The American Solution to the Armenian Question, 1918–1920," *Diplomatic History* 40, no. 4 (2016): 664–694.

35. I am using "liberal" here to connote a political system based upon individual rights and freedoms, particularly those guaranteed by citizens in a modern nation-state. Liberal, in this sense, should not be confused with contemporary progressive politics in the United States.

36. Tisa Wenger, "'We Are Guaranteed Freedom': Pueblo Indians and the Category of Religion in the 1920s," *History of Religions* 45, no. 2 (2005): 89–113; Tisa Wenger, "Indian Dances and the Politics of Religious Freedom, 1870–1930," *Journal of the American Academy of Religion* 79, no. 4 (2011): 850–878.

37. Raphael Lemkin, *Axis Rule in Occupied Europe: Laws of Occupation, Analysis of Government, Proposals for Redress* (Washington, DC: Carnegie Endowment for International Peace, 1944).

38. This right was further elaborated in the UN Declaration on the Elimination of All Forms of Intolerance and of Discrimination Based on Religion or Belief, which was ratified on November 25, 1981.

39. Michael Gunter, "What Is Genocide? The Armenian Case," *Middle East Quarterly* 20, no. 1 (2013): 37–46; Adam Jones, *Genocide: A Comprehensive Introduction* (New York: Routledge, 2006), 8–14; Jens Meierhenrich, *Genocide: A Reader* (New York: Oxford University Press, 2014), 3–55.

40. Milena Sterio, "The Karadžić Genocide Conviction: Inferences, Intent, and the Necessity to Redefine Genocide," *Emory International Law Review* 30, no. 2 (2017): 274.

41. "Universal Declaration of Human Rights," United Nations, accessed December 19, 2019, https://www.un.org/en/universal-declaration-human-rights/.

42. Saba Mahmood, *Religious Difference in a Secular Age: A Minority Report* (Princeton, NJ: Princeton University Press, 2015).

43. Henry Smith Leiper, *World Chaos or World Christianity? A Popular Interpretation of Oxford and Edinburgh 1937* (Chicago: Willett, Clark & Co., 1937); Geoffrey Wainwright, *The*

Ecumenical Moment: Crisis and Opportunity for the Church
(Grand Rapids, MI: Eerdmans Publishing Co., 1983); Brian
Stanley, *The World Missionary Conference, Edinburgh 1910*
(Grand Rapids, MI: Eerdmans Publishing Co., 2009). The role
of Vatican II should not be underestimated in the history of the
ecumenical movement, particularly the document *Unitas
redintegratio*. See Edmund Kee-Fook Chia, "Ecumenical
Pilgrimage toward World Christianity," *Theological Studies* 76,
no. 3 (2015): 503–530.

44. Hal Lindsey, *The Late Great Planet Earth* (Grand Rapids, MI:
Zondervan, 1970), 110–123.

45. To be clear, however, some conservative and fundamentalist
Christians had already begun organizing their own national
and international institutions in response to the World Council
of Churches. Carl McIntire, for example, established the
American Council of Christian Churches in 1941 and the
International Council of Christian Churches in 1947. Jill Gill,
*Embattled Ecumenism: The National Council of Churches, the
Vietnam War, and the Trials of the Protestant Left* (DeKalb, IL:
Northern Illinois University Press, 2011), 440.

46. Gill, *Embattled Ecumenism*, ch. 2.

47. Daniel Buda, "The World Council of Churches' Relationships
with Pentecostalism: A Brief Historical Survey and Some
Recent Perspectives on Membership Matters," *International
Review of Mission* 107, no. 1 (2018): 81–97.

48. McIntire's American Council of Christian Churches, for
example, published *How Red Is the Federal/National Council of
Churches?* (New York: American Council of Christian Churches)
in the early 1950s. For a brief overview of these decades, see
Butler, Wacker, and Balmer, *Religion in American Life*, 364–384.

49. Wilson, *Baptized in Blood*.

50. Daniel B. Lee, "The Great Racial Commission: Religion and
the Construction of White America," in *Race, Nation, and*

Religion in the Americas, ed. Henry Goldschmidt and Elizabeth McAlister (New York: Oxford University Press, 2004), 85–110.

51. Randall Balmer, "The Real Origins of the Religious Right," *Politico*, May 27, 2014, accessed December 19, 2019, https://www.politico.com/magazine/story/2014/05/religious-right-real-origins-107133.

52. Michael Barkun, *Religion and the Racist Right: The Origins of the Christian Identity Movement* (Chapel Hill, NC: UNC Press, 1997).

53. L. Nelson Bell, "A Southern Evangelical on Integration, August 17, 1955," in *Jerry Falwell and the Rise of the Religious Right*, ed. Matthew Avery Sutton (New York: Bedford/St. Martin's, 2013), 53; Curtis J. Evans, "White Evangelical Protestant Responses to the Civil Rights Movement," *Harvard Theological Review* 102, no. 2 (2009): 245–273.

54. Carl McIntire, "Letter of March 26, 1964 to President Lyndon Johnson," in Sutton, *Jerry Falwell and the Rise of the Religious Right*, 55–56.

55. Eugene D. Genovese, *A Consuming Fire: The Fall of the Confederacy in the Mind of the White Christian South* (Athens: University of Georgia Press, 1998), 96. On this point Genovese contrasts noticeably with Charles Raegan Wilson, who saw greater continuity between Antebellum and post-Reconstruction Southern life.

56. Kruse, *One Nation under God*; John Fea, *Was America Founded as a Christian Nation? A Historical Introduction* (Louisville, KY: Westminster John Knox, 2011).

57. Jeff Sharlet, *The Family: The Secret Fundamentalism at the Heart of American Power* (New York: HarperCollins, 2008); Molly Worthen, "The Chalcedon Problem: Rousas John Rushdoony and the Origins of Christian Reconstructionism," *Church History* 77, no. 2 (2008): 399–437.

58. Kruse, *One Nation under God*.

59. Portions of this section were taken from a review of a film adaptation of this book, published as Jason Bruner, "Tortured

for Christ in Trump's America," *Sacred Matters*, April 13, 2018, https://sacredmattersmagazine.com/tortured-for-christ-in -trumps-america/.

60. DC Talk and Voice of the Martyrs, *Jesus Freaks* (Minneapolis: Bethany House, 1999), 68.

61. Richard Wurmbrand, *Tortured for Christ* (Bartlesville, OK: Living Sacrifice Book Co., 1967), 139.

62. Wurmbrand, *Tortured for Christ*, 72–73.

63. Wurmbrand, 79, 82, 89–90, 124.

64. Wurmbrand, 73.

65. See also Richard Wurmbrand, *In God's Underground* (Bartlesville, OK: VOM Books, 1968, 2004).

66. Wurmbrand, *Tortured for Christ*, 138.

67. Wurmbrand, 80.

68. Melani McAlister, *The Kingdom of God Has No Borders: A Global History of American Evangelicals* (Oxford: Oxford University Press, 2018).

69. McAlister, *Kingdom of God*, 110–111.

70. It should be noted, however, that there are no discernable references to Christian communities such as Jehovah's Witnesses or Mormons.

71. Omri Elisha, "Saved by a Martyr: Evangelical Mediation, Sanctification, and the 'Persecuted Church,'" *Journal of the American Academy of Religion* 84, no. 4 (December 2016): 1056–1080.

72. McAlister, *Kingdom of God*, 109.

73. This organizing precedent was raised at several points in a conference organized by the Institute on Religion and Democracy that I attended in the Dirksen Senate Building in May 2018. Andrew Preston, "Defender of the Faith: The United States and World Christianity," in *Relocating World Christianity: Interdisciplinary Studies in Universal and Local Expressions of the Christian Faith*, ed. Joel Cabrita, David Maxwell, and Emma Wild-Wood (Leiden: Brill, 2017), 261–280; McAlister, *Kingdom of God*, ch. 8.

74. I am not here arguing that the Religious Right represents the totality of American conservatism, or that the history of American conservatism can only be explained or accounted for with respect to religion.

75. McIntire, "Letter of March 26, 1964 to President Lyndon Johnson," 55–56.

76. Kevin Kruse, *White Flight: Atlanta and the Making of Modern Conservatism* (Princeton, NJ: Princeton University Press, 2005).

77. "Brief of National Association of Evangelicals as Amicus Curiae in Support of Petitioner," in Sutton, *Jerry Falwell and the Rise of the Religious Right*, 61–62. One might note here the distinction between how the NAE presented these issues of biblical interpretation and belief with Genovese's critique, quoted above.

78. Stanley R. Rader, *Against the Gates of Hell: The Threat to Religious Freedom in America* (New York: Everest House, 1980), 275.

79. The text of this brief can be found in Rader, *Against the Gates of Hell*, 308–309.

80. "Title IX and Sex Discrimination," U.S. Department of Education, Office of Civil Rights, accessed December 19, 2019, https://www2.ed.gov/about/offices/list/ocr/docs/tix_dis.html.

81. Deborah L. Brake, *Getting in the Game: Title IX and the Women's Sports Revolution* (New York: NYU Press, 2010); Welch Suggs, *A Place on the Team: The Triumph and Tragedy of Title IX* (Princeton, NJ: Princeton University Press, 2005).

82. "*Grove City College v. Bell*—Facts and Case Summary," Administrative Office of the U.S. Courts, accessed December 19, 2019, https://www.uscourts.gov/educational-resources/educational-activities/grove-city-college-v-bell-facts-and-case-summary.

83. Quoted in Victoria Louise Jackson, "Title IX and the Big Time: Women's Intercollegiate Athletics at the University of North Carolina at Chapel Hill, 1950–1992" (PhD diss., Arizona State University, 2015), 196.

84. Jackson, "Title IX," 194–197.

85. See, for example, Carl F. H. Henry, "NCC Conference Urges Recognition of Red China," *Christianity Today* December 8, 1958; "Red China and World Morality," *Christianity Today* December 10, 1956; "The Communist Terror: Plight of the Korean Christians," *Christianity Today*, September 25, 1961.

86. Thomas Friedman, *The World Is Flat: A Brief History of the Twenty-First Century* (New York: Farrar, Straus, and Giroux, 2005).

87. Francis Fukuyama, "The End of History?" *National Interest* 16 (1989): 3–18; Samuel P. Huntington, *The Clash of Civilizations and the Remaking of World Order* (New York: Touchstone, 1996).

88. "Underground" here refers to the practice of working as missionaries in an informal or covert manner in countries in which missionary activity is either illegal or heavily proscribed.

89. McAlister, *Kingdom of God*, 146.

90. Moranian, "Armenian Genocide and American Missionary Efforts," 196.

91. Dana L. Robert, "Shifting Southward: Global Christianity since 1945," *International Bulletin of Missionary Research* 24, no. 2 (2000): 50–58; Dana L. Robert, *Christian Mission: How Christianity Became a World Religion* (Oxford: Wiley-Blackwell, 2009); Andrew Walls, *The Missionary Movement in Christian History: Studies in the Transmission of Faith* (Maryknoll, NY: Orbis Books, 1996).

92. Brian Stanley, *Christianity in the 20th Century: A World History* (Princeton, NJ: Princeton University Press, 2018).

93. Lamin Sanneh, *West African Christianity: The Religious Impact* (Maryknoll, NY: Orbis Books, 1983); Marthinus Louis Daneel, *Zionism and Faith-Healing in Rhodesia: Aspects of African Independent Churches* (The Hague: Mouton, 1970).

94. Klaus Koschorke, "Transcontinental Links, Enlarged Maps, and Polycentric Structures in the History of World Christianity," *Journal of World Christianity* 6, no. 1 (2016): 28–56.

95. Lamin Sanneh, *Disciples of All Nations: Pillars of World Christianity* (New York: Oxford University Press, 2008), xx.

96. Daniel Philpott and Timothy Samuel Shah, introduction to *Under Caesar's Sword: How Christians Respond to Persecution*, ed. Daniel Philpott and Timothy Samuel Shah (Cambridge: Cambridge University Press, 2018), 1–29.

97. Johnnie Moore, *The Martyr's Oath: Living for the Jesus They're Willing to Die For* (Carol Stream, IL: Tyndale House Publishers, 2017); Jason Bruner, "The Evangelical Search for Authenticity," *Marginalia Review of Books*, April 13, 2018.

98. Walls, *Missionary Movement*.

99. DC Talk and Voice of the Martyrs, *Jesus Freaks*, 80–82.

100. I use this example because it represents these tendencies in this kind of literature. I do not use it to imply that any similar instance necessarily occludes violence perpetuated by Christians.

101. David Platt, *Radical: Taking Your Faith Back from the American Dream* (Colorado Springs, CO: Multnomah, 2010); Dominic Sputo, *Heirloom Love: Authentic Christianity in This Age of Persecution* (self-published, 2018); Moore, *Martyr's Oath*; Rob Bell and Don Golden, *Jesus Wants to Save Christians: A Manifesto for the Church in Exile* (Grand Rapids, MI: Zondervan, 2008).

102. Voice of the Martyrs, *I am N Devotional* (Eastbourne: David Cook, 2016), 195.

103. David Limbaugh, *Persecution: How Liberals Are Waging War against Christianity* (Washington, DC: Regnery Publishing, 2003); Nina Shea, *In the Lion's Den* (Nashville: Broadman & Holman Publishers, 1997), 2.

104. Robert P. Jones, *The End of White Christian America* (New York: Simon and Schuster, 2017).

105. Thomas H. Kean, "The 9/11 Commission Report: Final Report of the National Commission on Terrorist Attacks upon the United States; Executive Summary," accessed December 19, 2019, https://govinfo.library.unt.edu/911/report/911Report_Exec .pdf.

106. While Saba Mahmood has perceptively analyzed the effects of the idea of "religious minority" with respect to Middle Eastern nation-states, one might also note the similarities with respect to how the United States has surveilled its Muslim citizens and residents, especially after 9/11. Mahmood, *Religious Difference*.

107. "Christmas under Siege: The Big Picture," Fox News, December 24, 2004, updated May 20, 2015, https://www.foxnews.com /story/christmas-under-siege-the-big-picture.

108. The allusion here is to cases such as that of the Masterpiece Cakeshop. The issue in question here was a conservative Christian baker's refusal to make a cake for a same-sex wedding ceremony based upon his religious objections to same-sex marriage. *Syllabus Masterpiece Cakeshop, Ltd., et al. v. Colorado Civil Rights Commission et al.*, U.S. Supreme Court, accessed December 19, 2019, https://www.supremecourt.gov /opinions/17pdf/16-111_j4el.pdf.

109. VOM, *I am N Devotional*, 15–16.

110. Jeffrey Goldberg, "Washington Discovers Christian Persecution," *New York Times Magazine*, December 21, 1997.

111. Paul Marshall, *Their Blood Cries Out: The Untold Story of Persecution Against Christians in the Modern World* (Dallas, TX: Word Publishing, 1997).

112. Philpott and Shah, ed., *Under Caesar's Sword*.

113. Russell Moore, "Why the Church Should neither Cave nor Panic about the Decision on Gay Marriage," *Washington Post*, June 26, 2015, https://www.washingtonpost.com/news/acts-of -faith/wp/2015/06/26/why-the-church-should-neither-cave-nor -panic-about-the-decision-on-gay-marriage/.

114. Michael Stone, "James Dobson Releases Radio Ad Endorsing Roy Moore," *Progressive Secular Humanist*, November 27, 2017, https://www.patheos.com/blogs/progressivesecularhumanist /2017/11/james-dobson-releases-radio-ad-endorsing-roy -moore/; Peter Beinart, "Breaking Faith," *Atlantic*, April 2017,

https://www.theatlantic.com/magazine/archive/2017/04
/breaking-faith/517785/. If too clear a line was drawn from
American evangelicals to support for Trump, researchers also
found that one of the key determinants of the strength of
evangelicals' political support was whether or not the person
actually attended a church regularly. They found non-
churchgoers who identified as evangelical to be significantly
more supportive of Donald Trump in the 2016 GOP
primaries.

115. Rod Dreher, *The Benedict Option: A Strategy for Christians in a
Post-Christian America* (New York: Penguin, 2017).

116. David Congdon, "No, the American Church Isn't in Exile,"
Sojourners, April 19, 2017, https://sojo.net/articles/no-american
-church-isn-t-exile.

117. Ed Mazza, "Jerry Falwell Jr. Calls Donald Trump the 'Dream
President' for Evangelicals," *Huffington Post*, April 30, 2017,
https://www.huffpost.com/entry/jerry-falwell-jr-dream
-president-trump_n_5906950fe4b05c3976807a08.

118. Samuel Smith, "Obama State Department Responsible for
Rise in Global Christian Persecution, Tony Perkins Says,"
Christian Post, January 13, 2017, https://www.christianpost
.com/news/obama-state-department-responsible-for-rise-in
-global-christian-persecution-tony-perkins-says-172969/.

119. Ben Kamisar, "Trump: 'We're Saying Merry Christmas
Again,'" *The Hill*, October 13, 2017, https://thehill.com
/homenews/administration/355303-trump-were-saying-merry
-christmas-again.

120. Allen, *Global War on Christians*.

121. Portions of this concluding section were first published as Jason
Bruner, "The Evangelical Search for Authenticity," *Marginalia
Review of Books*, April 13, 2018, https://marginalia.lareviewof
books.org/evangelical-search-for-authenticity/.

Chapter 4   A Global War on Christians?

1. Jacob Siegel, "Islamic Extremists Now Crucifying People in Syria—and Tweeting Out the Pictures," *Daily Beast*, April 30, 2014, https://www.thedailybeast.com/islamic-extremists-now -crucifying-people-in-syriaand-tweeting-out-the-pictures.

2. Valeria Cetorelli et al., "ISIS' Yazidi Genocide," *Foreign Affairs*, June 8, 2017, https://www.foreignaffairs.com/articles/syria/2017 -06-08/isis-yazidi-genocide.

3. Nicola Menzie, "History Magazine, VOM Highlight Persecu- tion of Modern Believers," *Christian Post*, June 25, 2014, https://www.christianpost.com/news/history-magazine-vom -highlight-persecution-of-modern-believers-cite-claim-that -christians-partly-to-blame-for-70-million-martyred-since -jesus-time.html.

4. "Subcommittee Hearing: The Persecution of Christians as a Worldwide Phenomenon," US House Foreign Affairs Com- mittee, February 11, 2014, https://www.youtube.com/watch?v =LP5Ji7x6hEg.

5. Michael Horowitz, introduction to *Their Blood Cries Out: The Untold Story of Persecution against Christians in the Modern World*, by Paul Marshall (Dallas: Word Publishing, 1997), xxi–xxiv.

6. Richard Wurmbrand, *Tortured for Christ* (Bartlesville, OK: Living Sacrifice Book Co., 1967); Nina Shea, *In the Lion's Den* (Nashville: Broadman & Holman Publishers, 1997), 1–12.

7. Kevin Kruse, *One Nation under God: How Corporate America Invented Christian America* (New York: Basic Books, 2015); Martin Marty, "A Judeo-Christian Looks at the Judeo- Christian Tradition," *Christian Century* 103, no. 29 (October 8, 1986): 858–860; Deborah Dash Moore, "Jewish GIs and the Creation of the Judeo-Christian Tradition," *Religion and American Culture* 8, no. 1 (1998): 31–51.

8. Horowitz, introduction to *Their Blood Cries Out*, xxiii.

9. As a counterpoint to this, see David Limbaugh, *Persecution: How Liberals Are Waging War against Christianity* (Washington, DC: Regnery Publishing, 2003).

10. Andrew Preston, "Defender of the Faith: The United States and World Christianity," in *Relocating World Christianity: Interdisciplinary Studies in Universal and Local Expressions of the Christian Faith*, ed. Joel Cabrita, David Maxwell, and Emma Wild-Wood (Leiden: Brill, 2017).

11. Marshall, *Their Blood Cries Out*, 7.

12. Marshall, 4.

13. DC Talk and Voice of the Martyrs, *Jesus Freaks* (Minneapolis: Bethany House, 1999), 17. In retelling her story, this book only includes the barest details in order to make the point that she fits an ancient martyrological type. Her name is not mentioned, probably because the story was so well known. But it later came to light that the story about Cassie was almost certainly not true and that another girl who was near Cassie is the one who was asked the question. That other girl survived the shooting. Misty Bernall, *She Said Yes: The Unlikely Martyrdom of Cassie Bernall* (New York: Pocket Books, 1999). For a discussion of the conflicting reports about who said "yes" at Columbine, see Dave Cullen, "Who Said 'Yes'?" *Salon*, September 30, 1999, https://www.salon.com/1999/09/30/bernall/.

14. Melani McAlister, *The Kingdom of God Has No Borders: A Global History of American Evangelicals* (Oxford: Oxford University Press, 2018), 165.

15. Quoted in Shea, *In the Lion's Den*, 100.

16. McAlister, *Kingdom of God*, 166–168.

17. Marshall, *Their Blood Cries Out*, ch. 2.

18. Robert Sieple, "The USCIRF Is Only Cursing the Darkness," *Christianity Today*, October 1, 2002.

19. Theodore Schleifer, "Donald Trump: 'I Think Islam Hates Us,'" CNN, March 10, 2016, https://www.cnn.com/2016/03/09/politics/donald-trump-islam-hates-us/index.html.

20. Marshall, *Their Blood Cries Out*, 4.

21. DC Talk and Voice of the Martyrs, *Jesus Freaks*, 15.

22. Todd M. Johnson and Gina Zurlo, "Christian Martyrdom as a Pervasive Phenomenon," *Society* 51 (2014): 681.

23. "Background of the Genocide against the Tutsi," n.d., Republic of Rwanda, National Commission for the Fight Against Genocide, accessed April 3, 2019, https://www.cnlg.gov.rw/index .php?id=80.

24. Timothy Longman, *Memory and Justice in Post-Genocide Rwanda* (Cambridge: Cambridge University Press, 2017); Jennie E. Burnet, *Genocide Lives in Us: Women, Memory, and Silence in Rwanda* (Madison: University of Wisconsin Press, 2012).

25. "Report of the Independent Inquiry into the Actions of the United Nations during the 1994 Genocide in Rwanda," December 15, 1999, accessed April 3, 2019, https://reliefweb.int /report/rwanda/report-independent-inquiry-actions-united -nations-during-1994-genocide-rwanda.

26. Human Rights Watch, "Numbers," from *Leave None to Tell the Story: Genocide in Rwanda*, (1999, modified July 29, 2017), accessed April 3, 2019, https://www.hrw.org/reports/1999/rwanda/Geno1-3 -04.htm. The data used in the documentary, in addition to related materials, can be found at https://genodynamics.weebly.com/.

27. Marijke Vanpoorten, "The Death Toll of the Rwandan Genocide: A Detailed Analysis for Gikongoro Province," *Population* 60, no. 4 (2005): 331–367. In 2014, the British Broadcasting Corporation (BBC) released a documentary containing controversial claims put forward by Christian Davenport and Allan Stam, who stated that there were only 200,000 Tutsi victims of the Rwandan Genocide. Davenport and Stam's comparatively low numbers were the result of a different method for determining the size of the Tutsi population in Rwanda in early 1994. Relying upon extrapolated numbers from a 1952 census (they considered census data from 1991 to be unreliable because it was conducted under the

auspices of a Hutu-controlled government), Davenport and Stam figured that the Tutsi population at the start of the genocide was 506,000. Subtracting 300,000 Tutsi genocide survivors from that number, they reached the conclusion that there were 200,000 victims. For Vanpoorten's refutation of the Davenport and Stam numbers, see Marijke Vanpoorten, "Rwanda: Why Claim That 200,000 Tutsi Died in the Genocide Is Wrong," *African Arguments,* October 27, 2014, https://africanarguments.org/2014/10/27/rwanda-why -davenport-and-stams-calculation-that-200000-tutsi-died-in -the-genocide-is-wrong-by-marijke-verpoorten/.

28. Longman, *Memory and Justice.*

29. Caritas, "Six Million Dead in Congo's War," February 24, 2010, https://www.caritas.org/2010/02/six-million-dead-in-congos-war/.

30. Benjamin Coughlin et al., "Mortality in the Democratic Republic of Congo: An Ongoing Crisis," International Rescue Committee, accessed December 19, 2019, https://www.rescue.org/sites/default /files/document/661/2006-7congomortalitysurvey.pdf.

31. Severine Autesserre, "The Trouble with Congo: How Local Disputes Fuel Regional Conflict," *Foreign Affairs* 87, no. 3 (2008): 94–110; Benjamin Coghlin et al., "Mortality in the Democratic Republic of the Congo: A Nationwide Survey," *Lancet* 367 (2006): 44–51; Michael Spagat et al., "Estimating War Deaths," *Journal of Conflict Resolution* 53, no. 6 (2009): 934–950.

32. Peter James Spielman, "Review of Congo War Halves Death Toll from 5.4 Million," Associated Press, January 20, 2010.

33. UNHCR, *Report of the Mapping Exercise Documenting the Most Serious Violations of Human Rights and International Humanitarian Law Committed within the Territory of the Democratic Republic of the Congo between March 1993 and June 2003,* August 2010.

34. Coghlin et al., "Mortality in the Democratic Republic of Congo."

35. Benjamin Coghlin et al., "Update on Mortality in the Democratic Republic of Congo: Results from a Third Nationwide Survey," *Disaster Medicine and Public Health Preparedness* 3, no. 2 (2009): 88–96.

36. Johnson and Zurlo, "Christian Martyrdom," 684n40. The figure of 20 percent derives from an earlier observation in 1982 that 20 percent of African Christians were "practicing" Christians. Ruth Alexander, "Are There Really 100,000 New Christian Martyrs Every Year?" BBC, November 12, 2013, https://www.bbc.com/news/magazine-24864587.

37. Johnson and Zurlo, "Christian Martyrdom," 681; emphasis in original.

38. Johnson and Zurlo, 681.

39. Thomas Schirrmacher, "A Response to the High Counts of Christian Martyrs per Year," *International Journal of Religious Freedom* 4, no. 2 (2011): 11.

40. J. J. Carney, *Rwanda before the Genocide* (New York: Oxford University Press, 2014).

41. "The Ntarama Church Massacre," *Rwandan Stories*, accessed April 21, 2019, http://www.rwandanstories.org/genocide/ntarama_church.html.

42. Scott Straus, *The Order of Genocide: Race, Power, and War in Rwanda* (Ithaca, NY: Cornell University Press, 2006).

43. "DR Congo: UN-Mandated Group Finds Evidence Rwanda, Army Aiding Rival Rebels," UN News, December 12, 2008, https://news.un.org/en/story/2008/12/285222-dr-congo-un-mandated-group-finds-evidence-rwanda-army-aiding-rival-rebels.

44. "Nearly 1 Million Christians Martyred for Their Faith in Last Decade," Fox News, July 6, 2017, https://www.foxnews.com/world/nearly-1-million-christians-reportedly-martyred-for-their-faith-in-last-decade.

45. Pew Research Center, "The Changing Global Religious Landscape," April 5, 2017, https://www.pewforum.org/2017/04/05/the-changing-global-religious-landscape, 35.

46. Timothy Longman, *Christianity and Genocide in Rwanda* (Cambridge: Cambridge University Press, 2009).

47. Waithera Junghae, "'Deny Christ or Die,' Boko Haram Tells Young Christian Woman," *Christian Post*, December 7, 2013, https://www.christianpost.com/news/nigeria-kills-13-boko -haram-militants-as-massacre-of-christians-continues-87555/; "Christian Militia Killed up to 1000 Muslims in Nigeria, Leader Claims," *Sydney Morning Herald*, May 8, 2004, https://www.smh.com.au/world/christian-militia-killed-up -to-1000-muslims-in-nigeria-leader-claims-20040508-gdivw5 .html.

48. "Nigeria Election: Riots over Goodluck Jonathan Win," BBC, April 18, 2011, https://www.bbc.com/news/world-africa -13107867.

49. Stoyan Zaimov, "Nigeria Kills 13 Boko Haram Militants as Massacre of Christians Continues," *Christian Post*, January 2, 2013, https://www.christianpost.com/news/nigeria-kills-13 -boko-haram-militants-as-massacre-of-christians-continues -87555/. Portions of this section were taken from Jason Bruner and Ryan Linde, "Eusebius and the Global War on Christians," *Sacred Matters*, June 2, 2014, https://sacredmattersmagazine .com/eusebius-and-the-global-war-on-christians/.

50. Moore, *The Martyr's Oath*, 13.

51. Moore, *The Martyr's Oath*, 90.

52. Gerard Chouin, Manuel Reinert, and Elodie Apard, "Body Count and Religion in the Boko Haram Crisis: Evidence from the Nigeria Watch Database," in *Boko Haram: Islamism, Politics, Security, and the State in Nigeria*, ed. Marc-Antoine Pérouse de Montclos (Leiden: African Studies Centre, 2014), 213–236. Their analysis, however, does not appear to factor in rates of conversions in these areas since the 1980s, which Darren Kew considers to be an important factor in the development of the violence. Darren Kew, "Why Nigeria Matters," *First Things*

(November 2007), accessed April 15, 2019, https://www
.firstthings.com/article/2007/11/why-nigeria-matters. See also
Akinola Ejodame Olojo, "Muslims, Christians, and Religious
Violence in Nigeria: Patterns and Mapping (June 2006–
May 2014)," IFRA-Nigeria Working Paper Series, no. 32
(November 11, 2014), accessed April 17, 2019, http://www
.nigeriawatch.org/media/html/WP3OLOJOFinal.pdf.

53. Moore, *The Martyr's Oath*, 108, 2, 138 (in order of quotation).

54. Moore, *The Martyr's Oath*, 110.

55. Jason Bruner, "The Evangelical Search for Authenticity,"
Marginalia Review of Books, April 13, 2018, https://marginalia
.lareviewofbooks.org/evangelical-search-for-authenticity/.

56. Moore, *The Martyr's Oath*, 110.

57. Linda Bordoni, "Pope to WCC: Ongoing Ecumenism of Blood
Urges Us to Go Forward," Vatican News, June 21, 2018,
https://www.vaticannews.va/en/pope/news/2018-06/pope
-francis-geveva-wcc.html.

58. Kate Shellnutt, "Russia's Newest Law: No Evangelizing
outside of Church," *Christianity Today*, July 8, 2016, https://
www.christianitytoday.com/news/2016/june/no-evangelizing
-outside-of-church-russia-proposes.html.

59. "The Enemy Is Shooting at Us!" Open Doors, December 13,
2013, https://www.opendoorsusa.org/christian-persecution
/stories/enemy-shooting-us/.

60. Jeff Thomas, "Exile," *World Watch Monitor*, April 18, 2014,
https://www.worldwatchmonitor.org/2014/04/exile/.

61. Tom O'Connor, "Iraqi Christians Face 'Death Sentence' as
Trump Prepares Mass Deportations," *Newsweek*, June 14, 2017,
https://www.newsweek.com/iraq-christians-trump-death
-sentence-deportation-625722; Callum Patton, "Mike Pence
Won't Be Meeting Any Christians on His Trip to Save
Christianity in the Middle East," *Newsweek,* December 18,
2017, https://www.newsweek.com/mike-pence-wont-be

-meeting-any-christians-his-trip-save-christianity-middle
-751334.

62. Schirrmacher, "Response to the High Counts of Christian
Martyrs."

63. Menzie, "History Magazine."

64. Jolyon Mitchell, *Martyrdom: A Very Short Introduction* (Oxford:
Oxford University Press, 2013).

65. "Number of Christian Martyrs Continues to Cause Debate,"
Open Doors, November 14, 2013, https://www.opendoorsusa
.org/take-action/pray/number-of-christian-martyrs-continues
-to-cause-debate/.

66. Adam Beckett, "Christians Are the Most Persecuted Religious
Group in the World, Says Pew Report," *Church Times*, June 29,
2018, https://www.churchtimes.co.uk/articles/2018/29-june
/news/world/christians-are-the-most-persecuted-religious
-group-in-the-world-says-report.

67. Pew Research Center, "Global Uptick in Government
Restrictions on Religion in 2016," June 21, 2016, accessed
April 17, 2019, https://www.pewforum.org/2018/06/21/global
-uptick-in-government-restrictions-on-religion-in-2016/. See
also Pew Research Center, "Religious Hostilities Reach
Six-Year High," January 14, 2014, https://www.pewforum.org
/2014/01/14/religious-hostilities-reach-six-year-high/; and Pew
Research Center, "Rising Restrictions on Religion—One-
Third of the World's Population Experiences an Increase,"
August 9, 2011, https://www.pewforum.org/2011/08/09/rising
-restrictions-on-religion2/.

68. National Counterterrorism Center, "Report on Terror 2011,"
March 12, 2012, https://fas.org/irp/threat/nctc2011.pdf, 14.

69. United Nations Office on Drugs and Crime, "Global Study on
Homicide 2013," accessed December 19, 2019, https://www.unodc
.org/documents/gsh/pdfs/2014_GLOBAL_HOMICIDE
_BOOK_web.pdf.

70. Physicians for Social Responsibility, "Body Count: Casualty Figures after 10 Years of the 'War on Terror'—Iraq, Afghanistan, Pakistan," March 2015, accessed April 13, 2019, https://www.psr.org/wp-content/uploads/2018/05/body-count.pdf; G. Burnham et al., "Mortality after the 2003 Invasion of Iraq: A Cross-Sectional Cluster Sample Survey," *Lancet* 368, no. 9545 (2006): 1421–1428. See also Iraq Family Health Survey Study Group, "Violence-Related Mortality in Iraq from 2002 to 2006," *New England Journal of Medicine* 358 (2008): 484–493; Madelyn Hsaio-Rei Hicks et al., "Violent Deaths of Iraqi Civilians, 2003–2008: Analysis by Perpetrator, Weapon, Time, and Location," *PLoS Med* 8, no. 2 (2011): e1000415; Neta C. Crawford, "Human Cost of the Post-9/11 Wars: Lethality and the Need for Transparency," Costs of War, Brown University (November 2018), accessed April 13, 2019, https://watson.brown.edu/costsofwar/files/cow/imce/papers/2018/Human%20Costs%2C%20Nov%208%20 2018%20CoW.pdf. For a review of Iraq mortality studies, see Christine Tapp et al., "Iraq War Mortality Estimates: A Systematic Review," *Conflict and Health* 2, no. 1 (2008).

71. Megan Specia, "How Syria's Death Toll Is Lost in the Fog of War," *New York Times*, April 13, 2018, https://www.nytimes.com/2018/04/13/world/middleeast/syria-death-toll.html.

72. "Ethnic Cleansing in Central African Republic, No Genocide: U.N. Inquiry," Reuters, January 5, 2015, https://www.reuters.com/article/us-centralafrica-inquiry/ethnic-cleansing-in-central-african-republic-no-genocide-u-n-inquiry-idUSKBN0KH2BM20150108.

73. "Up to 15,000 Killed in Libya War: U.N. Expert," Reuters, June 9, 2011, https://www.reuters.com/article/us-libya-un-deaths/up-to-15000-killed-in-libya-war-u-n-rights-expert-idUSTRE7584UY20110609.

74. Louis Charbonneau, "U.N. Says Darfur Dead May Be 300,000 as Sudan Denies," Reuters, April 22, 2008, https://www.reuters

.com/article/us-sudan-darfur-un/u-n-says-darfur-dead-may-be
-300000-as-sudan-denies-idUSN2230854320080422.

75. Nikolaus Grubeck, "Civilian Harm in Somalia: Creating an
Appropriate Response," Campaign for Innocent Victims in
Conflict, November 23, 2011, https://civiliansinconflict.org
/publications/research/civilian-harm-somalia-creating
-appropriate-response/, 17–18. The death toll for the famine that
struck Somalia in this period was itself estimated at 260,000.
For the sake of this analysis, I take the famine to be a deriva-
tive catastrophe that is related to both Ethiopia's prior invasion
(starting in 2006) and the prevention of aid by some armed
groups. Associated Press, "Somalia: Famine Toll in 2011 Was
Larger Than Previously Reported," *New York Times*, April 29,
2013, https://www.nytimes.com/2013/04/30/world/africa
/somalia-famine-toll-in-2011-was-larger-than-previously
-reported.html?ref=world&pagewanted=print.

76. Francesco Checchi and W. Courtland Robinson, "Mortality
among Populations of Southern and Central Somalia Affected
by Severe Food Insecurity and Famine during 2010–2012,"
FEWS NET, May 2, 2013. Estimates for comparable deaths in
Indonesia are difficult to assess. Edward Aspinall estimates
that the separatist movement in Aceh between 1998 and 2005
killed approximately 10,000 people. A study by the International Organization for Migration (IOM), however, states that
there were 155,473 people "widowed" during the conflict and an
additional 184,021 children orphaned at some point during the
conflict. See Edward Aspinall, *Islam and Nation: Separatist
Rebellion in Aceh, Indonesia* (Stanford, CA: Stanford University
Press, 2009); IOM, "Meta Analysis; Vulnerability, Stability,
Displacement and Reintegration: Issues Facing the Peace
Process in Aceh, Indonesia," August 2008, accessed April 13,
2019, https://www.iom.int/jahia/webdav/site/myjahiasite
/shared/shared/mainsite/activities/countries/docs/usaid_meta
_analysis.pdf. For an estimated Arab Spring death toll, see

Jessica Rettig, "Death Toll of 'Arab Spring,'" *US News and World Report*, November 8, 2011, https://www.usnews.com /news/slideshows/death-toll-of-arab-spring; "Chad's Spiralling Conflict," Al Jazeera, February 2, 2008, https://web .archive.org/web/20080207035718/http://english.aljazeera.net /NR/exeres/55C5792F-6112-427D-92C1-69A2E5C38785.htm; "Mali Conflict and Aftermath: Compendium of Human Rights Watch Reporting, 2012–2017," Human Rights Watch, New York, 2017.

77. Nick Cumming-Bruce, "United Nations Investigators Accuse ISIS of Genocide over Attacks on Yazidis," *New York Times*, March 19, 2015, https://www.nytimes.com/2015/03/20/world /middleeast/isis-genocide-yazidis-iraq-un-panel.html.

78. "MEPs Call for Urgent Action to Protect Religious Minorities against ISIS," News European Parliament, February 4, 2016, https://www.europarl.europa.eu/news/en/press-room /20160129IPR11938/meps-call-for-urgent-action-to-protect -religious-minorities-against-isis.

79. "House Unanimously Passes Fortenberry ISIS Genocide Resolution," press release, Congressman John Fortenberry, March 15, 2016, https://fortenberry.house.gov/media-center /press-releases/house-unanimously-passes-fortenberry-isis -genocide-resolution.

80. Matthew Rosenberg, "Citing Atrocities, John Kerry Calls ISIS Actions Genocide," *New York Times*, March 17, 2016, https:// www.nytimes.com/2016/03/18/world/middleeast/citing -atrocities-john-kerry-calls-isis-actions-genocide.html.

81. Rt. Rev. Philip Mounstephen, "Bishop of Truro's Independent Review for the Foreign Secretary of FCO Support for Persecuted Christians," accessed December 19, 2019, https://christian persecutionreview.org.uk/interim-report/.

82. President Donald J. Trump, "Executive Order Protecting the Nation from Foreign Terrorist Entry into the United States," January 27, 2017, https://www.whitehouse.gov/presidential

-actions/executive-order-protecting-nation-foreign-terrorist
-entry-united-states/.

83. Shea, *In the Lion's Den*.

84. Amanda Holpuch, "US Judge Halts Deportation of More Than
100 Iraqi Christians," *Guardian*, June 22, 2017, https://www
.theguardian.com/us-news/2017/jun/22/iraq-deportation-us
-judge-halts-detroit-ice-raid.

85. Associated Press, "US Decries ISIS 'Genocide' of Christians,
Other Groups," NBC News, August 15, 2017, https://www
.nbcnews.com/news/us-news/u-s-decries-islamic-state
-genocide-christians-other-groups-n792866.

86. Charles Jaret, "Troubled by Newcomers: Anti-Immigrant
Attitudes and Action during Two Eras of Mass Immigration to
the United States," *Journal of American Ethnic History* 18, no. 3
(1999): 9–39.

87. "Indonesia," USCIRF 2013 Annual Report, accessed April 15,
2019, https://www.uscirf.gov/sites/default/files/resources
/Indonesia%202013.pdf; Asia Banyan, "We Decide If You Are
Muslim or Not," *Economist*, June 10, 2010, https://www
.economist.com/banyan/2010/06/10/we-decide-whether-youre
-muslim-or-not.

88. "Situation of Baha'is in Iran," Baha'i International Community,
accessed April 17, 2019, https://www.bic.org/focus-areas/situation
-iranian-bahais/current-situation; "World Watch List: Iran,"
Open Doors, accessed April 17, 2019, https://www.opendoorsusa
.org/christian-persecution/world-watch-list/iran/.

89. Cathy Lynn Grossman, "Americans Value Religious Freedom,
but Mostly for Christians," *USA Today*, December 31, 2015,
https://www.usatoday.com/story/news/2015/12/31/americans
-value-religious-freedom-but-mostly-christians/78130098/.

90. Robert D. Kaplan, "In Defense of Empire," *Atlantic*, April 2014.

91. Trump, "Executive Order Protecting the Nation from Foreign
Terrorist Entry."

92. Christopher White, "New Poll Shows Anti-Christian Persecution a 'Very Severe' Global Concern," *Crux Now*, March 21, 2019, https://cruxnow.com/global-church/2019/03/21 /new-poll-shows-anti-christian-persecution-a-very-severe -global-concern/.

93. Schirrmacher, "Response to the High Counts of Christian Martyrs."

94. Daniel Philpott and Timothy Samuel Shah, eds., *Under Caesar's Sword: How Christians Respond to Persecution* (Cambridge, UK: Cambridge University Press, 2018).

95. "Number of Christian Martyrs Continues to Cause Debate," Open Doors, November 14, 2013, https://www.opendoorsusa .org/take-action/pray/number-of-christian-martyrs-continues -to-cause-debate/.

96. Terrence McCoy, "'Soldiers of Jesus': Armed Neo-Pentecostals Torment Brazil's Religious Minorities," *Washington Post*, December 8, 2019, https://www.washingtonpost.com/world/the _americas/soldiers-of-jesus-armed-neo-pentecostals-torment -brazils-religious-minorities/2019/12/08/fd74de6e-fff0-11e9-8501 -2a7123a38c58_story.html.

97. Patton, "Mike Pence Won't Be Meeting Any Christians."

98. Kirsten Powers, "The New Age of Christian Martyrdom," *Daily Beast*, January 3, 2014, https://www.thedailybeast.com /the-new-age-of-christian-martyrdom.

99. Stoyan Zaimov, "Christian Group Praises US Gov't's Decision to Help Save Kidnapped School Girls in Nigeria," *Christian Post*, May 8, 2014, https://www.christianpost.com/news /christian-group-praises-us-govts-decision-to-help-save -kidnapped-schoolgirls-in-nigeria-119363/.

100. Associated Press, "Pope Urges Christian Unity," Fox News, December 10, 2015, https://www.foxnews.com/world/pope -urges-christian-unity-when-they-kill-a-christian-they-dont -ask-are-you-catholic.

Chapter 5   The Global Politics of the Suffering Body of Christ

1. "The Latest: Trump Announces Details of NKorea Summit," *Washington Post*, May 10, 2018, https://www.washingtonpost.com/world/national-security/the-latest-trump-announces-details-of-nkorea-summit/2018/05/10/762160fa-54c9-11e8-a6d4-ca1d035642ce_story.html.

2. Ayesha Ramachandran, *The Worldmakers: Global Imagining in Early Modern Europe* (Chicago: University of Chicago Press, 2015), 14.

3. "'Tortured for Christ' Richard Wurmbrand," YouTube, accessed December 26, 2019, https://www.youtube.com/watch?v=bqdPkDPMCwk.

4. Susan Sontag, *On Regarding the Pain of Others* (London: Penguin Books, 2019).

5. Vincanne Adams, "Metrics of the Global Sovereign: Numbers and Stories in Global Health," in *Metrics: What Counts in Global Health*, ed. Vincanne Adams (Durham, NC: Duke University Press, 2017), 19–54.

6. Ramachandran, *Worldmakers*, 15.

7. Nimi Wariboko, *Nigerian Pentecostalism* (Rochester, NY: University of Rochester Press, 2014); Kate Bowler, *Blessed: A History of the American Prosperity Gospel* (New York: Oxford University Press, 2013).

8. Elizabeth Shakman Hurd, *Beyond Religious Freedom: The New Politics of Religion* (Princeton, NJ: Princeton University Press, 2015).

9. Michael Barnet and Janice Gross Stein, *Sacred Aid: Faith and Humanitarianism* (New York: Oxford University Press, 2012).

10. Omri Elisha, "Saved by a Martyr: Evangelical Mediation, Sanctification, and the 'Persecuted Church.'" *Journal of the American Academy of Religion* 84, no. 4 (December 2016): 1056–1080.

11. Karl Rahner, a prominent twentieth-century Catholic theologian, developed the notion of "anonymous Christian" to describe those who had not heard the Christian gospel but might nevertheless have salvation through Christ. See Lucas Lamadrid, "Anonymous or Analogous Christians? Rahner and Von Balthasar on Naming the Non-Christian," *Modern Theology* 11, no. 3 (1995): 363–384.

12. Physicians for Social Responsibility, "Body Count: Casualty Figures after 10 Years of the 'War on Terror'—Iraq, Afghanistan, Pakistan," March 2015, accessed December 19, 2019, https://www.psr.org/wp-content/uploads/2018/05/body-count.pdf.

13. Lauren Frances Turek, "To Support a 'Brother in Christ': Evangelical Groups and U.S.-Guatemalan Relations during the Ríos Montt Regime," *Diplomatic History* 39, no. 4 (2015): 689–719.

14. Jennifer McEntee and Mica Rosenberg, "U.S. Says It Will Separate Families Crossing Border Illegally," Reuters, May 7, 2018, https://www.reuters.com/article/us-usa-immigration-children/u-s-cements-plans-to-separate-families-crossing-border-illegally-idUSKBN1I82AB.

15. Daniel Burke, "100 Evangelical Leaders Sign Ad Denouncing Trump's Refugee Ban," CNN, February 8, 2017, https://www.cnn.com/2017/02/08/politics/evangelicals-ad-trump/index.html.

16. Andrew Preston, "Defender of the Faith: The United States and World Christianity," in *Relocating World Christianity: Interdisciplinary Studies in Universal and Local Expressions of the Christian Faith*, ed. Joel Cabrita, David Maxwell, and Emma Wild-Wood (Leiden: Brill, 2017), 261–280.

17. Hurd, *Beyond Religious Freedom*.

18. Thomas Schirrmacher raises a similar point regarding the use of high rates of martyrdom. Schirrmacher, "A Response to the High Counts of Christian Martyrs per Year," *International Journal of Religious Freedom* 4, no. 2 (2011): 9–13.

19. Jon Sobrino, *The Principle of Mercy: Taking the Crucified People from the Cross* (Maryknoll, NY: Orbis Books, 1994); Ernesto

Cardenal, "I Cry in the Night from the Torture Chamber (Psalm 129)," in *Mission Trends No. 3: Third World Theologies*, ed. Gerald H. Anderson and Thomas F. Stransky (Grand Rapids, MI: Eerdmans Publishing Co., 1976), 39–40. For a Black theology of liberation, see James H. Cone, *The Cross and the Lynching Tree* (Maryknoll, NY: Orbis Books, 2018); and James H. Cone, *A Black Theology of Liberation*, 40th anniversary ed. (Maryknoll, NY: Orbis Books, 2010).

Bibliography

Adams, Vincanne. "Metrics of the Global Sovereign: Numbers and Stories in Global Health." In *Metrics: What Counts in Global Health*, edited by Vincanne Adams, 19–54. Durham, NC: Duke University Press, 2017.

"The Address of Q. Sept. Tertullian to Scapula Tertullus." Translated by Sir David Dalrymple. Accessed April 1, 2020. http://www.tertullian.org/articles/dalrymple_scapula.htm.

Alexander, Ruth. "Are There Really 100,000 New Christian Martyrs Every Year?" BBC, November 12, 2013. https://www.bbc.com/news/magazine-24864587.

Allen, S. J., and Emilie Amt. Introduction to *The Crusades: A Reader*, edited by S. J. Allen and Emilie Amt, xv–xxii. Toronto: University of Toronto Press, 2014.

Allen Jr., John. *The Global War on Christians: Dispatches from the Front Lines of Anti-Christian Persecution*. New York: Image, 2013.

"Americans in Armenia." *Daily Inter Ocean*, December 15, 1894.

"Apology of Patriarch Timothy of Baghdad before the Caliph Mahdi." In *Readings in World Christian History*, vol. 1, *Earliest Christianity to 1453*, edited by John W. Coakley and Andrea Sterk, 231–242. Maryknoll, NY: Orbis Books, 2009.

Aspinall, Edward. *Islam and Nation: Separatist Rebellion in Aceh, Indonesia*. Stanford, CA: Stanford University Press, 2009.

Associated Press. "Pope Urges Christian Unity." Fox News, December 10, 2015. https://www.foxnews.com/world/pope-urges

-christian-unity-when-they-kill-a-christian-they-dont-ask-are
-you-catholic.

———. "Somalia: Famine Toll in 2011 Was Larger Than Previously
Reported." *New York Times*, April 29, 2013. https://www.nytimes
.com/2013/04/30/world/africa/somalia-famine-toll-in-2011-was
-larger-than-previously-reported.html?ref=world&pagewanted
=print.

———. "US Decries ISIS 'Genocide' of Christians, Other Groups."
NBC News, August 15, 2017. https://www.nbcnews.com/news
/us-news/u-s-decries-islamic-state-genocide-christians-other
-groups-n792866.

Athanasius of Alexandria. *Life of Anthony of Egypt*. In *Readings in
World Christian History*, vol. 1, *Earliest Christianity to 1453*, edited
by John W. Coakley and Andrea Sterk, 131–144. Maryknoll, NY:
Orbis Books, 2009.

Autesserre, Severine. "The Trouble with Congo: How Local
Disputes Fuel Regional Conflict." *Foreign Affairs* 87, no. 3 (2008):
94–110.

"Background of the Genocide against the Tutsi." Republic of Rwanda,
National Commission for the Fight Against Genocide. Accessed
April 3, 2019. https://www.cnlg.gov.rw/index.php?id=80.

Balakian, Peter. *The Burning Tigris: The Armenian Genocide and
America's Response*. New York: HarperCollins, 2003.

Balmer, Randall. "The Real Origins of the Religious Right."
Politico, May 27, 2014. https://www.politico.com/magazine/story
/2014/05/religious-right-real-origins-107133.

Banyan, Asia. "We Decide If You Are Muslim or Not." *Economist*,
June 10, 2010. https://www.economist.com/banyan/2010/06/10
/we-decide-whether-youre-muslim-or-not.

Barkun, Michael. *Religion and the Racist Right: The Origins of the
Christian Identity Movement*. Chapel Hill, NC: UNC Press, 1997.

Barnet, Michael, and Janice Gross Stein. *Sacred Aid: Faith and
Humanitarianism*. New York: Oxford University Press, 2012.

Bartlett, Robert. *Why Can the Dead Do Such Great Things?* Princeton, NJ: Princeton University Press, 2015.

Baumeister, Theofried. "Martyrdom and Persecution in Early Christianity." In *Martyrdom Today*, edited by Johanes-Baptist Metz and Edward Schillebeeckx, 3–8. Edinburgh: T&T Clark, 1983.

Beckett, Adam. "Christians Are the Most Persecuted Religious Group in the World, Says Pew Report." *Church Times*, June 29, 2018. https://www.churchtimes.co.uk/articles/2018/29-june/news/world/christians-are-the-most-persecuted-religious-group-in-the-world-says-report.

Beinart, Peter. "Breaking Faith." *Atlantic*, April 2017. https://www.theatlantic.com/magazine/archive/2017/04/breaking-faith/517785/.

Bell, L. Nelson. "A Southern Evangelical on Integration, August 17, 1955." In *Jerry Falwell and the Rise of the Religious Right*, edited by Matthew Avery Sutton, 51–54. New York: Bedford/St. Martin's, 2013.

Bell, Rob, and Don Golden. *Jesus Wants to Save Christians: A Manifesto for the Church in Exile.* Grand Rapids, MI: Zondervan, 2008.

Bernall, Misty. *She Said Yes: The Unlikely Martyrdom of Cassie Bernall.* New York: Pocket Books, 1999.

Bevans, Stephen B., and Roger P. Schroeder. *Constants in Context: A Theology of Mission for Today.* Maryknoll, NY: Orbis Books, 2004.

Blum, Edward. *Reforging the White Republic: Race, Religion, and American Nationalism, 1865–1989.* Baton Rouge: Louisiana State University Press, 2015.

Bordoni, Linda. "Pope to WCC: Ongoing Ecumenism of Blood Urges Us to Go Forward." Vatican News, June 21, 2018. https://www.vaticannews.va/en/pope/news/2018-06/pope-francis-geveva-wcc.html.

Bowersock, Glen W. *Martyrdom and Rome.* Cambridge: Cambridge University Press, 2002.

Bowler, Kate. *Blessed: A History of the American Prosperity Gospel.* New York: Oxford University Press, 2013.

Boyarin, Daniel. "Martyrdom and the Making of Christianity and Judaism." *Journal of Early Christian Studies* 6, no. 4 (1998): 577–627.

Boyd, Lydia. *Preaching Prevention: Born-Again Politics and the Moral Politics of AIDS in Uganda.* Athens: Ohio University Press, 2015.

Brake, Deborah. *Getting in the Game: Title IX and the Women's Sports Revolution.* New York: NYU Press, 2010.

Brown, Raymond E. *An Introduction to the New Testament.* New York: Doubleday, 1997.

Bruner, Jason. "The Evangelical Search for Authenticity." *Marginalia Review of Books*, April 13, 2018. https://marginalia .lareviewofbooks.org/evangelical-search-for-authenticity/.

———. "Tortured for Christ in Trump's America." *Sacred Matters*, April 13, 2018. https://sacredmattersmagazine.com/tortured-for -christ-in-trumps-america/.

———. "Uganda's President Will Sign Anti-Gay Bill. How Did the Nation Get to This Point?" *Religion and Politics*, February 19, 2014. https://religionandpolitics.org/2014/02/18/ugandas -president-will-sign-anti-gay-bill-how-did-the-nation-get-to -this-point/.

Bruner, Jason, and Ryan Linde. "Eusebius and the Global War on Christians." *Sacred Matters*, June 2, 2014. https://sacredmatters magazine.com/eusebius-and-the-global-war-on-christians/.

Buc, Philippe. *Holy War, Martyrdom, and Terror: Christianity, Violence, and the West.* Philadelphia: University of Pennsylvania Press, 2015.

Buda, Daniel. "The World Council of Churches' Relationships with Pentecostalism: A Brief Historical Survey and Some Recent Perspectives on Membership Matters." *International Review of Mission* 107, no. 1 (2018): 81–97.

Burke, Daniel. "100 Evangelical Leaders Sign Ad Denouncing Trump's Refugee Ban." CNN, February 8, 2017. https://www .cnn.com/2017/02/08/politics/evangelicals-ad-trump/index .html.

Burnet, Jennie E. *Genocide Lives in Us: Women, Memory, and Silence in Rwanda*. Madison: University of Wisconsin Press, 2012.

Burnham, G., R. Lafta, S. Doocy, and L. Roberts. "Mortality after the 2003 Invasion of Iraq: A Cross-Sectional Cluster Sample Survey." *Lancet* 368, no. 9545 (2006): 1421–1428.

Bushur, James G. "Ignatius of Antioch's Letter to the Romans: The Passionate Confession of Christian Identity." *Logia* 2, no. 1 (2015): 13–18.

Butler, Jon, Grant Wacker, and Randall Balmer, *Religion in American Life: A Short History*. New York: Oxford University Press, 2003.

Cabrita, Joel, David Maxwell, and Emma Wild-Wood, eds. *Relocating World Christianity: Interdisciplinary Studies in Universal and Local Expressions of the Christian Faith*. Leiden: Brill, 2017.

Cameron, Euan. "Medieval Heretics as Protestant Martyrs." In *Martyrs and Martyrologies*, edited by Diana Wood, 185–208. Oxford: Blackwell, 1993.

Cardenal, Ernesto. "I Cry in the Night from the Torture Chamber (Psalm 129)." In *Mission Trends No. 3: Third World Theologies*, edited by Gerald H. Anderson and Thomas F. Stransky, 39–40. Grand Rapids, MI: Eerdmans Publishing Co., 1976.

Caritas. "Six Million Dead in Congo's War." February 24, 2010. https://www.caritas.org/2010/02/six-million-dead-in-congos-war/.

Carney, J. J. *Rwanda before the Genocide*. New York: Oxford University Press, 2014.

Castelli, Elizabeth. *Martyrdom and Memory: Early Christian Culture Making*. New York: Columbia University Press, 2004.

Cavanaugh, William T. "Destroying the Church to Save It: Intra-Christian Persecution and the Modern State." In *Witness of the Body: The Past, Present, and Future of Christian Martyrdom*, edited by Michael L. Budde and Karen Scott, 125–150. Grand Rapids, MI: Eerdmans Publishing Co., 2011.

Cetorelli, Valeria, Isaac Sasson, Nazar Shabila, and Gilbert Burnham. "ISIS' Yazidi Genocide." *Foreign Affairs*, June 8, 2017.

https://www.foreignaffairs.com/articles/syria/2017-06-08/isis
-yazidi-genocide.

"Chad's Spiralling Conflict." Al Jazeera, February 2, 2008. https://
web.archive.org/web/20080207035718/http://english.aljazeera
.net/NR/exeres/55C5792F-6112-427D-92C1-69A2E5C38785.htm.

Chadwick, Henry. *The Early Church*. New York: Penguin Books, 1967.

"The Changing Global Religious Landscape." Pew Research Center,
April 5, 2017. https://www.pewforum.org/2017/04/05/the-changing
-global-religious-landscape/.

Charbonneau, Louis. "U.N. Says Darfur Dead May Be 300,000 as
Sudan Denies." Reuters, April 22, 2008. https://www.reuters
.com/article/us-sudan-darfur-un/u-n-says-darfur-dead-may-be
-300000-as-sudan-denies-idUSN2230854320080422.

Checchi, Francesco, and W. Courtland Robinson. "Mortality
among Populations of Southern and Central Somalia Affected
by Severe Food Insecurity and Famine during 2010–2012."
FEWS NET, May 2, 2013.

Chia, Edmund Kee-Fook. "Ecumenical Pilgrimage toward World
Christianity." *Theological Studies* 76, no. 3 (2015): 503–530.

Chouin, Gerard, Manuel Reinert, and Elodie Apard. "Body Count
and Religion in the Boko Haram Crisis: Evidence from the
Nigeria Watch Database." In *Boko Haram: Islamism, Politics,
Security, and the State in Nigeria*, edited by Marc-Antoine Pérouse
de Montclos, 213–236. Leiden: African Studies Centre, 2014.

"Christian Militia Killed up to 1000 Muslims in Nigeria, Leader
Claims." *Sydney Morning Herald*, May 8, 2004. https://www.smh
.com.au/world/christian-militia-killed-up-to-1000-muslims-in
-nigeria-leader-claims-20040508-gdivw5.html.

"Christmas under Siege: The Big Picture." Fox News, December 24,
2004, updated May 20, 2015. https://www.foxnews.com/story
/christmas-under-siege-the-big-picture.

Claster, Jill N. *Sacred Violence: The European Crusades to the Middle
East, 1095–1396*. Toronto: University of Toronto Press, 2009.

Clement of Alexandria. "Stromata." Accessed April 1, 2020, http://www.earlychristianwritings.com/text/clement-stromata -book4.html.

Coghlin, Benjamin, Richard J. Brennan, Pascal Ngoy, David Dofara, Brad Otto, and Mark Clements. "Mortality in the Democratic Republic of the Congo: A Nationwide Survey." *Lancet* 367 (2006): 44–51.

Coghlin, Benjamin, Pascal Ngoy, Flavien Mulumba, Colleen Hardy, Valerie Nkamgang Bemo, Tony Stewart, Jennifer Lewis, and Richard Brennan. "Mortality in the Democratic Republic of Congo: An Ongoing Crisis." International Rescue Committee. Accessed December 19, 2019. https://www.rescue .org/sites/default/files/document/661/2006-7congomortality survey.pdf.

———. "Update on Mortality in the Democratic Republic of Congo: Results from a Third Nationwide Survey." *Disaster Medicine and Public Health Preparedness* 3, no. 2 (2009): 88–96.

"The Communist Terror: Plight of the Korean Christians." *Christianity Today*, September 25, 1961.

Cone, James H. *A Black Theology of Liberation.* 40th anniversary ed. Maryknoll, NY: Orbis Books, 2010.

———. *The Cross and the Lynching Tree.* Maryknoll, NY: Orbis Books, 2018.

Congdon, David. "No, the American Church Isn't in Exile." *Sojourners*, April 19, 2017. https://sojo.net/articles/no-american -church-isn-t-exile.

Cooke, John Esten. *The Life of Stonewall Jackson.* New York: Charles B. Richardson, 1863.

Cowdrey, H.E.J. "Pope Urban II's Preaching of the First Crusade." In *The Crusades*, edited by Thomas E. Madden, 15–31. Oxford: Blackwell, 2002.

Cox, Daniel, and Robert P. Jones. "Majority of Americans Oppose Transgender Bathroom Restrictions." Public Religion Research

Institute. March 10, 2017. https://www.prri.org/research/lgbt
-transgender-bathroom-discrimination-religious-liberty/.

Craver, Earlene. "On the Boundary of White: The Cartozian
Naturalization Case and the Armenians, 1923–1925." *Journal of
American Ethnic History* 28, no. 2 (2009): 30–56.

Crawford, Neta C. "Human Cost of the Post-9/11 Wars: Lethality
and the Need for Transparency." Costs of War, Brown University. November 2018. https://watson.brown.edu/costsofwar/files
/cow/imce/papers/2018/Human%20Costs%2C%20Nov%208%20
2018%20CoW.pdf.

Cullen, Dave. "Who Said 'Yes'?" *Salon*, September 30, 1999.
https://www.salon.com/1999/09/30/bernall/.

Cumming-Bruce, Nick. "United Nations Investigators Accuse ISIS
of Genocide over Attacks on Yazidis." *New York Times*,
March 19, 2015. https://www.nytimes.com/2015/03/20/world
/middleeast/isis-genocide-yazidis-iraq-un-panel.html.

Dailey, Alice. *The English Martyr from Reformation to Revolution.*
South Bend, IN: University of Notre Dame Press, 2012.

Daneel, Marthinus Louis. *Zionism and Faith-Healing in Rhodesia:
Aspects of African Independent Churches.* The Hague: Mouton, 1970.

DC Talk and Voice of the Martyrs. *Jesus Freaks.* Minneapolis:
Bethany House, 1999.

"The Deeds of the Franks." *The Crusades: A Reader*, edited by S. J. Allen
and Emilie Ant, 56–57. Toronto: University of Toronto Press, 2014.

De La Torre, Miguel, and Gaston Espinosa, eds. *Rethinking
Latino(a) Religion and Identity.* Cleveland: Pilgrim Press, 2006.

De Voragine, Jacobus. *The Golden Legend.* Medieval Sourcebooks,
Fordham University. Accessed December 20, 2019. https://
sourcebooks.fordham.edu/basis/goldenlegend/.

———. "Here Followeth the Life of S. Blasé, and First of His
Name." In *The Golden Legend*, vol. 3. Medieval Sourcebooks,
Fordham University. Accessed December 20, 2019. https://
sourcebooks.fordham.edu/basis/goldenlegend/GoldenLegend
-Volume3.asp.

———. "The Passion of Our Lord." In *The Golden Legend*, vol. 1. Medieval Sourcebooks, Fordham University. Accessed December 20, 2019. https://sourcebooks.fordham.edu/basis /goldenlegend/GoldenLegend-Volume1.asp#The%20Passion%20 of%20our%20Lord.

"Documents on the Sack of Constantinople." In *The Crusades: A Reader*, edited by S. J. Allen and Emilie Ant, 228–234. Toronto: University of Toronto Press, 2014.

Dogan, Mehmet Ali. "American Board of Commissioners for Foreign Missions (ABCFM) and 'Nominal Christians': Elias Riggs (1810–1901) and American Missionary Activities in the Ottoman Empire." PhD diss., University of Utah, 2013.

"DR Congo: UN-Mandated Group Finds Evidence Rwanda, Army Aiding Rival Rebels." UN News, December 12, 2008. https:// news.un.org/en/story/2008/12/285222-dr-congo-un-mandated -group-finds-evidence-rwanda-army-aiding-rival-rebels.

Dreher, Rod. *The Benedict Option: A Strategy for Christians in a Post-Christian America*. New York: Penguin, 2017.

Dyck, C. J. "The Suffering Church in Anabaptism." *Mennonite Quarterly Review* 59 (1985): 5–23.

Ehrman, Bart D. *The New Testament: A Historical Introduction to the Early Christian Writings*, 6th ed. New York: Oxford University Press, 2016.

Elisha, Omri. "Saved by a Martyr: Evangelical Mediation, Sanctification, and the 'Persecuted Church.'" *Journal of the American Academy of Religion* 84, no. 4 (December 2016): 1056–1080.

"The Enemy Is Shooting at Us!" Open Doors, December 13, 2013. https://www.opendoorsusa.org/christian-persecution/stories /enemy-shooting-us/.

"Ethnic Cleansing in Central African Republic, No Genocide: U.N. Inquiry." Reuters, January 5, 2015. https://www.reuters.com /article/us-centralafrica-inquiry/ethnic-cleansing-in-central -african-republic-no-genocide-u-n-inquiry -idUSKBN0KH2BM20150108.

Eusebius of Caesarea. *Church History*. New Advent. Accessed March 15, 2020. http://www.newadvent.org/fathers/250105.htm.

———. *The Life of the Blessed Emperor Constantine*. Ancient History Sourcebook. Fordham University. Accessed March 15, 2020. https://sourcebooks.fordham.edu/basis/vita-constantine.asp.

Evans, Curtis J. "White Evangelical Protestant Responses to the Civil Rights Movement." *Harvard Theological Review* 102, no. 2 (2009): 245–273.

"Eyewitness to a Beheading." *The Voice of the Martyrs, Persecution Blog*. Updated November 18, 2008. https://www.persecutionblog .com/2008/11/eyewitness-to-a-beheading.html.

Faupel, John Francis. *African Holocaust: The Story of the Uganda Martyrs*. Nairobi: Paulines Publications Africa, 2007.

Fea, John. *Was America Founded as a Christian Nation? A Historical Introduction*. Louisville, KY: Westminster John Knox, 2011.

Fowl, Stephen. "The Primacy of the Witness of the Body to Martyrdom in Paul." In *Witness of the Body: The Past, Present, and Future of Christian Martyrdom*, edited by Michael L. Budde and Karen Scott, 43–60. Grand Rapids, MI: Eerdmans Publishing Co., 2011.

Friedman, Thomas. *The World Is Flat: A Brief History of the Twenty-First Century*. New York: Farrar, Straus, and Giroux, 2005.

Fukuyama, Francis. "The End of History?" *National Interest* 16 (1989): 3–18.

Gabrielian, Mugurdich Chojhauji. *Armenia, a Martyr Nation: A Historical Sketch of the Armenian People from Traditional Times to the Present Tragic Days*. New York: Fleming H. Revell, 1916.

"Galerius and Constantine: Edicts of Toleration 311/313." Ancient History Sourcebook. Fordham University. Accessed March 15, 2020. https://sourcebooks.fordham.edu/source/edict-milan.asp.

Genovese, Eugene D. *A Consuming Fire: The Fall of the Confederacy in the Mind of the White Christian South*. Athens: University of Georgia Press, 1998.

Gill, Jill. *Embattled Ecumenism: The National Council of Churches, the Vietnam War, and the Trials of the Protestant Left.* DeKalb, IL: Northern Illinois University Press, 2011.

Goldberg, Jeffrey. "Washington Discovers Christian Persecution." *New York Times Magazine,* December 21, 1997.

Grabill, Joseph L. *Protestant Diplomacy and the Near East: Missionary Influence on American Policy, 1810–1927.* Minneapolis: University of Minnesota Press, 1971.

Gregerson, Linda. "The Commonwealth of the Word: New England, Old England, and the Praying Indians." In *Empires of God: Religious Encounters in the Early Modern Atlantic,* edited by Linda Gregerson and Susan Juster, 70–84. Philadelphia: University of Pennsylvania Press, 2011.

Gregory, Brad S. "Persecution or Prosecution, Martyrs or False Martyrs? The Reformation Era, History, and Theological Reflection." In *Witness of the Body: The Past, Present, and Future of Christian Martyrdom,* edited by Michael L. Budde and Karen Scott, 107–124. Grand Rapids, MI: Eerdmans Publishing Co., 2011.

———. *Salvation at Stake: Christian Martyrdom in Early Modern Europe.* Cambridge, MA: Harvard University Press, 1999.

———. *The Unintended Reformation: How a Religious Revolution Secularized Society.* Cambridge, MA: Harvard University Press, 2012.

Griffith, Sidney H. *The Church in the Shadow of the Mosque: Christians and Muslims in the World of Islam.* Princeton, NJ: Princeton University Press, 2012.

Gross, Abraham. *Spirituality and Law: Courting Martyrdom in Christianity and Judaism.* New York: University Press of America, 2005.

Grossman, Cathy Lynn. "Americans Value Religious Freedom, but Mostly for Christians." *USA Today,* December 31, 2015. https://www.usatoday.com/story/news/2015/12/31/americans-value-religious-freedom-but-mostly-christians/78130098/.

"*Grove City College v. Bell*—Facts and Case Summary." Administrative Office of the US Courts. Accessed December 19, 2019. https://www.uscourts.gov/educational-resources/educational-activities/grove-city-college-v-bell-facts-and-case-summary.

Grubeck, Nikolaus. "Civilian Harm in Somalia: Creating an Appropriate Response." Campaign for Innocent Victims in Conflict, November 23, 2011. https://civiliansinconflict.org/publications/research/civilian-harm-somalia-creating-appropriate-response/.

Gunter, Michael. "What Is Genocide? The Armenian Case." *Middle East Quarterly* 20, no. 1 (2013): 37–46.

Hall, Stuart G. "Women among the Early Martyrs." In *Martyrs and Martyrologies*, edited by Diana Wood, 1–21. London: Blackwell Publishers, 1993.

Harlow, Luke E. "The Civil War and the Making of Conservative American Evangelicalism." In *Turning Points in the History of American Evangelicalism*, edited by Heath W. Carter and Laura Rominger Porter, 107–132. Grand Rapids, MI: Eerdmans Publishing Co., 2017.

Hartunian, Abraham H. *To Neither Laugh nor Weep: A Memoir of the Armenian Genocide*. Boston: Beacon Press, 1968.

Hatch, Nathan O. *The Democratization of American Christianity*. New Haven, CT: Yale University Press, 1989.

Hendrix, Scott. *Recultivating the Vineyard: The Reformation Agendas of Christianization*. Louisville, KY: Westminster John Knox, 2004.

Henry, Carl F. H. "NCC Conference Urges Recognition of Red China." *Christianity Today*, December 8, 1958.

Holpuch, Amanda. "US Judge Halts Deportation of More Than 100 Iraqi Christians." *Guardian*, June 22, 2017. https://www.theguardian.com/us-news/2017/jun/22/iraq-deportation-us-judge-halts-detroit-ice-raid.

Hooper, John, and Stephen Bates. "Dismay and Anger as Pope Declares Protestants Cannot Have Churches." *Guardian*, July 11,

2007. https://www.theguardian.com/world/2007/jul/11
/catholicism.religion.

Horowitz, Michael. Introduction to *Their Blood Cries Out: The Untold Story of Persecution against Christians in the Modern World*, by Paul Marshall, xxi–xxiv. Dallas, TX: Word Publishing, 1997.

"House Unanimously Passes Fortenberry ISIS Genocide Resolution." Press release. Congressman John Fortenberry. March 15, 2016. https://fortenberry.house.gov/news/press-releases/house-unanimously-passes-fortenberry-isis-genocide-resolution.

Hsaio-Rei Hicks, Madelyn, Hamit Dardagan, Gabriela Guerrero Serdán, Peter M. Bagnall, John A. Sloboda, and Michael Spagat. "Violent Deaths of Iraqi Civilians, 2003–2008: Analysis by Perpetrator, Weapon, Time, and Location." *PLoS Med* 8, no. 2 (2011): e1000415.

Human Rights Watch. "Numbers." In *Leave None to Tell the Story: Genocide in Rwanda*. 1999; modified July 29, 2017. https://www.hrw.org/reports/1999/rwanda/Geno1-3-04.htm.

Huntington, Samuel P. *The Clash of Civilizations and the Remaking of World Order*. New York: Touchstone, 1996.

Hurd, Elizabeth Shakman. *Beyond Religious Freedom: The New Politics of Religion*. Princeton, NJ: Princeton University Press, 2015.

"Indonesia." USCIRF 2013 Annual Report. Accessed April 15, 2019. https://www.uscirf.gov/sites/default/files/resources /Indonesia%202013.pdf.

IOM. "Meta Analysis; Vulnerability, Stability, Displacement, and Reintegration: Issues Facing the Peace Process in Aceh, Indonesia." August 2008. Accessed April 13, 2019. https://www.iom.int/jahia/webdav/site/myjahiasite/shared/shared/mainsite /activities/countries/docs/usaid_meta_analysis.pdf.

Iraq Family Health Survey Study Group. "Violence-Related Mortality in Iraq from 2002 to 2006." *New England Journal of Medicine* 358 (2008): 484–493.

Irvin, Dale T., and Scott W. Sunquist, *History of the World Christian Movement*, vol. 1, *Earliest Christianity to 1453*. Maryknoll, NY: Orbis Books, 2001.

Jackson, Victoria Louise. "Title IX and the Big Time: Women's Intercollegiate Athletics at the University of North Carolina at Chapel Hill, 1950–1992." PhD diss., Arizona State University, 2015.

Jaret, Charles. "Troubled by Newcomers: Anti-Immigrant Attitudes and Action during Two Eras of Mass Immigration to the United States." *Journal of American Ethnic History* 18, no. 3 (1999): 9–39.

Jenkins, Philip. *The Next Christendom: The Coming of Global Christianity*. Oxford: Oxford University Press, 2002.

Johnson, Todd M., and Gina A. Zurlo. "Christian Martyrdom as a Pervasive Phenomenon." *Society* 51 (2014): 679–685.

Johnson, Todd M., and Gina A. Zurlo, eds. *World Christian Database*. Leiden/Boston: Brill, 2020.

Jones, Adam. *Genocide: A Comprehensive Introduction*. New York: Routledge, 2006.

Jones, Robert P. *The End of White Christian America*. New York: Simon and Schuster, 2017.

Junghae, Waithera. "'Deny Christ or Die,' Boko Haram Tells Young Christian Woman." *Christian Post*, December 7, 2013. https:// www.christianpost.com/news/nigeria-kills-13-boko-haram -militants-as-massacre-of-christians-continues-87555/.

Kamisar, Ben. "Trump: 'We're Saying Merry Christmas Again.'" *The Hill*, October 13, 2017. https://thehill.com/homenews/adminis tration/355303-trump-were-saying-merry-christmas-again.

Kaplan, Robert D. "In Defense of Empire." *Atlantic*, April 2014.

Kean, Thomas H. "The 9/11 Commission Report: Final Report of the National Commission on Terrorist Attacks upon the United States; Executive Summary." Accessed December 19, 2019. https://govinfo.library.unt.edu/911/report/911Report _Exec.pdf.

Kew, Darren. "Why Nigeria Matters." *First Things*, November 2007. https://www.firstthings.com/article/2007/11/why-nigeria-matters.

Klein, Thoralf. "Media Events and Missionary Periodicals: The Case of the Boxer War, 1900–1901." *Church History* 82, no. 2 (2013): 399–404.

Koschorke, Klaus. "Transcontinental Links, Enlarged Maps, and Polycentric Structures in the History of World Christianity." *Journal of World Christianity* 6, no. 1 (2016): 28–56.

Kruse, Kevin. *One Nation under God: How Corporate America Invented Christian America*. New York: Basic Books, 2015.

———. *White Flight: Atlanta and the Making of Modern Conservatism*. Princeton, NJ: Princeton University Press, 2005.

Laderman, Charlie. "Sharing the Burden? The American Solution to the Armenian Question, 1918–1920." *Diplomatic History* 40, no. 4 (2016): 664–694.

Lamadrid, Lucas. "Anonymous or Analogous Christians? Rahner and Von Balthasar on Naming the Non-Christian." *Modern Theology* 11, no. 3 (1995): 363–384.

"The Latest: Trump Announces Details of NKorea Summit." *Washington Post*, May 10, 2018. https://www.washingtonpost.com/world/national-security/the-latest-trump-announces-details-of-nkorea-summit/2018/05/10/762160fa-54c9-11e8-a6d4-ca1d035642ce_story.html.

Lee, Daniel B. "The Great Racial Commission: Religion and the Construction of White America." In *Race, Nation, and Religion in the Americas*, edited by Henry Goldschmidt and Elizabeth McAlister, 85–110. New York: Oxford University Press, 2004.

Leemans, Johan, and Peter Gemeinhardt. *Christian Martyrdom in Late Antiquity (300–450 AD): History and Discourse, Tradition and Identity*. Berlin: De Gruyter, 2012.

Leiper, Henry Smith. *World Chaos or World Christianity? A Popular Interpretation of Oxford and Edinburgh 1937*. Chicago: Willett, Clark & Co., 1937.

Lemkin, Raphael. *Axis Rule in Occupied Europe: Laws of Occupation, Analysis of Government, Proposals for Redress.* Washington, DC: Carnegie Endowment for International Peace, 1944.

"The Letter of Ignatius to the Romans." In *The New Testament and Other Early Christian Writings: A Reader*, edited by Bart D. Ehrman, 328–330. Oxford: Oxford University Press, 1998.

"Letters of Innocent III." In *The Crusades: A Reader*, edited by S. J. Allen and Emilie Ant, 216–220. Toronto: University of Toronto Press, 2014.

"Letters of Pliny the Younger and the Emperor Trajan." *Frontline* ("From Jesus to Christ"). Translated by William Whiston. Accessed April 1, 2020. https://www.pbs.org/wgbh/pages/frontline/shows/religion/maps/primary/pliny.html.

Limbaugh, David. *Persecution: How Liberals Are Waging War against Christianity.* Washington, DC: Regnery Publishing, 2003.

Lindberg, Carter. *The European Reformations.* New York: John Wiley & Sons, 2011.

Lindsey, Hal. *The Late Great Planet Earth.* Grand Rapids, MI: Zondervan, 1970.

Loades, David. "John Foxe and the Traitors: The Politics of the Marian Persecution (Presidential Address)." In *Martyrs and Martyrologies*, edited by Diana Wood, 231–244. Oxford: Blackwell, 1993.

Longman, Timothy. *Christianity and Genocide in Rwanda.* Cambridge: Cambridge University Press, 2009.

———. *Memory and Justice in Post-Genocide Rwanda.* Cambridge: Cambridge University Press, 2017.

Lynch, Joseph H. *Early Christianity: A Brief History.* New York: Oxford University Press, 2010.

Mahmood, Saba. *Religious Difference in a Secular Age: A Minority Report.* Princeton, NJ: Princeton University Press, 2015.

Malcom, Allison O. "Anti-Catholicism and the Rise of Protestant Nationhood in North America, 1830–1871." PhD diss., University of Illinois at Chicago, 2011.

"Mali Conflict and Aftermath: Compendium of Human Rights
Watch Reporting, 2012–2017." Human Rights Watch, New
York, 2017.

Marshall, Paul. *Their Blood Cries Out: The Untold Story of Persecution
against Christians in the Modern World.* Dallas, TX: Word
Publishing, 1997.

Marty, Martin. "A Judeo-Christian Looks at the Judeo-Christian
Tradition." *Christian Century* 103, no. 29 (October 8, 1986):
858–860.

"The Martyrdom of Saints Perpetua and Felicitas." *From Jesus
to Christ.* Accessed April 1, 2020. http://www.pbs.org/wgbh
/pages/frontline/shows/religion/maps/primary/perpetua.html.

Mazza, Ed. "Jerry Falwell Jr. Calls Donald Trump the 'Dream
President' for Evangelicals." *Huffington Post*, April 30, 2017.
https://www.huffpost.com/entry/jerry-falwell-jr-dream
-president-trump_n_590695ofe4b05c3976807a08.

McAlister, Melani. *The Kingdom of God Has No Borders: A Global
History of American Evangelicals.* Oxford: Oxford University
Press, 2018.

McCoy, Terrence. "'Soldiers of Jesus': Armed Neo-Pentecostals
Torment Brazil's Religious Minorities." *Washington Post*,
December 8, 2019. https://www.washingtonpost.com/world/the
_americas/soldiers-of-jesus-armed-neo-pentecostals-torment
-brazils-religious-minorities/2019/12/08/fd74de6e-fff0-11e9-8501
-2a7123a38c58_story.html.

McEntee, Jennifer, and Mica Rosenberg. "U.S. Says It Will
Separate Families Crossing Border Illegally." Reuters, May 7,
2018. https://www.reuters.com/article/us-usa-immigration
-children/u-s-cements-plans-to-separate-families-crossing
-border-illegally-idUSKBN1I82AB.

McIntire, Carl. "Letter of March 26, 1964 to President Lyndon
Johnson." In *Jerry Falwell and the Rise of the Religious Right: A
Brief History with Documents*, edited by Matthew Avery Sutton,
55–56. Boston, MA: Bedford/St. Martin's, 2013.

Meierhenrich, Jens. *Genocide: A Reader.* New York: Oxford University Press, 2014.

Menzie, Nicola. "History Magazine, VOM Highlight Persecution of Modern Believers." *Christian Post*, June 25, 2014. https://www.christianpost.com/news/history-magazine-vom-highlight-persecution-of-modern-believers-cite-claim-that-christians-partly-to-blame-for-70-million-martyred-since-jesus-time.html.

"MEPs Call for Urgent Action to Protect Religious Minorities against ISIS." News European Parliament, February 4, 2016. https://www.europarl.europa.eu/news/en/press-room/20160129IPR11938/meps-call-for-urgent-action-to-protect-religious-minorities-against-isis.

Middleton, Paul. "Enemies of the (Church and) State: Martyrdom as a Problem for Early Christianity." *Annali Di Storia Dell'esegesi* 29, no. 2 (December 2012): 161–181.

Miller, Donald, and Lorna Touryan Miller. *Survivors: An Oral History of the Armenian Genocide.* Berkeley: University of California Press, 1999.

"Mission Board Told of Turkish Horrors." *New York Times*, September 17, 1915.

Mitchell, Jolyon. *Martyrdom: A Very Short Introduction.* Oxford: Oxford University Press, 2013.

Monger, David. "Networking against Genocide during the First World War: The International Network behind the British Parliamentary Report on the Armenian Genocide." *Journal of Transatlantic Studies* 16, no. 3 (2018): 295–316.

Moore, Deborah Dash. "Jewish GIs and the Creation of the Judeo-Christian Tradition." *Religion and American Culture* 8, no. 1 (1998): 31–51.

Moore, Johnnie. *The Martyr's Oath: Living for the Jesus They're Willing to Die For.* Carol Stream, IL: Tyndale House Publishers, 2017.

Moore, Russell. "Why the Church Should neither Cave nor Panic about the Decision on Gay Marriage." *Washington Post*, June 26,

2015. https://www.washingtonpost.com/news/acts-of-faith/wp
/2015/06/26/why-the-church-should-neither-cave-nor-panic
-about-the-decision-on-gay-marriage/?utm_term=.fc9fa6d0acca.

Moranian, Suzanne E. "The Armenian Genocide and American
Missionary Efforts." In *America and the Armenian Genocide of
1915*, edited by Jay Winter, 185–213. Cambridge: Cambridge
University Press, 2004.

Morris, Colin. "Martyrs on the Field of Battle before and during
the First Crusade." In *Martyrs and Martyrologies*, edited by
Diana Wood, 93–104. Oxford: Blackwell, 1993.

Moss, Candida R. *The Myth of Persecution: How Early Christians
Invented a Story of Martyrdom*. New York: HarperOne, 2014.

Mounstephen, Rt. Rev. Philip. "Bishop of Truro's Independent
Review for the Foreign Secretary of FCO Support for Persecuted Christians." 2019. Accessed December 19, 2019. https://
christianpersecutionreview.org.uk/interim-report/.

Murray, David. "Spreading the Word: Missionaries, Conversion,
and Circulation in the Northeast." In *Spiritual Encounters:
Interactions between Christianity and Native Religions in
Colonial America*, edited by Nicholas Griffiths and Fernando
Cervantes, 43–64. Birmingham: University of Birmingham
Press, 1999.

National Commission for the Fight against Genocide. "Background
of the Genocide against the Tutsi." Accessed April 3, 2019.
https://www.cnlg.gov.rw/index.php?id=80.

National Counterterrorism Center. "Report on Terror 2011."
March 12, 2012. https://fas.org/irp/threat/nctc2011.pdf.

"Nearly 1 Million Christians Martyred for Their Faith in Last
Decade." Fox News, July 6, 2017. https://www.foxnews.com
/world/nearly-1-million-christians-reportedly-martyred-for
-their-faith-in-last-decade.

"Nigeria Election: Riots over Goodluck Johnathan Win." BBC,
April 18, 2011. https://www.bbc.com/news/world-africa-13107867.

Noll, Mark A. *America's God: From Jonathan Edwards to Abraham Lincoln*. New York: Oxford University Press, 2005.

"The Ntarama Church Massacre." *Rwandan Stories*. Accessed April 21, 2019. http://www.rwandanstories.org/genocide/ntarama_church.html.

"Number of Christian Martyrs Continues to Cause Debate." Open Doors, November 14, 2013. https://www.opendoorsusa.org/take-action/pray/number-of-christian-martyrs-continues-to-cause-debate/.

O'Connor, Tom. "Iraqi Christians Face 'Death Sentence' as Trump Prepares Mass Deportations." *Newsweek*, June 14, 2017. https://www.newsweek.com/iraq-christians-trump-death-sentence-deportation-625722.

Olojo, Akinola Ejodame. "Muslims, Christians, and Religious Violence in Nigeria: Patterns and Mapping (June 2006–May 2014)." IFRA-Nigeria Working Paper Series, no. 32, November 11, 2014. http://www.nigeriawatch.org/media/html/WP3OLOJOFinal.pdf.

Patton, Callum. "Mike Pence Won't Be Meeting Any Christians on His Trip to Save Christianity in the Middle East." *Newsweek*, December 18, 2017. https://www.newsweek.com/mike-pence-wont-be-meeting-any-christians-his-trip-save-christianity-middle-751334.

Penn, Michael Philip. *Envisioning Islam: Syriac Christians and the Early Muslim World*. Oakland: University of California Press, 2015.

———. *When Christians First Met Muslims: A Sourcebook of the Early Syriac Writings on Islam*. Oakland: University of California Press, 2015.

Peterson, Derek R. *Ethnic Patriotism and the East African Revival: A History of Dissent, c. 1935–1972*. Cambridge: Cambridge University Press, 2012.

Pew Research Center. "The Changing Global Religious Landscape." April 5, 2017. https://www.pewforum.org/2017/04/05/the-changing-global-religious-landscape/.

———. "Global Uptick in Government Restrictions on Religion in 2016." June 21, 2016. https://www.pewforum.org/2018/06/21 /global-uptick-in-government-restrictions-on-religion-in -2016/.

———. "How Does Pew Research Center Measure the Religious Composition of the U.S.?" July 5, 2018. https://www.pewforum .org/2018/07/05/how-does-pew-research-center-measure-the -religious-composition-of-the-u-s-answers-to-frequently-asked -questions/.

———. "Religious Hostilities Reach Six-Year High." January 14, 2014. https://www.pewforum.org/2014/01/14/religious-hostilities -reach-six-year-high/.

———. "Rising Restrictions on Religion—One-Third of the World's Population Experiences an Increase." August 9, 2011. https:// www.pewforum.org/2011/08/09/rising-restrictions-on-religion2/.

Philpott, Daniel, and Timothy Samuel Shah. Introduction to *Under Caesar's Sword: How Christians Respond to Persecution*, edited by Daniel Philpott and Timothy Samuel Shah, 1–29. Cambridge: Cambridge University Press, 2018.

Philpott, Daniel, and Timothy Samuel Shah, eds. *Under Caesar's Sword: How Christians Respond to Persecution*. Cambridge, UK: Cambridge University Press, 2018.

Physicians for Social Responsibility. "Body Count: Casualty Figures after 10 Years of the 'War on Terror'—Iraq, Afghanistan, Pakistan." March 2015. https://www.psr.org/wp-content/uploads /2018/05/body-count.pdf.

Platt, David. *Radical: Taking Your Faith Back from the American Dream*. Colorado Springs, CO: Multnomah, 2010.

Powers, Kirsten. "The New Age of Christian Martyrdom." *Daily Beast*, January 3, 2014. https://www.thedailybeast.com/the-new -age-of-christian-martyrdom.

Preston, Andrew. "Defender of the Faith: The United States and World Christianity." In *Relocating World Christianity: Interdisciplinary Studies in Universal and Local Expressions of the Christian*

Faith, edited by Joel Cabrita, David Maxwell, and Emma Wild-Wood, 261–280. Leiden: Brill, 2017.

Rader, Stanley R. *Against the Gates of Hell: The Threat to Religious Freedom in America*. New York: Everest House, 1980.

Ramachandran, Ayesha. *The Worldmakers: Global Imagining in Early Modern Europe*. Chicago: University of Chicago Press, 2015.

"Red China and World Morality." *Christianity Today*, December 10, 1956.

"Report of the Independent Inquiry into the Actions of the United Nations during the 1994 Genocide in Rwanda." December 15, 1999. https://reliefweb.int/report/rwanda/report-independent -inquiry-actions-united-nations-during-1994-genocide-rwanda.

Rettig, Jessica. "Death Toll of 'Arab Spring.'" *US News and World Report*, November 8, 2011. https://www.usnews.com/news /slideshows/death-toll-of-arab-spring.

Rivinius, Karl J. "The Boxer Movement and Christian Missions in China." *Mission Studies* 7, no. 2 (1990): 189–217.

Robert, Dana L. *Christian Mission: How Christianity Became a World Religion*. Oxford: Wiley-Blackwell, 2009.

———. "Shifting Southward: Global Christianity since 1945." *International Bulletin of Missionary Research* 24, no. 2 (2000): 50–58.

Rosenberg, Matthew. "Citing Atrocities, John Kerry Calls ISIS Actions Genocide." *New York Times*, March 17, 2016. https:// www.nytimes.com/2016/03/18/world/middleeast/citing-atrocities -john-kerry-calls-isis-actions-genocide.html.

Runciman, Sir Steven. "Byzantium and the Crusades." In *The Crusades*, edited by Thomas E. Madden, 211–220. Oxford: Blackwell, 2002.

Sanneh, Lamin. *Disciples of All Nations: Pillars of World Christianity*. New York: Oxford University Press, 2008.

———. *West African Christianity: The Religious Impact*. Maryknoll, NY: Orbis Books, 1983.

Satlow, Michael L. *How the Bible Became Holy*. New Haven, CT: Yale University Press, 2015.

Scherz, China. *Having People, Having Heart: Charity, Sustainable Development, and Problems of Dependence in Central Uganda.* Chicago: University of Chicago Press, 2014.

Schirrmacher, Thomas. "A Response to the High Counts of Christian Martyrs per Year." *International Journal of Religious Freedom* 4, no. 2 (2011): 9–13.

Schleifer, Theodore. "Donald Trump: 'I Think Islam Hates Us.'" CNN, March 10, 2016. https://www.cnn.com/2016/03/09 /politics/donald-trump-islam-hates-us/index.html.

Schreiter, Robert J. *The New Catholicity: Theology between the Global and Local.* Maryknoll, NY: Orbis Books, 1997.

Sharlet, Jeff. *The Family: The Secret Fundamentalism at the Heart of American Power.* New York: HarperCollins, 2008.

Shea, Nina. *In the Lion's Den.* Nashville: Broadman & Holman Publishers, 1997.

Shellnutt, Kate. "Russia's Newest Law: No Evangelizing outside of Church." *Christianity Today*, July 8, 2016. https://www .christianitytoday.com/news/2016/june/no-evangelizing-outside -of-church-russia-proposes.html.

Siegel, Jacob. "Islamic Extremists Now Crucifying People in Syria—and Tweeting Out the Pictures." *Daily Beast*, April 30, 2014. https://www.thedailybeast.com/islamic-extremists-now -crucifying-people-in-syriaand-tweeting-out-the-pictures.

Sieple, Robert. "The USCIRF Is Only Cursing the Darkness." *Christianity Today*, October 1, 2002.

Singh, Stacy. "Christians #1 Most Persecuted, and Rising." *The Stand.* May 29, 2015. https://afa.net/the-stand/faith/2015/05 /christians-the-1-most-persecuted-and-rising/.

"Situation of Baha'is in Iran." Baha'i International Community. Accessed April 17, 2019. https://www.bic.org/focus-areas /situation-iranian-bahais/current-situation.

Smith, Samuel. "Obama State Department Responsible for Rise in Global Christian Persecution, Tony Perkins Says." *Christian*

Post, January 13, 2017. https://www.christianpost.com/news /obama-state-department-responsible-for-rise-in-global -christian-persecution-tony-perkins-says-172969/.

Sobrino, Jon. *The Principle of Mercy: Taking the Crucified People from the Cross.* Maryknoll, NY: Orbis Books, 1994.

Sontag, Susan. *On Regarding the Pain of Others.* London: Penguin Books, 2019.

Spagat, Michael, Andrew Mack, Tara Cooper, and Joakim Kreutz. "Estimating War Deaths: An Arena of Contestation." *Journal of Conflict Resolution* 53, no. 6 (2009): 934–950.

Specia, Megan. "How Syria's Death Toll Is Lost in the Fog of War." *New York Times*, April 13, 2018. https://www.nytimes.com/2018 /04/13/world/middleeast/syria-death-toll.html.

Spielman, Peter James. "Review of Congo War Halves Death Toll from 5.4 Million." Associated Press, January 20, 2010.

Spivey, Robert A., D. Moody Smith, and C. Clifton Black. *Anatomy of the New Testament*, 7th ed. Minneapolis: Fortress Press, 2013.

Sputo, Dominic. *Heirloom Love: Authentic Christianity in This Age of Persecution.* Self-published, 2018.

Stanley, Brian. *Christianity in the 20th Century: A World History.* Princeton, NJ: Princeton University Press, 2018.

———. *The World Missionary Conference, Edinburgh 1910.* Grand Rapids, MI: Eerdmans Publishing Co., 2009.

Stanwood, Owen. "Catholics, Protestants, and the Clash of Civilizations in Early America." In *The First Prejudice: Religious Tolerance and Intolerance in Early America*, edited by Chris Beneke and Christopher S. Grenda, 218–240. Philadelphia: University of Pennsylvania Press, 2010.

Sterio, Milena. "The Karadžić Genocide Conviction: Inferences, Intent, and the Necessity to Redefine Genocide." *Emory International Law Review* 30, no. 2 (2017): 271–298.

Stowell, Daniel W. *Rebuilding Zion: The Religious Reconstruction of the South, 1863–1877.* New York: Oxford University Press, 1998.

Straus, Scott. *The Order of Genocide: Race, Power, and War in Rwanda*. Ithaca, NY: Cornell University Press, 2006.

Su, Anna. "Woodrow Wilson and the Origins of the International Law of Religious Freedom." *Journal of the History of International Law* 15, no. 2 (2013): 235–267.

"Subcommittee Hearing: The Persecution of Christians as a Worldwide Phenomenon." US House Foreign Affairs Committee, February 11, 2014. https://www.youtube.com/watch?v=LP5Ji7x6hEg.

Suggs, Welch. *A Place on the Team: The Triumph and Tragedy of Title IX*. Princeton, NJ: Princeton University Press, 2005.

Sun, Anna. "Counting Confucians: Who Are the Confucians in Contemporary East Asia?" *Newsletter of the Institute for Advanced Studies in Humanities and Social Sciences of National Taiwan University*, 2009.

Sutton, Matthew Avery, ed. *Jerry Falwell and the Rise of the Religious Right*. New York: Bedford/St. Martin's, 2013.

Syllabus Masterpiece Cakeshop, Ltd., et al. v. Colorado Civil Rights Commission et al., U.S. Supreme Court. Accessed December 19, 2019. https://www.supremecourt.gov/opinions/17pdf/16-111 _j4el.pdf.

Tapp, Christine, Frederick M. Burkle Jr., Kumanan Wilson, Tim Takaro, Gordon H. Guyatt, Hani Amad, and Edward J. Mills, "Iraq War Mortality Estimates: A Systematic Review." *Conflict and Health* 2, no. 1 (2008).

Thomas, Jeff. "Exile." *World Watch Monitor*, April 18, 2014. https://www.worldwatchmonitor.org/2014/04/exile/.

Thompson, T. Jack. *Light on Darkness? Missionary Photography of Africa in the Nineteenth and Early Twentieth Centuries*. Grand Rapids, MI: Eerdmans Publishing Co., 2012.

"Title IX and Sex Discrimination." U.S. Department of Education, Office of Civil Rights. Accessed December 19, 2019. https://www2.ed.gov/about/offices/list/ocr/docs/tix_dis.html.

Torrance, Iain R. *Christology after Chalcedon: Severus of Antioch and Sergius the Monophysite*. Eugene, OR: Wipf and Stock, 1998.

"'Tortured for Christ' Richard Wurmbrand." YouTube. Accessed December 26, 2019. https://www.youtube.com/watch?v =bqdPkDPMCwk.

Trump, President Donald J. "Executive Order Protecting the Nation from Foreign Terrorist Entry into the United States." January 27, 2017. https://www.whitehouse.gov/presidential-actions/executive -order-protecting-nation-foreign-terrorist-entry-united-states/.

Turek, Lauren Francis. "To Support a 'Brother in Christ': Evangelical Groups and U.S.-Guatemalan Relations during the Ríos Montt Regime." *Diplomatic History* 39, no. 4 (2015): 689–719.

UNHCR. *Report of the Mapping Exercise Documenting the Most Serious Violations of Human Rights and International Humanitarian Law Committed within the Territory of the Democratic Republic of the Congo between March 1993 and June 2003.* August 2010.

United Nations Office on Drugs and Crime. "Global Study on Homicide 2013." Accessed December 19, 2019. https://www .unodc.org/documents/gsh/pdfs/2014_GLOBAL_HOMICIDE _BOOK_web.pdf.

"Universal Declaration of Human Rights." United Nations. Accessed December 19, 2019. https://www.un.org/en/universal -declaration-human-rights/.

"Up to 15,000 Killed in Libya War: U.N. Expert." Reuters, June 9, 2011. https://www.reuters.com/article/us-libya-un-deaths/up-to -15000-killed-in-libya-war-u-n-rights-expert -idUSTRE7584UY20110609.

Vanpoorten, Marijke. "The Death Toll of the Rwandan Genocide: A Detailed Analysis for Gikongoro Province." *Population* 60, no. 4 (2005): 331–367.

———. "Rwanda: Why Claim That 200,000 Tutsi Died in the Genocide Is Wrong." *African Arguments*, October 27, 2014. https://africanarguments.org/2014/10/27/rwanda-why-davenport -and-stams-calculation-that-200000-tutsi-died-in-the-genocide -is-wrong-by-marijke-verpoorten/.

Voice of the Martyrs. *I am N Devotional*. Eastbourne: David Cook, 2016.

Wainwright, Geoffrey. *The Ecumenical Moment: Crisis and Opportunity for the Church*. Grand Rapids, MI: Eerdmans Publishing Co., 1983.

Wallace, Jeremy David. "Virtue and Knowledge as the Hermeneutical Key for Unlocking Maximus the Confessor's *Quaestiones ad Thalassium*." PhD diss., Princeton Theological Seminary, 2013.

Walls, Andrew. *The Missionary Movement in Christian History: Studies in the Transmission of Faith*. Maryknoll, NY: Orbis Books, 1996.

Ward, Kevin. "Tukutendereza Yesu: The Balokole Revival in Uganda." Dictionary of African Christian Biography. Accessed April 1, 2019. https://dacb.org/histories/uganda-tukutendereza-yesu/.

Ware, Bishop Kallistos. *The Orthodox Way*. Crestwood, NY: St. Vladimir's Seminary Press, 1995.

Wariboko, Nimi. *Nigerian Pentecostalism*. Rochester, NY: University of Rochester Press, 2014.

Wenger, Tisa. "Indian Dances and the Politics of Religious Freedom, 1870–1930." *Journal of the American Academy of Religion* 79, no. 4 (2011): 850–878.

———. "'We Are Guaranteed Freedom': Pueblo Indians and the Category of Religion in the 1920s." *History of Religions* 45, no. 2 (2005): 89–113.

White, Christopher. "New Poll Shows Anti-Christian Persecution a 'Very Severe' Global Concern." *Crux Now*, March 21, 2019. https://cruxnow.com/global-church/2019/03/21/new-poll-shows -anti-christian-persecution-a-very-severe-global-concern/.

White, L. Michael. *From Jesus to Christianity*. San Francisco: HarperOne, 2005.

Wiedmann, F. "Rushing Judgment? Willfulness and Martyrdom in Early Christianity." *Union Seminary Quarterly Review* 53, no. 1 (1999): 61–69.

Wilken, Robert Louis. *Christians as the Romans Saw Them.* New Haven, CT: Yale University Press, 2003.

———. *The First Thousand Years: A Global History of Christianity.* New Haven, CT: Yale University Press, 2012.

Wilson, Charles Raegan. *Baptized in Blood: The Religion of the Lost Cause, 1965–1920.* Athens, GA: University of Georgia Press, 2009.

Wintour, Patrick, and Harriet Sherwood. "Jeremy Hunt Orders Global Review into Persecution of Christians." *Guardian*, December 26, 2018. https://www.theguardian.com/world/2018/dec/26/jeremy-hunt -orders-global-review-into-persecution-of-christians.

Wolffe, John. "Anti-Catholicism in Britain and the United States, 1830–1860." In *Evangelicalism: Comparative Studies of Popular Protestantism in North America, the British Isles, and Beyond, 1700–1990,* edited by Mark A. Noll, David W. Bebbington, and George A. Rawlyk, 179–197. Oxford: Oxford University Press, 1994.

Womack, Deanna Feree. *Protestants, Gender, and the Arab Renaissance in Late Ottoman Syria.* Edinburgh: Edinburgh University Press, 2015.

Workman, Herbert B. *Persecution in the Early Church.* New York: Oxford University Press, 1980.

"World Watch List: Iran." Open Doors. Accessed April 17, 2019. https://www.opendoorsusa.org/christian-persecution/world -watch-list/iran/.

Worthen, Molly. "The Chalcedon Problem: Rousas John Rushdoony and the Origins of Christian Reconstructionism." *Church History* 77, no. 2 (2008): 399–437.

Wright, Katherine Fairfax, and Malika Zouhali-Worrall, dirs. *Call Me Kuchu.* Cinedigm Corp., 2012.

Wurmbrand, Richard. *In God's Underground.* Bartlesville, OK: VOM Books, 2004.

———. *Tortured for Christ.* Bartlesville, OK: Living Sacrifice Book Co., 1967.

Wuthnow, Robert. *Inventing American Religion: Polls, Surveys, and the Tenuous Quest for a Nation's Faith.* Oxford: Oxford University Press, 2015.

Zaborowski, Jason R. *The Coptic Martyrdom of John of Phanijōit: Assimilation and Conversion to Islam in Thirteenth-Century Egypt.* Leiden: Brill, 2005.

Zaimov, Stoyan. "Christian Group Praises US Gov't's Decision to Help Save Kidnapped School Girls in Nigeria." *Christian Post*, May 8, 2014. https://www.christianpost.com/news/christian -group-praises-us-govts-decision-to-help-save-kidnapped -schoolgirls-in-nigeria-119363/.

———. "Nigeria Kills 13 Boko Haram Militants as Massacre of Christians Continues." *Christian Post*, January 2, 2013. https:// www.christianpost.com/news/nigeria-kills-13-boko-haram -militants-as-massacre-of-christians-continues-87555/.

Index

freedom and, 155–156; spiritual obligation *vs.*, 139–140; under Trump, 137

Foxe, John, 59, 88, 130

Foxe's Book of Martyrs, 59–60, 98, 113, 130

Francis, Pope, 130

Gaffney, Frank, 144

Galatians, Epistle to, 10, 25, 146

Galerius, 38

gay marriage, 104, 185n108

gender discrimination, 92–93

genocide: Armenian, 73–74, 96, 113; origin of term, 77; Rwandan, 118–121, 189n27; Yazidi, 136–137

Genovese, Eugene, 83

Gesta Francorum, 50–51

Global War on Christians, The (Allen), 130

Gnostics, 40, 62

Goldberg, Jeffrey, 102

Golden Legend, The (Jacobus de Voraigne), 53–57

Goldstein, Joshua, 121–122

Gospels, 22–24. *See also specific Gospels*

Gravell, Richard, 60

Great Persecution, 38

Grove City College v. Bell, 92–93

Guatemala, 154

Habyarimana, Juvenal, 118

Hagia Sophia, 52

Hartunian, Abraham, 72–73

Hebrews, Epistle to, 27–28

Helms, Jesse, 93

Holocaust, 77–78

Hooper John, 59–60

Horowitz, Michael, 110, 144

HRW. *See* Human Rights Watch (HRW)

human rights, 75–80

Human Rights Watch (HRW), 119

Humbert, Cardinal, 49

Hus, Jan, 57

I am N (Voice of the Martyrs), 101

Ignatius, 30–31

Imagining, as term, viii

Indonesia, 138

Innocent III, Pope, 52

Institute on Religion and Democracy (IRD), 111, 144, 150–151, 153

International Religious Freedom Act (IRFA), 114–115

In the Lion's Den (Shea), 102, 111

Invisible Children, 164n9

"I Pledge Allegiance to the Lamb" (Boltz), 112

Iran, 138

Iraq, 108, 134–135, 137, 153, 155, 158

Iraq War, 154

IRD. *See* Institute on Religion and Democracy (IRD)

IRFA. *See* International Religious Freedom Act (IRFA)

Iron Curtain, 84, 89, 110

Isaiah, Book of, 27

Isho'yahb III, 44

Islam, 39–48, 71, 114–115, 127–130, 133–134. *See also entries at* Muslim

Islamic State (ISIS), 101, 108, 129, 136–137, 139, 145

Jackson, Stonewall, 69

Jackson-Vanik Amendment, 89

Jacobites, 42

Jacob of Edessa, 42

Jacob of Serug, 42

Jacobus de Voraigne, 53–57

Jehovah's Witnesses, 131

Jesus Freaks (Voice of the Martyrs), 98–99, 113

Jesus to the Communist World, 87

Jews, 77–78, 109–110

About the Author

JASON BRUNER is an associate professor of global Christianity in the School of Historical, Philosophical, and Religious Studies at Arizona State University in Tempe. He is the author of *Living Salvation in the East African Revival in Uganda*.